ReFocus: The Films of Lucrecia Martel

ReFocus: The International Directors Series

Series Editors: Robert Singer, Stefanie Van de Peer, and Gary D. Rhodes

Board of Advisors:
Lizelle Bisschoff (University of Glasgow)
Stephanie Hemelryck Donald (University of Lincoln)
Anna Misiak (Falmouth University)
Des O'Rawe (Queen's University Belfast)

ReFocus is a series of contemporary methodological and theoretical approaches to the interdisciplinary analyses and interpretations of international film directors, from the celebrated to the ignored, in direct relationship to their respective culture – its myths, values, and historical precepts – and the broader parameters of international film history and theory.

Titles in the series include:

edinburghuniversitypress.com/series/refocint

ReFocus:
The Films of Lucrecia Martel

Edited by Natalia Christofoletti Barrenha,
Julia Kratje and Paul R. Merchant

EDINBURGH
University Press

Edinburgh University Press is one of the leading university presses in the UK. We publish academic books and journals in our selected subject areas across the humanities and social sciences, combining cutting-edge scholarship with high editorial and production values to produce academic works of lasting importance. For more information visit our website: edinburghuniversitypress.com

Edinburgh University Press Ltd
The Tun – Holyrood Road
12 (2f) Jackson's Entry
Edinburgh EH8 8PJ

Typeset in 11/13 Ehrhardt MT by
IDSUK (DataConnection) Ltd, and
printed and bound by CPI Group (UK) Ltd,
Croydon, CR0 4YY

A CIP record for this book is available from the British Library

ISBN 978 1 4744 8522 7 (hardback)
ISBN 978 1 4744 8524 1 (webready PDF)
ISBN 978 1 4744 8525 8 (epub)

Contents

Figures

Notes on Contributors

Gonzalo Aguilar is full professor of Brazilian literature at the Universidad de Buenos Aires, and a researcher at the Argentine National Scientific and Technical Research Council (CONICET). He directs the Master's programme in literatures of Latin America at the Universidad Nacional de San Martín. He is the author of several books, including *Hélio Oiticica, a asa branca do êxtase: arte brasileira de 1964–1980* (2016), *Más allá del pueblo. Imágenes, indicios y políticas del cine* (2015), *Episodios cosmopolitas en la cultura argentina* (2009), *Otros mundos. Un ensayo sobre el nuevo cine argentino* (2006; translated into English, 2008) and *Poesía concreta brasileña. Las vanguardias en la encrucijada modernista* (2003; translated into Portuguese, 2005). With David Oubiña, he co-authored *El cine de Leonardo Favio* (1993), and with Emiliano Jelicié, *Borges va al cine* (2010). In 2021, he curated the exhibition *Madalena Schwartz: As metamorfoses* at the Instituto Moreira Salles, São Paulo, and at the Museo de Arte Latinoamericano de Buenos Aires, alongside Samuel Titán Jr.

Ana Amado obtained her PhD in Humanities from the University of Leiden. She was a professor at the Universidad de Buenos Aires and a visiting professor at a number of universities in Argentina, Latin America and worldwide. During her Guggenheim Fellowship term, she researched the relationship between political insurgency and popular imagination as seen in the visual arts of Argentina. Among her publications are *La imagen justa. Cine argentino y política (1980–2007)* (2009), *Lazos de familia. Herencias, cuerpos, ficciones* (2004) and *Espacio para la igualdad. El ABC de un periodismo no sexista* (1996). She also contributed numerous chapters to anthologies in her field, as well as articles and essays to specialist and popular periodicals.

Adriana Amante holds a PhD in Literature from the Universidad de Buenos Aires. She is full professor and teaches nineteenth-century Argentine literature at UBA. She is also a professor at New York University in Buenos Aires, on the Master's programme in history and architecture and urban culture at Universidad Torcuato Di Tella and on the Master's programme in creative writing at Universidad Nacional de Tres de Febrero. She has been visiting researcher at the New York University and at the University of London, and visiting professor at the University of California, Berkeley. She is the author of *Poéticas y políticas del destierro. Argentinos en Brasil en la época de Rosas* (2010) and the editor of the volume on Sarmiento in the *Historia crítica de la literatura argentina* (2012). She co-authored *Absurdo Brasil* (2000), and has translated Pessoa's and Machado de Assis's works from Portuguese into Spanish. She directs a project on calligraphic, typographic and visual culture in South American literature.

Natalia Christofoletti Barrenha is an independent film researcher and programmer specialising in Latin American cinema. She conducted postdoctoral research at the Universidade Estadual de Campinas and was Visiting Fellow at the KU Leuven and the Univerzita Komenského v Bratislave. She is the author of *Espaços em conflito. Ensaios sobre a cidade no cinema argentino contemporâneo* (2019) and *A experiência do cinema de Lucrecia Martel: Resíduos do tempo e sons à beira da piscina* (2014; translated into Spanish, 2020).

Emilio Bernini holds a PhD in Literature from the Universidad de Buenos Aires. He directs the Research and Postgraduate Department of the Universidad del Cine. Among other texts, he has published *Después del nuevo cine. Diez miradas en torno al cine argentino contemporáneo* (2018), *Cine y Filosofía. Las entrevistas de Fata Morgana* (2015), *El matadero. Ensayos de transposición. Literatura/Cine argentinos* (2010) and *Silvia Prieto, un film sin atributos* (2008). He directs the magazine *Kilómetro III. Ensayos sobre cine* and the book series *Biblioteca Kilómetro III*.

Mônica Campo is associate professor in the History Department at the Universidade Federal de Uberlândia. She holds a PhD in Cultural History from Universidade Estadual de Campinas, has participated in several international congresses and is a frequent contributor to academic journals. Jointly with Carla Barros, she is the coordinator of Festival Curta (C)Errado, currently on its third edition.

Nora Catelli has a BA in Literature from the Universidad Nacional de Rosario and a PhD in Hispanic Philology. She currently teaches Literary Theory and Comparative Literature at the Universidad de Barcelona. Her work in literary criticism has been published in *La Vanguardia*, *El País* and several European magazines. She has written various essays about genres and authors in modern European and American literature, and has published *Cartas a mujeres* by Virginia Woolf (2001) and written the prologues for Franz Kafka's *Diaries* and *Letter to His Father* (2001). She has written *Desplazamientos necesarios. Lecturas de literatura argentina* (2021), *La tarea del traductor* (2021), *El espacio autobiográfico* (1991) and, in collaboration with Marietta Gargatagli, *El tabaco que fumaba Plinio. Escenas de la traducción en España y América: Relatos, leyes y reflexiones sobre los otros* (1998).

Damyler Cunha is assistant professor at the Universidade Federal de Sergipe. She currently teaches on the cinema and audiovisual course in the Social and Communication Department, and researches the usage of music and sound in cinema. She has a PhD from the Universidade São Paulo with the thesis *O uso da música e do som no filme experimental latino-americano: As experiências de Glauber Rocha em* Pátio *(Brasil, 1959) e Hugo Santiago em* Invasión *(Argentina, 1969)*.

Ana Forcinito is professor of Latin American literatures and cultures, and the holder of the Arsham and Charlotte Ohanessian Chair in the College of Liberal Arts, University of Minnesota. She is the author of *Óyeme con los ojos: Cine, mujeres, voces, visiones* (2018), *Intermittences: Memory, Justice and the Poetics of the Visible* (2018), *Los umbrales del testimonio: Entre las naraciones de los sobrevivientes y las marcas de la posdictadura* (2012) and *Memorias y nomadías: Géneros y cuerpos en los márgenes del posfeminismo* (2004). She has edited seven books and volumes, *Migraciones, derechos humanos y acciones locales* (2020), *Poner el cuerpo. Rescatar y visibilizar las marcas sexuales y de género de los archivos dictatoriales* (2017) and *Human Rights and Latin American and Iberian Cultures* (2009), among others.

Julia Kratje has a PhD in Social Sciences from the Universidad de Buenos Aires. She is a researcher at the Argentine National Scientific and Technical Research Council (CONICET), and teaches at UBA and at the Universidad Nacional de las Artes. She is the author of *Al margen del tiempo. Deseos, ritmos y atmósferas en el cine argentino* (2019) and editor of *De cuerpo entero. Debates feministas y campo cultural en Argentina 1960–1980* (2021), *Espejos oblicuos. Cinco miradas sobre feminismo y cine contemporáneo* (2020) and *El asombro y la audacia. El cine de María Luisa Bemberg* (2020).

Alejandra Laera is full professor of Argentine literature at the Universidad de Buenos Aires, and principal researcher at the Argentine National Scientific and Technical Research Council (CONICET). She is the author of *Ficciones del dinero. Argentina, 1890–2001* (2014) and of *El tiempo vacío de la ficción. Las novelas argentinas de Eduardo Gutiérrez y Eugenio Cambaceres* (2004), as well as the director of *El brote de los géneros* (Emecé, 2010), the third volume of *Historia crítica de la literatura argentina*. She edited *Una historia de la imaginación* *literaria en la Argentina* (2019), and has co-edited various collections, among them *El valor de la cultura. Arte, literatura y mercado en América Latina* (2007). She currently directs the *Viajeras/Viajeros* series for the Fondo de Cultura Económica, and with Mónica Szurmuk, is preparing the *Cambridge History of Argentinean Literature*.

Deborah Martin is Professor of Latin American film and culture in the Department of Spanish, Portuguese and Latin American Studies at University College London. She has published widely on Latin American cinema, including the books *The Child in Contemporary Latin American Cinema* (2019) and *The Cinema of Lucrecia Martel* (2016). She is currently working on Latin American eco-cinema.

Paul R. Merchant is senior lecturer in Latin American film and visual culture at the University of Bristol. He is the author of *Remaking Home: Domestic Spaces in Argentine and Chilean Film, 2005–2015* (2022) and the co-editor of *Latin American Culture and the Limits of the Human* (2020). His most recent research, funded by the Arts and Humanities Research Council, explores visual and audiovisual responses to the Pacific Ocean in Chile and Peru.

Dianna C. Niebylski is professor of Latin American Literature and Cultural Studies in the Department of Hispanic and Italian Studies at the University of Illinois Chicago. Her research centres on three general areas: bodies and sexuality in contemporary Latin American women's fiction, poverty and violence in Latin American literature, and humour and laughter in women's fiction. Among her publications are the books *Pobreza y precariedad en el imaginario latinoamericano actual* (co-edited with Stephen Buttes, 2017), *Latin American Icons: Fame across Borders* (co-edited with Patrick O'Connor, 2014), *Sergio Chejfec: Trayectorias de una escritura* (edited volume, 2012) and *Humoring Resistance: Laughter and the Excessive Body in Latin American Women's Fiction* (2004).

David Oubiña has a PhD in Literature from the Universidad de Buenos Aires. He is a researcher at the Argentine National Scientific and Technical Research Council (CONICET) and teaches at UBA. He has been a visiting researcher at the University of London, and visiting professor at the University of Bergen, New York University and the University of California, Berkeley. He is editor of *Las Ranas (art, essay and translation)* and *Revista de cine*. His books include *Ceremonias de lo invisible. Apuntes sobre el cine y la guerra* (2020), *El silencio y sus bordes. Modos de lo extremo en la literatura y el cine* (2011), *Una juguetería filosófica: Cine, cronofotografía y arte digital* (2009), *Estudio crítico sobre La ciénaga, de Lucrecia Martel* (2007) and *Filmología: Ensayos con el cine* (2000).

Mariana Souto is assistant professor of audiovisual studies at the Universidade de Brasília. She has a PhD in Communication from the Universidade Federal de Minas Gerais, and is the author of *Infiltrados e invasores: Uma perspectiva comparada sobre as relações de classe no cinema brasileiro* (2019). Her postdoctoral work was at the Universidade de São Paulo, and she was a FAPESP scholar. She is currently researching comparative methodologies in cinema.

Malena Verardi has a PhD in Art History and Theory, a Master's degree in Discourse Analysis and a Bachelor's degree in Combined Arts from the Universidad de Buenos Aires. She is a researcher for the Argentine National Scientific and Technical Research Council (CONICET) and a lecturer in film history at UBA. She has led several research projects for the scientific programming UBACyT (Secretariat of Science and Technology of the University of Buenos Aires) and published numerous articles in magazines that specialise in film analysis.

Acknowledgements

Putting together a volume of essays during a global pandemic does not sound like an easy task, particularly when the editors are located in three different countries and the lives of all of the contributors have been upended by the spread of Covid-19 in 2020 and 2021. The fact that the process of editing this book has remained such a pleasure is due to the remarkable efforts of a large number of people.

Our thanks must first go to Lucrecia Martel, not only for the dazzling, challenging and mysterious films that she has given to the world, but also for being such a thoughtful and generous interlocutor.

We are very grateful to the editors of *ReFocus: The International Directors Series*, Robert Singer, Stefanie Van de Peer and Gary D. Rhodes, for their unwavering encouragement and helpful feedback since the earliest days of this project. At Edinburgh University Press, Gillian Leslie, Richard Strachan and Sam Johnson have all helped to make the publication process as smooth as possible, and we are very thankful for their efforts in these complicated times.

Many people have assisted with obtaining copies of films, the acquisition of rights and the reproduction of images, among them Benjamín Domenech and Brenda Erdei at Rei Cine, Vania Catani at Bananeira Filmes, Sebastián A. Pérez at Lita Stantic Producciones, Michelle Petit de Meurville at ENERC, Mariana Amieva and Marília-Marie Goulart. We are very grateful to them all.

Our thanks are also due to Mariana Casullo Amado, Liza Casullo Amado, Gerardo Yoel, Victoria Álvarez and Virginia Flôres. Natalia Christofoletti Barrenha would like to thank Adriana Nanci Christofoletti, Agustín Masaedo, Bruno Christofoletti Barrenha, Cynthia Tompkins, Daniel Maggi, Diego Cordes, Fernando Passos, Miriam Gárate, Nadia Lie, Susana Santos Rodrigues and Tiago de Luca. Julia Kratje would like to thank Marina Etcheverrigaray and Ricardo Kratje.

A book would of course be nothing without its authors, and the editors cannot thank them enough for their insights, patience and persistence as we have worked together to make this volume a reality.

CHAPTER I

Metamorphosis and Persistence: An Introduction

Natalia Christofoletti Barrenha, Julia Kratje and Paul R. Merchant

The name 'Lucrecia Martel' has, over the course of a career spanning more than thirty years, found itself associated with a strangely consistent set of epithets. The Argentine film director and her work are described as 'opaque', 'enigmatic', 'ambiguous' and 'beguilingly peculiar' – indeed, all of these adjectives occur in just one article in *Variety*, published in 2020.[1] Some of this language, particularly in its manifestations in the anglophone press, can be attributed to the exoticisation of a Latin American woman who has achieved the status of global *auteur* more often reserved for men hailing from the Global North. Yet there is no doubt that Martel's body of work is in many senses unusual: alongside features that have won critical acclaim across the world are to be found short films, including one made for a clothing brand, and the art direction of a concert tour.

An indication of Martel's remarkable global status can be seen in a mural in Montevideo, Uruguay. The vast majority of neighbourhood cinemas in Uruguay, as in Argentina and elsewhere, have been demolished or converted into supermarkets, garages or churches, at the same time as a boom in internationally funded multiplexes and the removal of policies that encourage cultural diversity and protect cultural heritage. Yet in the heart of Montevideo can be found the Cinemateca Uruguaya, the last of the old cinemas on the city's famed Avenida 18 de Julio to remain standing, thanks to its faithful audience. In April 2017, during the Tourism Week introduced by the secular state to coincide with the Christian Holy Week, and in the context of the 35th Festival Cinematográfico Internacional del Uruguay (Uruguay International Film Festival), the facade of this temple of cinema was renovated with a one-off mural, created by an artistic collective. From left to right, gazing straight at the viewer, and holding a megaphone, a crow, a surrealist door and a photo camera respectively, the figures of Federico Fellini, Alfred Hitchcock, Luis Buñuel and Lucrecia Martel emerge from on high. As in religious prints, each has a halo, indicating their divine nature. Under the slogan 'Festival empieza con Fe' ('Festival begins with Faith'),[2] the profane devotion to cinema and its saints – the directors – was accompanied by prayers and commandments. 'Oh Saint Lucrecia, patron of Argentine cinema and apostle of Latin American film, open your scripts to us, and let us enter your Swamp ['Ciénaga'] so that we become soaked in reality', intones a fragment that canonises Martel in the pantheon of universal filmmakers, with her cat-eye glasses and strikingly red nails.

In addition to such popular expressions of admiration, Martel's films have received critical acclaim, prestigious awards and significant scholarly attention, both in her native Argentina and among scholars of global cinema. Yet to date no one volume has set out to provide a comprehensive view of Martel's work (whether in fiction, documentary or essayistic short film) and of the range of critical responses it can generate. The chapters in this collection are authored by some of the most prominent scholars of Martel's films and by emergent voices, and offer a fresh set of perspectives (alongside two translations of landmark essays not previously available in English) that build on existing critical trends and suggest promising new avenues for research.

Figure 1.1 Mural at the Cinemateca Uruguaya, in Montevideo: Fellini, Hitchcock, Buñuel and Martel. Photo by Mariana Amieva

A CAREER IN EVASION

Martel was born in 1966 in Salta, a province on the border with Bolivia in the north-west of Argentina, about 1,500 km away from Buenos Aires. She was the second child among seven siblings and liked to stage Western films using her brothers and sisters as actors, while she operated a heavy camera that their father had bought to record his large family. Nobody had paid much attention to the machine, but Martel was curious about how it worked, read the user guide, as she liked to do with new tools, and went ahead with putting her freshly acquired knowledge into practice. As she has mentioned in several interviews,[3] the filming experiences during her adolescence were fundamental for forming her gaze, even though she did not immediately realise it. The whole process of recording, understanding what was happening, and coming across things that were so different from what she was used to seeing on television began to interest her. The mundanity of domestic life, of chats between the mother, the children and the visitors, and the irrelevant facts of everyday existence drew Martel's attention towards the off-screen world, the drift of the dialogues and the appearance of events that she thought she had not filmed but were there, on the edge of the frame.

Despite having discovered something that fascinated her, she never imagined that her future would be related to it. Martel has remarked that her approach to the cinema as a possible career was the result of a misunderstanding:[4] when she was a teenager, she followed the massive success of the Argentine blockbuster and Oscar nominee *Camila* (1984), directed by María Luisa Bemberg and produced by Lita Stantic, who used to appear on television, radio, everywhere, talking about the feature. She then registered the making of films as a form of women's work, a universe inhabited and led by them. From a conventional middle-class, provincial home, where Catholicism was embraced and practised in non-orthodox ways, intertwined with popular beliefs, she studied in an ultra-Catholic and elitist local school, chosen because it was the only place where she could learn Latin and Ancient Greek – a passion discovered through an uncle who was a priest. At the age of nineteen, after enrolling in different courses in different cities, she decided to go to Buenos Aires to study advertising. A new degree course at that time, it was taught only at a Catholic university, which made Martel, entirely disengaged from the Church at that moment, back out. She eventually began her studies in social communication at the University of Buenos Aires (another new course, launched after the dictatorship years that had badly harmed the press and its professionals) while also attending the Animation Film School at the Avellaneda Institute of Cinematographic Art. Shortly afterwards, she would join the very selective National School of Film Experimentation and Production (ENERC, in its Spanish acronym), maintained by the National Institute of Cinema and Audiovisual Arts (INCAA).

When she arrived at ENERC, it had been hit by a lack of funds due to a severe economic crisis, and amidst the shortage of equipment, materials and staff, Martel and her colleagues improvised and experimented producing independent short films, learning by themselves and among themselves. *The 56/El 56* (1988), *24th Floor/Piso 24* (1989) and *Red Kisses/Besos rojos* (1991) are among those collective exercises, copies of which are not now available. The first film signed by Martel as a writer and director was *You Won't Get Her, Bastard/No te la llevarás, maldito* (1989), a two-minute university assignment with no dialogue about the revenge dreamt up by a boy against his mother's boyfriend, in which she combines animation and live action via agile editing. It was followed by *The Other/La otra* (1989), a joyful documentary on the world of transvestites also developed during her period at ENERC.

The song that Martel chose for the opening and closing sequences of *The Other* demonstrates, once again, her ability to grasp the sensitive fibres of popular culture and, like a puppet master, to make them dance among the dense layers of a film's audiovisual weave. That song, *Se dice de mí* ('They Say About Me'), is an endearing choice, one that evokes modes of feeling, thinking and acting that are deeply rooted in the collective imaginary of the Río de la Plata, across generations. Written in 1943, with lyrics by the Argentine Ivo Pelay and music by the Uruguayan Francisco Canaro, it was Tita Merello's performance of the song in *Mercado de abasto* (Lucas Demare, 1955) that cemented its place in popular culture. Merello's rustic timbre and rich contralto register, which brims with humour and determination, imbues the lyrics with rage and joyful abandon. 'Se dicen muchas cosas, / mas si el bulto no interesa / ¿Por qué pierden la cabeza ocupándose de mí?' ('Many things are said, / but if the shape doesn't matter / why do you lose your heads talking about me?'): this is the challenge that Merello daringly issues to her spectators (both diegetic and beyond the screen). This sensuous performance becomes part of *The Other* through Merello's voice, to which a man playfully lip-syncs in a modest kitchen, without make-up, holding a *mate* gourd like a microphone. Martel's short focuses on a small group of transvestites who recount their experiences, intercut with archive footage. The ten minutes of the film showcase a multitude of ways of inhabiting sex and gender, mixing artifice and nature, through pleasurable bodies that transgress binary distinctions between man and woman, masculine and feminine. 'They may chatter, / they may talk / and whisper, and bray / but the ugliness God gave me / has been the envy of many women / and they won't say I've fooled myself / because I've always been modest', the song and the film conclude.[5] 'Yo soy así' ('That's how I am').

Dead King/Rey Muerto (1995) was Martel's first film produced in a more professional environment. Its script was selected in the first edition of *Short Stories/Historias breves*, a competition organised by INCAA to fund short films and nurture young filmmakers. Alongside Martel, Daniel Burman, Paula

Figure 1.2 A scene from *The Other*, a short film directed by Martel during her studies at ENERC

Hernández and Ulises Rosell were among the awardees. The set of ten shorts was released in cinemas (something uncommon for the format), was critically acclaimed and drew the audience's attention to this generation, becoming a landmark in the renewal of Argentine cinema in the mid-1990s that became known, at least by critics, as *Nuevo Cine Argentino* (New Argentine Cinema). New Argentine Cinema emerged driven by a series of factors, such as the creation of a law to promote and fund the audiovisual sector, the reactivation of a reserved screen quota in cinemas for Argentine films, the appearance and reopening of various film schools, and easier access to equipment due to exchange rate convertibility between the Argentine peso and the US dollar. These developments led to a rapid reactivation of the audiovisual sector, which became more dynamic than ever before.

It is no surprise, then, that the formal characteristics of New Argentine Cinema are marked by the social and institutional upheavals that transformed the world of work and urban space in the 1990s, intensifying consumption, rendering audiovisual media and information networks omnipresent, and changing how sexuality was experienced. Yet the films also evince a desire to break with the traditions of industrial cinema, by eroding the boundary between documentary and fiction, involving new and non-professional actors, and using unconventional methods of financing and distribution. The films' aesthetic characteristics, both by choice and by necessity, bear the marks of low-budget productions: hand-held cameras, for instance, or black and white footage. New Argentine Cinema films moreover eschew the large-scale political (and often metaphorical) narratives of directors like Eliseo Subiela or Luis Puenzo. Instead, the works of Pablo Trapero, Adrián Caetano, Martín

Rejtman, Lisandro Alonso and others deal with marginal communities and small-scale, personal and unresolved narratives.

The success of *Dead King* (which also travelled to several international film festivals) led Martel to work in television, where she was part of the team of the documentary series *D.N.I.* (1995) and the cutting-edge children's show *Magazine For Fai* (1995–9), which was created by the Argentine musician, actor and entertainer Mex Urtizberea, and broadcast on Cablín, the first dedicated children's television channel in Latin America. Set in the 1950s, *Magazine For Fai* has become an object of cult interest for adults. The programme imagines a world dominated by a corporation led by the pitiless Orwell For Fai. In this world, a cast of boys and girls between six and fifteen years old interact with Urtizberea on the basis of minimal script prompts, which then give way to improvisation games. While working in television, Martel also directed the documentaries *Encarnación Ezcurra* and *The Outbuildings/Las dependencias*, both part of *Six Women/Seis mujeres*, a six-episode series dedicated to exploring the life and work of six female Argentine personalities, broadcast in 1999. The series was produced by, among others, Lita Stantic, and was the first contact between the filmmaker and the legendary producer, thus leading to their partnership on *The Swamp/La ciénaga* (2001).

Martel was having great difficulties getting financial support for *The Swamp*, an assembly of situations and characters inspired by family scenes and memories, provincial gossip and popular tales (elements that run through all her feature films). Stantic suggested sending the script to the Sundance Institute, which backed the project, opening up the path for other partners from Argentina, Europe and Japan. *The Swamp* premiered as part of the main competition at the 51st Berlin International Film Festival in February 2001 and won the Alfred Bauer Prize, which aimed to recognise 'films that open up new perspectives in the field of cinematic art', as described at the Berlinale website archives. In March, *The Swamp* was featured at the 16th Mar del Plata Film Festival, and from April, it was screened in Argentine movie theatres, reaching a national box office of about 130,000 viewers[6] – not a phenomenon, but a significant figure for a debut filmmaker with such a demanding film.

The prize at the Berlinale and international critical prestige made things easier for Martel in the journey to her second feature, *The Holy Girl/La niña santa* (2004). She was invited to the Cinéfondation residency, promoted by the Cannes Film Festival, and the Spanish director Pedro Almodóvar joined Stantic as a co-producer. The film received support from the prestigious Hubert Bals Fund, among other national and international institutions. *The Holy Girl* competed for the Palme d'Or at the 57th edition of Cannes, *The New York Times* included it amongst the ten best film releases in the United States that year, and it achieved 110,000 spectators in Argentina. Since then, Martel has been invited constantly to participate in film festival juries, deliver lectures and teach workshops worldwide.

Her third feature, *The Headless Woman/La mujer sin cabeza* (2008), also opened in Cannes. The film had a cold critical reception during its press screening, a reaction largely disseminated through the media. This fact severely harmed its international distribution, and even in Argentina the film barely exceeded 30,000 viewers. Shortly thereafter, Martel would need to deal with another setback: the cancellation of her next project, an adaptation of the mythical sci-fi Argentine comic *The Eternaut/El Eternauta* (1957–9, written by Héctor Germán Oesterheld and drawn by Francisco Solano López), due to a disagreement with the producers and rights-holders. After a while out of the spotlight, Martel started to receive substantial attention again. Although her work has never ceased to be prominent and steadily explored in academia, from 2010 onwards film festivals, film museums and cultural institutions at large began to request her presence. *The Headless Woman* was seen as unfairly misunderstood, and retrospectives of the frequently so-called Salta Trilogy popped up from Sarajevo to Harvard. In 2012, the renowned magazine *Cinema Scope*, celebrating its fiftieth issue, listed 'The Best 50 Filmmakers Under 50', and Martel was there, praised in an article signed by the distinguished Thai director Apichatpong Weerasethakul.

Despite the continued excitement around her name, Martel would only release a new feature in 2017, at the 74th Venice International Film Festival: *Zama*, based on the homonymous novel by the Argentine writer Antonio Di Benedetto, published in 1956. Set in the late eighteenth century, it necessitated a more complex production structure that involved eight countries and several challenges throughout its process, especially regarding funding. Eventually, the film had a major enthusiastic critical reception internationally and enjoyed tremendous recognition in Argentina, where it was chosen to represent the country for the Goya and Oscar awards, gained almost 100,000 viewers, and was the most successful film at national ceremonies such as the Premios Sur and Cóndor de Plata. *Zama* represented a true film-event for both the cultural and cinematographic fields, giving rise to an engaging documentary filmed during the shoot (*Light Years/Años luz*, Manuel Abramovich, 2017), and a book that describes fascinating scenes and anecdotes about the film (*The Monkey in the Whirlpool/El mono en el remolino*, Selva Almada, 2017).

Alongside these features, Martel has also directed several more recent short films. The documentary *The City That Flees/La ciudad que huye* (2006) was produced within the international initiative *The Burgeoning City/La ciudad en ciernes*.[7] During 2006 and 2007, in different cities in Spain and Latin America, the project promoted seminars and exhibitions to draw attention to the right to the city and the relationship between urbanism and human rights. Martel's

short explores the phenomenon of gated communities in Buenos Aires, which
for the filmmaker are remarkable and improbable. An on-screen anecdote
confirms this: 'Twenty years ago, scouting locations for a short film, we came
across a gated community. What an absurd idea! This is not going to work, we
thought.' The incredulity in discovering, many years later, the extent to which
such an idea *has* worked contaminates the film with amazement, reinforcing
the illogic of these islands of wealth surrounded by poor suburbs.

In an unstable shot, the opening scene depicts a private guard closing a
gate to the crew, a situation that will be repeated more than once: gates, grids,
guards, barbed wire, prohibitive signs, menacing voices. *The City That Flees*
demonstrates the impossibility of making a film about a *country* (as the gated
communities are called in Argentina, after the English term 'country club'),
while managing to capture the very essence of one. The camera is never allowed
to enter: the barriers that obstruct people's circulation also obstruct the film.
The boundaries are rigid and non-negotiable (despite the attempts to 'natu-
ralise' them with the inclusion of climbing plants or trees). Where there are
no material borders, there are the security personnel, vigilant, as are the cameras. Maps, statistics and satellite images replace the lack of internal footage, so
that the short adopts a quasi-scientific documentary mode that belies its highly
political content. A narrator traces a brief history of this type of urbanisation:
the loss of state interest in influencing the development of the city started in the
dictatorship in the 1970s, deepened with the neoliberal mood of the 1990s, and
resulted in the dismantling of the public transport network and the expansion of
the highways. Together, these factors paved the way for real estate speculation
and the privatisation of many sectors of life.

These enclaves with golf courses and polo pitches, shopping malls and
bilingual schools grew as fast as the social divide in Argentina at the end of the
twentieth century. What *The City That Flees* keenly shows is that this gulf can
be the width of a street, and as a result even more stark. The neighbours living
across the road from the gated communities inhabit an entirely different landscape. When depicting this disparity, Martel splits the screen, and manages
the rhythm of editing so that these differing images never appear at the same
time, side by side. Despite the visible poverty outside the *country*, there is life,
movement, colour and cheerful voices, in contrast to the nauseous travelling
shot of the endless grey wall that surrounds the gated neighbourhood. Here, as
in her other works, Martel displays a capacity to bend cinematic form in order
to create a sense of what cannot be seen.

Following *The City That Flees*, Martel directed a series of commissioned
shorts that are still more unusual and unsettling. *Fish/Pescados* (2010) is a mesmerising and funny experiment involving chatty koi carp dreaming that they
were once a car driving on a rainy night, which was made for Notodofilmfest
(a Spanish online film festival). Martel collaborated with Argentine electro-folk
musician Juana Molina to give voice to her characters. The eerie sensation that

emanates from *Fish* is developed in *Muta* (2011), where Martel embraces the horror genre after having flirted with it in her previous features. Verging on science fiction, *Muta* is the second film in the ongoing *Women's Tales* series, conceived by the Italian fashion company Miu Miu (part of the Prada conglomerate) in partnership with the Venice International Film Festival. Since 2011, the luxurious brand has invited both promising and established women filmmakers worldwide (Agnès Varda, Ava DuVernay, Hiam Abbas, Naomi Kawase and Mati Diop are among them) to create shorts in which the only condition is that the actors wear Miu Miu clothing.

New Argirópolis/Nueva Argirópolis (2010) and *Leagues/Leguas* (2015) bring to the foreground the marginalisation of indigenous communities and the different ways in which they are often (and violently) disconnected from Argentine citizenship. The former belongs to the anthology *25 Looks, 200 Minutes/25 miradas, 200 minutos*, for which the National Secretariat of Culture invited twenty-five filmmakers to produce shorts as part of the celebrations of the Bicentennial of the 1810 May Revolution (which ended effective Spanish rule in Argentina). The latter is part of the feature *The Empty Classroom/El aula vacía*, which explores the school dropout crisis across Latin America, and was the result of a collaborative effort by leading filmmakers from the region under the creative direction of Gael García Bernal.

Over the course of her career, Martel has moved ever closer to the struggle of indigenous people in the north of Argentina, using her status as a renowned public figure in the region in order to be politically active alongside them. Since 2010, she has been working on the documentary *Chocobar* (working title), which explores the causes and consequences of the murder of indigenous leader Javier Chocobar in Tucumán in 2009. Although the images of his homicide circulated widely, the killers were convicted only in 2018, before being eventually released in 2020. In a few statements about the film publicised so far,[8] Martel explains that she departs from the history of the Chocobar murder to reflect upon the construction of racist and oppressive discourses that allow crimes like this to continue in Argentina in particular and in Latin America in general.

AI is another short commissioned by a film festival: it is the trailer for the 2019 Viennale. Here, Martel works with her well-known passion for YouTube, gathering and heavily manipulating footage found on the platform. The film is organised around a very brief excerpt from a popular and disturbing interview conducted in 1961 with a catatonic schizophrenic under treatment. The director reframes the image, keeping only a close-up of the interviewee, mutating him into a talking head, while blurring his face with a pixelated effect, which is commonly used to hide someone's identity, as well as being a symbol of low-quality digital archives. Just one eye is left out of this intervention; a restless eye that seems trapped among those several small squares. The film's succinct title leads the spectator to believe that they are watching some kind of artificial intelligence. This suspicion is bolstered by the disembodied, machinic voice and the subject's affirmation that 'I am not completely like other people.' However, the frightening and cryptic soundtrack in the background does not allow straightforward judgements. Glimpses of other videos suddenly assault the film: caressing hands, people playing the piano, famous ASMR sessions. As Ross McDonnell asks, would that be a dysfunction in the machine's data set, or algorithmically generated hallucinations?[9] Then, an inquisitive, insistent inquiry emerges: 'What is it you are trying to do with your life?' What human has never encountered this question hanging over their lives? To this very human affliction, we hear in reply another very human expression: the pursuit of a desire – 'Play the piano for people.' One cannot help thinking about *Zama* when watching *AI*. The phrase 'What is it you are trying to do with your life?' echoes from one film to the other. In the aforementioned article by McDonnell, Martel herself – always generous in providing insightful keys to delving into her work and world – gives a clue that could link Don Diego to *AI*'s mysterious character: 'This particular futuristic monster of the short film has melancholy not for music, but for hands.' Hands that Zama also lacks at the end of his journey.

Martel has also been involved with projects in areas beyond cinema. In 2015, she directed the recording of the audio-short story collection *Audio Library/Audioteca*, a project supported by the Argentine Ministry of Culture. Curated by the literary critic and screenwriter Graciela Speranza, the compilation gathered thirty short stories – which cross geographies and diverse generations of Argentine writers, from Sara Gallardo to Ricardo Piglia, from Hebe Uhart to César Aira, among others – narrated by thirty eminent actors. Released very discreetly, the anthology was available online for a brief period but published again on several platforms in 2020, when it garnered greater attention.

In 2018, the filmmaker directed the music video for Julieta Laso's song *Fantasmas* ('Ghosts'), which was the flagship release from her album *Martingala*. Ghosts are a recurrent figure in Martel's oeuvre: among their various manifestations, they move the tree branches on the side of the road in *The Holy Girl*, they live with Don Diego in a decrepit lodging in *Zama*, and they haunt both Vero and Aunt Lala in *The Headless Woman*. As in the films, in the music video she does not depict traditional ghosts but makes them present in a subtle way, a ghostly form of filming. The camera is not steady, but instead smoothly floats, while the ambience is old-fashioned and infused with a sort of smoke. Bathed in a faded light, Laso sings in the foreground, other women dance languidly around her, and shadows sporadically cross over their bodies. There are no direct cuts: instead, the images evolve through dozens of slow and gentle superpositions of the same situation. From the combination of these elements, Laso and the other characters acquire an ethereal nature as if they were spectres trapped in this glamorous decadent space.

In 2019, Martel paired with another singer, the renowned Icelandic artist Björk, joining as the theatrical director of her concert *Cornucopia*, conceived from the album *Utopia* (2017). This ambitious sensory techno-acoustic spectacle,

Figure 1.3 Lucrecia Martel with Daniel Giménez Cacho and Matheus Nachtergaele during the filming of *Zama*. Photo by Eugenio Fernández Abril. © Rei Cine SRL, Bananeira Filmes Ltda, El Deseo DA SLU, Patagonik Film Group SA

underscored by a poignant socio-political message about the need for environmental action, was produced by The Shed (an innovative arts venue in New York) as part of its inauguration activities, and toured another nine cities (Mexico City, Brussels, Esch-sur-Alzette, London, Glasgow, Dublin, Oslo, Copenhagen and Stockholm) throughout that year.

THIS VOLUME

This biographical sketch may give the impression of an artist who is difficult to pin down, and whose interests are constantly shifting and evolving. Indeed, the article in *Variety* with which we began suggests that a seemingly deliberate ambiguity and resistance to categorisation are two of the driving forces behind the vast attention that Martel's work has received from film critics and scholars alike. It would be impossible to do justice to the full range of existing writing on Martel within the limitations of this format and in any case the authors of the chapters that follow are careful to acknowledge their debt to previous critical approaches, even as they suggest original and innovative readings. This volume nonetheless hopes to broaden and renew the conversation about this remarkable filmmaker, not least by drawing overdue attention to the formal

diversity of her output, and at the same time identifying philosophical, political and aesthetic threads that run through her oeuvre. One such thread is a
fascination with 'limit points' of all kinds: the limits of language, the limits of
sensory perception, and the limits of empathy and affect. Rather than being
viewed as an indicator of opacity, ambiguity or evasion, this insistent questioning of the limits of cinema might be seen as a liberating act.

In this vein, in the following chapter, originally published in Spanish in
2004, Ana Amado reveals the way in which Martel's first feature-length film
frees its spectators from a temporality bound to the illusion of an unbroken
chain of events. The temporal regime of *The Swamp* expresses itself through
multiple durations and heterogeneous velocities; gestures, attitudes and postures that, as Amado demonstrates, are different for adults, with their dulled
senses, to what they are for children and adolescents, who are animated by a
sensorial potency. This is not an anecdotal point, tied to the plot, but rather a
question of how narrative is affected by bodily presence, and how symptoms
linked to traumatic and persistent historical processes, linking distinct generations, are exposed. In order to understand how Martel constructs a dramatic
minimalism through shots that emphasise the act of *precipitation*, Amado offers
a daring and pioneering reading of the poetics of sedentarism, which presents
bodies that are static to the point of collapse. This approach stands in contrast
to the poetics of nomadism in evidence in a series of contemporaneous films
from Argentina. Amado notes, moreover, points of connection with women
filmmakers who insist on showing, in detail, behaviours and rhythms that indicate a feminine subjectivity in crisis. The course of events and the characters'
pathways stray from the conventions of realism in an entropic movement, a
whirlwind that takes us towards the interiors where conflicts implode.

Remarking that Martel's distrust of traditional film music and her own minimalist use of diegetic music in her films has led to a general inattentiveness to
the musical content of the director's films, Dianna C. Niebylski examines the
fragments of the five cumbias and the folk song heard in *The Swamp* to argue
that they provide additional layers of signification without reducing or compro-
mising the indirectness and open-endedness that characterises Martel's style.
Positioned at the crossroads of film music theory and ethnomusicology, and
focusing on the cumbia genre that became and is still synonymous with *carnaval*
in Northern Argentina, the essay examines both the importance of rhythm and
the ways in which the lyrics extend the film's preoccupation with ethnic prejudice and with gender conflict. Additionally, the chapter also explores instances
where the music fissures the image with political footnotes.

Sound is indeed inevitable when watching a film, as Ana Forcinito states.
In Martel's work, especially in the shorts *Fish, New Argirópolis* and *Muta*, the
disjunction between images and the modulation of voices, whispers and echoes
creates an interweaving that gives body to that which cannot be seen, precisely

because it points us towards what is invisible, or has been made invisible, and to the difficulty of seeing what is taken for granted. Yet this acoustic work does not remove the barriers of classism, racism, sexism or the dominant visual regime by amplifying the audible or by aiming for sonic transparency. Instead, as Forcinito persuasively argues, Martel's cinema explores the difficulty of hearing or understanding clearly. These films do not claim to recover an archive of buried or forgotten collective memories in order to triumphantly display them. They do, however, perceive normative cultural and affective patterns, which are lost from view precisely because they have become part of daily life. These works generate discomfort in the face of the unknown, stemming from an encounter with marginal, almost unintelligible languages and resonances, and leading to confusion and to multisensorial experiences.

It might be said, then, that Martel focuses neither on the clearly audible nor on deepest silence; she does not aim either to frame the visible or to evoke the order of the invisible. Her aesthetic and political preoccupations are not to be found at those extremes, but rather in the channels that flow between them: in multiple forms of silencing and rendering (in)visible. In other words, Martel's cinema is characterised by unbalanced processes, tricks of light, infinite nuances, *glissandi* and mutations, which by pointing to the double-sided nature of perspective make clear its profound ambivalence. In this way, the limits and excesses of ordinary perception also reveal the restrictions associated with being human. Rather than definitive states, the spectator is presented with a series of metamorphoses, which always occur in the realm of the mundane and the routine; they are never supernatural. The opacity and technical virtuosity of Martel's sounds and images not only break with synchronous and coherent representation; they show how far *we ourselves* are made up of incoherent and asynchronous experiences. An anti-Cartesian cinema, then? Probably, since it is never a question of evidence, or of clear and distinct perception. A cinema that is, nonetheless, rational? Perhaps, in that it shows a methodical suspicion of magical thinking and of the dictates of the senses, which are themselves far from innocent. Going against the grain of prefabricated interpretative frameworks, the cinema of Martel shakes up the litany of appearances.

The *monstrous* is at the heart of Martel's conception of fiction, as Mariana Souto and Mônica Campo observe. Think, for instance, of the characters: whether they are men, women, adolescents or children, it is not psychological or sociological difference that marks them out, but their ambiguous relationship to customs and morals. In *Muta*, for example, the creatures can be understood as figures in transformation between chameleonic and automatised states, both human and non-human, which create a sense of mystery and of estrangement. Unlike advertisements for women's clothing, which aim to increase consumption, the short film Martel made for Miu Miu shows bodies shunning their wardrobe, their stilettos, their false eyelashes.

Emilio Bernini examines this experimental quality of Martel's work, viewing it as an autotelic activity, freed from commercial imposition and the constraints of industrial parameters for certain audiovisual formats, such as television series or feature films. By undertaking a thorough review of historical avant-gardes and experimental cinema movements, Bernini finds an illuminating way to rethink the aesthetic radicalism of *Dead King* and *You Won't Get Her, Bastard*, alongside Martel's other short films.

Martel's is a politically committed mode of experimentation: committed to the project of undoing the received wisdom that organises daily family life in a world marked by racism and capitalism, overflowing with chauvinist pedagogy. In this vein, Gonzalo Aguilar argues that in *The Holy Girl*, Martel's second feature, the *apoyada*, the act of pressing one's body against another, acts as a rite of initiation that men try to impose on women, in order to reaffirm their sense of dominion. This bodily performance orders spaces according to relations of power and subordination. Women can be in public space on the condition that their bodies can be touched: Martel's film turns this rule, and the subsequent scene of assault, into a mirror that reflects numerous conflicts. Aguilar explores the contradictory traits of masculinity that lie behind the structure of patriarchy, and shows how the gap between images, sounds, intentions, actions and reactions exposes the flaws in that same structure.

In the final shot of *The Holy Girl*, the two friends swim alongside each other as they hum a song. This sisterly gesture reveals the potency of a feminine affectivity that takes flight in *Cornucopia*, Björk's show. Alejandra Laera immerses herself in the futurist fantasies and the dense sensorial realisms that resulted from this collaboration, in order to propose a stimulating reading of the idea (and act) of *bio-community*. *Cornucopia* invites us to rethink the notion of utopia as a natural, sensorial phenomenon, a proposed transformation that is shaped by forms of ecological care and rooted in the inequality and exclusion suffered by indigenous communities.

This should not be surprising: in Martel's narratives, any approach to reality comes with a critical view of social dynamics. The upper- and middle-class families of the north-western Argentine province of Salta come under frequent scrutiny, bearing as they do the marks of the civic, military and ecclesiastical dictatorship. In Malena Verardi's analysis, Martel's third feature *The Headless Woman* pushes the notion of indeterminacy to an extreme, within a narrative that condenses class arrogance and impunity. At a distance from the suffocating reality that dulls the senses of the protagonist, the film gives body to the disturbing universe around her by placing, in each frame, filters and layers that separate the gaze from its object. At the same time, the process of erasing incriminating evidence is revealed by a lens that shows the details of habitual mechanisms of denial and complicity. Martel's minimalism is in this sense something of a trick, in that her films do not exhibit a clear-cut reality, but rather a world shocked into definition by the spectres that inhabit it.

The insistent use of close-ups and tight frames means that the off-screen world, in Martel's films, is full of sounds that cause physical and psychological distress for the characters, and are no more agreeable to the spectator. For Damyler Cunha, both in *The Headless Woman* and in *Zama*, these absent presences lead to an intensifying sense of vertigo in the face of an uncontrollable element like an accident, an illness or another's decision.

In Adriana Amante's reading, Martel's cinema is an act of thinking, played out in the time that such a process requires. For that same reason, it is an essayistic endeavour, a kind of writing that manifests both as materiality and as duration: it is the process of happening. It is cinema as fluctuation, as a mobile and ever-changing form, distinct from hegemonic narratives that offer plots with a beginning, central crisis and dénouement. This perspective allows Amante to trace an unfamiliar route through Martel's work, from the machine-like music of *Fish* and *Muta* to the (lack of) communication and (il)legible languages of *New Argirópolis* and *Leagues*, and the documentaries about Encarnación Ezcurra and Silvina Ocampo that Martel made in 1999. Throughout, Amante pays particular attention to the practice of eavesdropping or furtive listening, which becomes crucial in *The Holy Girl*.

How to reconstruct a past scarred by conquest? How to bring to life the ghosts of a colony? How to give bodily form to fantastical gossip? These ethical and aesthetic questions lie behind Nora Catelli's succinct and incisive reflections on *Zama* and on certain Spanish reactions to it, originally published in Spain in 2018. The novel by Antonio Di Benedetto, the writings of Félix de Azara, and Juan José Saer's *The Witness/El entenado* are signposts that point Martel towards the imagining of lived experiences of the colonial past, the unsettling of official versions of history, and the weaving of a story made up of dreams, delays and acts of violence.

Attempting a visual image of the past also implies considering the uses and potential meanings of the colour palette. For Deborah Martin, the tonalities of *Zama* challenge the subjective and corporeal boundaries of colonial white masculinity, and at the same time they create an enunciative position for a subaltern voice. Intense colour, typically associated with otherness (whether feminine, 'oriental', primitive or queer), is often devalued, or seen as superficial, secondary or cosmetic. *Zama*, conversely, presents tropical *tableaux* that, when combined with Martel's soundscapes, create a reality that oscillates between the time of the colony, a time of travel and of waiting, and the polyvalent temporalities of indigenous cosmovisions.

When filming from a position of privilege, aiming to represent the experience of an entirely distinct culture is an impossible endeavour, and one that is moreover linked to the Europeanising cultural projects that have marked the history of Latin America. This is not Martel's aim or desire: her cinematic is more closely related to that found in horror film, whose mechanisms foment tension between what is shown and what is insinuated beyond the frame.

David Oubiña's chapter offers an analysis of horror as the mark of a difference that has been repressed and that returns in an uncontrolled, disturbing and threatening form. This dynamic can be traced through Martel's four features and several of her shorts, allowing Oubiña to position indecision as crucial to Martel's way of seeing: the camera never loses its capacity to observe, even as it seems to become infected by the perplexity and confusion of the characters. This perspective, Oubiña suggests, determines a form of realism that is sometimes negligent, sometimes indolent, and sometimes stirs up trouble.

Martel tells a story about a time when, while out walking with her nephew, they saw a man living on the street. Her nephew, astonished, began to ask who he was, why he was there, and what had happened to him. When she told him that the man lived on the street, her nephew immediately wanted to take him home, give him food: in short, to look after him. The boy's immediate response to understanding the situation was a desire to act in the most obvious and humane manner. And yet these actions are (almost) never undertaken. This anecdote is telling: incomprehension in the face of an exploited and plundered world, a gaze that does not become accustomed to brutal social inequalities, and the ability to render strange the habitual forms of perceiving the world around us are some of the aesthetic and ethical pillars of Martel's own practice. Each of these pillars is evidence in the interview that closes this volume, in which the director offers new ways of looking back over her work, and forwards to her new projects.

NOTES

1. Lodge, G. (2020), 'Locarno: Lucrecia Martel's Work-in-Progress Caps an Unusual Career', *Variety*, 7 August 2020, <https://variety.com/2020/film/global/locarno-lucrecia-martels-work-in-progress-caps-an-unusual-career-1234728610/> (last accessed 29 April 2021).
2. The wordplay in Spanish is difficult to capture in translation. 'Fe', in addition to meaning 'faith', sounds like the phoneme 'efe', which is used to represent the letter 'F' in speech.
3. Christofoletti Barrenha, N. (2014), *A experiência do cinema de Lucrecia Martel: Resíduos do tempo e sons à beira da piscina*, São Paulo: Alameda Casa Editorial, p. 99. Oubiña, D. (2007), *Estudio crítico sobre La ciénaga, de Lucrecia Martel*, Buenos Aires: Picnic Editorial, p. 56. Portillo, L. (2014), 'Lucrecia Martel'. Interview conducted within the Academy's Visual History Program Collection, administered by the Academy Foundation's Oral History Projects Department, <https://pstlala.oscars.org/interview/lucrecia-martel/> (last accessed 6 March 2021).
4. Bettendorff, P. and A. Pérez Rial (2014), 'Artilugios de pensamiento: Entrevista a Lucrecia Martel', in P. Bettendorff and A. Pérez Rial (eds), *Tránsitos de la mirada: Mujeres que hacen cine*, Buenos Aires: Libraria, pp. 179–96 (p. 195). Yemayel, M. (2018), 'El ojo extraterrestre', *Gatopardo*, 3 June 2018, <https://gatopardo.com/revista/entrevista-lucrecia-martel/> (last accessed 5 March 2021).
5. 'Podrán decir, / podrán hablar / Y murmurar, y rebuznar / Mas la fealdad que Dios me dio / Mucha mujer me la envidió / Y no dirán que me engrupí / Porque modesta siempre fui.'

6. All box office figures are from INCAA reports, <fiscalizacion.incaa.gov.ar/index_estadisticas_peliculas.php> (last accessed 14 April 2021).

7. See <http://derechoalaciudad.org/> (last accessed 21 April 2021).

8. GPS Audiovisual (2020), 'CHOCOBAR – Presentación de Lucrecia Martel en el Festival de Locarno 2020', YouTube, 14 August 2020, <https://www.youtube.com/watch?v=8O4R3lazLAI> (last accessed 25 April 2021).

9. McDonnell, R. (2020), 'Machine Eye: Lucrecia Martel Discusses AI', *Notebook Mubi*, 23 October 2020, <https://mubi.com/notebook/posts/lucrecia-martel-discusses-ai> (last accessed 14 November 2020).

CHAPTER 2

Speeds, Generations and Utopias: On *The Swamp*

Ana Amado

Time has a stellar role as a succession, as the chronological order or duration of a story, but it can also sediment into a density or thickness different from the targeted vector model. A one-way direction which the temporal convention takes from the human biographical story, nestled between birth and death, and by which time, in cooperation with space and point of view, is subjected to a normalisation and a standardisation of stories and images which are eminently desirable for captive viewers. This is particularly true in film, where space and point of view are literal concepts and require the mediation of movement and, particularly, of staging to ensure the fluidity of a malleable syntax, the illusion of seamless continuity. It is based on this summation of dependences, this indirect representation of temporality, on which Gilles Deleuze reflects as a matter of 'emancipation', of liberation of the image *from* time, and its indirect representation inasmuch as it depends on movement, space and staging to conquer a *direct* temporal representation. This, of course, does not entail doing away with movement, which is central to cinema, but transforming it into an abnormal movement, an 'aberrant' movement, as Deleuze describes it based on its effect of jamming fluidity, of transforming the link between present and past into a conflictive relation, of alluding to the real not as a mirror but as something full of tension and mystery.

This 'aberrant' movement, translated by different alteration ranges, whether it be in spatial layouts, in the dissipation of narrative centres, due to unexpected connections or unpredictable directions, causes the idea of time to emerge directly, unshackled from all syntactic dependencies, and that independence turns it into a problem which is related not only to film, but also to philosophy. Deleuze's 'time-image' is a conceptual distillation in which both fields flow together, film and philosophy, and which the author expands in multiple possibilities and variations.[1] In a similar register, Georges Didi-Huberman's 'symptom-image' extends the above notion, stressing the dysfunctional or paradoxical traits of images when they enable untargeted or discordant movements, to the point of turning time into a process, rather than a regulator of the story.[2] The 'symptom' is that which becomes evident when the normal course of representation is assaulted by 'counter-times' capable of changing the chronological story. It should be mentioned, however, that this does not refer to a mere alteration of the linear succession of events. Narrating several characters and actions simultaneously by means of cross-cutting is now a commonplace and no less arbitrary operation, well on its way to becoming a new convention: in place of the debased narrative device of the flashback, there is an interrupted present. These 'counter-times' refer instead to a temporal regime of images more complex and impure than one attained merely through a simple artifice of staging procedures. Such complexity and impurity can be seen in a film like *The Swamp/La ciénaga* (2001), for instance, with a world which is still or facing extinction, segregated by a series of spatial and temporal collisions, among which stands out, in principle, the unprecedented equation between bodies and temporality.

Deleuze places the body in the series of the time-image not only because it offers a glimpse, he says, of people's inner self — a statement inevitably illustrated by Michelangelo Antonioni's cinema — but for the synthesis of past experiences which can be established therein. His definitions portray the body as a surface of sorts on which the signs of a lived life are inscribed, a potential document which reveals the link between the past and the present, a virtual coexistence of times in gestures and telling everyday attitudes, almost instinctive, and a 'before' and 'after' of the body.

Among Argentine films, *The Swamp* may be the one that enables us to perceive an exceptional sense of temporality, expressed precisely through attitudes and body postures, through the ritualised repetition of the most mundane and trivial actions; that is, through the direct theatricalisation of bodies, whose positions would appear themselves to determine the plot, which is subjected to the slow cadence of stillness and repetition, but also to other rhythms and *speeds*. It could be said that *The Swamp* entails a double speed, to the degree that each generation of protagonists (i.e. adults, and children and teenagers) gives its gestures and movements a different speed. Indeed, this effect of multiple durations, of heterogeneous times born from the combination of physical presence, spatial movements and positions, stands in stark contrast to contemporary policies of image, with their redundant exaltation of marginal or juvenile bodies with reckless, violent, inconsequential or hysterical gestures, with their doses of objection or conflict, but almost always as vehicles for 'reality' or sociology. *The Swamp*, instead, is among those movies which fully trust the power of bodies and gestures not as an anecdotal tether, but in their ability to shape the shot (and to do that from impossible axes, as we shall see), or even to go through the shot and expose themselves as a 'symptom'. If the in-vogue phenomenological Vulgate favours the body as the channel for experience, as the synthesis of an authenticity which is plausible in cinema, resorting to movement, to actions and sensations, those premises assume in Lucrecia Martel their best meaning, to the degree that the presence of the body affects the narrative, more than the mere visual. Rather than furnishing an iconic vision, bodies in *The Swamp* carry the very logic of representation, they instil into the tale their enigmatic, deviant side, and they disorient the units of film grammar which typically take any physical performance and its materiality for an indicator of realism.

A digression is warranted here to rescue female filmmakers' insistence on showing body attitudes as a sign of women's states of mind. In their movies − perhaps not only in theirs, but they represent the majority in this trend − women are shown as revealing a subjectivity in crisis, in the search for their own individuality, their own temporality, together with specific ways of reacting against an era, with attitudes which almost inevitably manifest themselves in private, in the intimate exchange of encounters, which is not restricted to the domestic sphere. As the Latin American heiresses of Agnès Varda or Chantal Akerman − and also of Antonioni, it could be said − female characters are nomads traversing not only places but ages, situations, in films such as those by Mexican director María Novaro; Sandra Gugliotta, who set her urban migratory version in *A Lucky Day/Un día de suerte* (2002); Paula Hernández, in *Inheritance/Herencia* (2001), even though it did so as latency; Celina Murga, in *Ana and the Others/Ana y los otros* (2003); Albertina Carri, in *The Blonds/Los rubios* (2003); and this list, surely incomplete, should not leave out Eduardo Milewicz's *Life According to Muriel/La vida según Muriel* (1997), which pioneered geographic displacement fuelled by existential crisis.

At the opposite pole of transhumance, *The Swamp* is sedentary, with characters reduced to a cloistered life and the repetition of domestic routines, in a fictional world outlined along strict coordinates. If, in narrative terms, family sagas show a tendency towards a horizontality laid out by the chain of actions and emotions, in this case, that progression of successive links is replaced by an entropic movement, a type of inward, imploding movement. With a 'story' that is imprecise or barely glimpsed in the transience of movements, of lateral actions, of the informative resource of a gesture or a posture, narration can only stem from those traits which are material, physical, but also psychic, which make up the miniature world of family societies. Martel adopts the meticulous lens of the anthropologist focused on all details, as if taking them from her memory to show them as symptoms together with the rhythm of sleep, latencies and crises. No hierarchy comes through among important or minuscule events, as if accepting the Benjaminian idea that the story (actually, history) is ultimately segregated by the slightest manifestations of existence.

This dramatic minimalism resorts for its construction to basic time and place data. There is a chronological time: the story takes place during the summer, during the days of carnival, a permanent off-camera reality in which that time of masks and liberation of the bodies takes place, available to a social class which is not that of the protagonists' families: the poor. And, if the carnival dance is updated in images, the goal is not to show the confluence or harmonic coexistence which recent Argentine filmmaking constantly imagines for festive spaces, but the radical (and, this case, literal) clash, from which the upper-class boy emerges wounded, among characters from both sides of the social border. Martel focuses on the social matter which she seeks to describe, the middle class (including its codes of exclusion), and if she approaches subordinate bodies from the perspective and the desire of her teenage protagonist, she leaves them at the margins, alone with their rituals and smells. The field of the visible defines places: domestic interiors and nature, which vie to be the stages of that fabric of viscosity and survival made of the gestures and attitudes of men and women, of children and teenagers who circle the latency of a catastrophe to whose signs they appear impervious.

The stillness, the inertia, the acute perception of an annulled time which these elements convey have, then, no other outlet than physical attraction, and therefore converge in the concept of *precipitation*: something appears to drag everything and everyone down. In *The Swamp*, the precipitation, the downfall, unfurls fictionally, inasmuch as all narrative procedures attempt to tie themselves to the law of gravity. And it also becomes an allegory of fiction, which flows out from the title of the film to the image of the mire which hopelessly sucks in humans and animals.

Figure 2.1 *The Swamp.* © Lita Stantic Producciones

'We must always expect things to happen in conformity with the laws of gravity unless there is supernatural intervention', wrote Simone Weil (a German philosopher and mystic who converted to Catholicism and is admired by Lucrecia Martel, according to an interview) in *Gravity and Grace*. Weil deploys in this book the multiple relationships between time and space, linking them to the high and the low, which from her perspective relate to heaven and earth. Analysing from this spatial and physical standpoint the interpersonal relationships and family conflicts in *King Lear*, for instance, Weil does not hesitate to label them a tragedy of gravity. In this line, Martel assumes in *The Swamp* that the transmission of unease (or of any other movement towards doom or salvation) has physical gravity as its inevitable law. And also that the rules of thermodynamics are functional as a means to translate the world – the world seen from the model of family relations, in this case as a human mechanism doomed to move down, rather than up. 'If we think we gain this deliverance by means of our own energy, we will be like a cow pulling at a hobble and thus falling onto its knees',[3] says Simone Weil in one of her radiant images, in which she blends the immaterial with the laws of physics.

In this equation of lightness – a lightness which, like Weil, Martel appears to associate with the light or grace of hope, faith in the miracle or mere belief – and heaviness, with its collapsing movement, *The Swamp* favours the latter with the pulley of bodies. The prominence granted to gestures, movements, body attitudes and the rhythm of their position in the shot, which turns the most trivial of positions into choreography, finally, with the symbolic power of a story that unfolds between two downfalls (that of a mother toppled by alcohol and that of a child who dies). From one downfall to the next, adults and children collapse onto the ground, or into puddles, or into deck chairs, beds and foul pools, or onto piercing objects which tear their flesh or maim them, as if the impossibility of being upright or always lying down was their true realisation or a revelation of sorts.

The horizontal nature of the shot's format is matched by a horizontal image field. By choosing this horizontal or tilted axis for the postures of bodies, Martel manages to pivot them outside of the vertical, dominant and sublimating condition (after all, the phallus, as a virtual object and imaginary basis for all representation, is designated in an erect position) and references them from sub-human fixations, near animal-like positions: a somewhat similar operation to the body regulations of Samuel Beckett, who challenges the privileges of verticality with characters who are always sitting or just lying down, a direct expression of tiredness. With her choice of a horizontal, *tilted* perspective, Martel attempts a pedagogy of perception of a world which has crumbled, or exploded, and can only be glimpsed in disconnected fragments: a perception which, in turn, places bodies and their positions not as an aesthetic liturgy, but as social and political testimonies of the present. Unlike the bodies from the

Latin American films of the seventies, with vertical bodies which defy the law of gravity (though the exception of Glauber Rocha's cinema should be pointed out, with characters who frequently have their trances and public and private conflicts down on the ground), Martel's do not convey utopias, but pure defeat. This one possible interpretation of the relation between the body and the series of time I pointed out at the beginning, through the condensation it offers of before and after, that is, what remains in it from past experiences and what would appear to herald what is to come. *The Swamp* shows both directions, the traces of the past and the perception of the future in all attitudes of neglect and fatigue. And we can also see the order of time when they reveal the individual and the social they are made of and when they let time shine through in the space between two arrangements of bodies, in the interstice between them. I believe these reasons explain why bodies in *The Swamp* fail to be snared by the new mannerisms, among which the line of movement, the journey, the urban drifts, the pointless transits, to name but a few examples, would be the most noticeable. Rather, they stand out by the singular nature of their *horizontality*.

The time-image can be born from this paradoxical relation, in which stillness is segregated by bodies and attitudes, while space is absent. All the characters of the various generations depicted in *The Swamp* are, one way or another, attentive to a premonition, to the despair of waiting, to a *beyond* which

Figure 2.2 *The Swamp.* © Lita Stantic Producciones

can be geographic (travelling or not to Bolivia to buy school supplies) or heavenly (the apparitions of the Virgin seen by a young neighbour). If every event is related to an alien place, which works as the vessel for a vain expectation or something as shocking as a miracle or a belief, the problem is defined based on an outside point. The image centre is also a response to that other place which is ultimately the location for the point of view of an external observation, that of the narration, which only occasionally matches the internal view of Momi, a teenage character who, in the game of imperceptible oppositions between sleep and wakefulness, is the only one who identifies the details of a 'problem', or sees 'too much', even though she will ultimately accept her failure as a seer when attempting to see the material traces of a miracle.

However, there are differences both subtle and significant which affect the cog-like repetition of elements and alter the passive organisation of those components: variations translated by the genealogical times which coexist in the present of the hills of Salta, which are expressed through two speeds or rhythms. On the one hand, we have the world of adults, ruled by alcohol's unsteady movement. They do not stumble, but conquer a posture, that of alcoholics, which is associated with the cloister which heralds paralysis, as the route that takes the mother from room to room and ultimately to the circuit of her bed. Children and teenagers, on the other hand, take movement back. They play pretend and replicate the world of adults, they create their own world inside the larger world with the same elements, but with a different rhythm. Even though they adopt different combinations, lying in the mother's bed, alone or hugging in twos and threes, they offer a different view of what happens on the ground or when lying down, they abruptly interrupt the lethargy of movement with an unexpected sense of speed and violence in the awkward movements of their races and chases. Temporality, held still and subjected to the law of gravity, is interrupted or 'crossed' by these ephemeral explosions in which time is expressed as speed, linked solely to the rhythms of childhood.

Opposed to adults as a block of numbed perceptions (they would appear incapable of noticing falls, wounds on themselves and others, or even the rain against their skin), the bodies of children are astonishing at *communicating*, crossing as a loud and promiscuous entity the exterior spaces (the woods, the garden, the town streets, when they run from the water balloons: the apparitions of children energise the internal movement of shots), or disturbing the domestic stillness with unbridled gestures and shrill voices. In any event, in *The Swamp*, their vulnerable bodies are the only source of the unexpected and the disarray of the present.

'A playing child invents the conditions of his knowledge and history', claims Walter Benjamin.[4] There is a state of experience in their relation to the world and things, situated between the tactile and olfactory power of children — which becomes a way to survive — different from the numb existence of adults.

Where the latter establish a radical divide with their environment (with children, family, friends and objects), children re-establish a relation to the world, to the outdoors, with peers, with the other. Theirs is a different type of spatial perception, which incorporates the idea of *trajectory*, a concept held by Paul Virilio as the ideal way of recovering the physical, psychic and cultural space lost to technological globalisation.[5] The *trajectivity* put forward by Virilio as the unavoidable foundation for the relationship between subject and object is, in *The Swamp*, an idea insinuated − partially, perhaps as the single utopia − only in the generation of children and teenagers, but as an energy without direction, inherently uncontrollable and ultimately taken over by inertia. Between the two types of trajectories (downwards, subject to the law of gravity with the annulment of time, or in the horizontal nature of the sudden movement of children as a recovery of speed and space within the objective temporal coordinates required by the existence of the world and others), characters in *The Swamp* remain, however, trapped between the promise of life and a terrifying threat to this plenitude. Thus, the clash between the speed of children's movements and the sluggishness of matter is won by the latter. Matter lumps together, like the fermented pool water, and obstructs itself in a pure accumulation of debris. And in that accumulation of materialities (in the matter of bodies and ruined things, in the games of children, in language habits, in decadent behaviours), something emerges which is like the prehistory of a culture, as if every person was, in his or her way, the trace or the remnant of that past.

The past (which in *The Swamp* is, based on the above, a psychological indicator, rather than a dramatic one) resorts to language as well to be evoked and passed by the adults to the new generations. 'Children are political prisoners', said Deleuze, less optimistically than Benjamin as regards inheritances. Children, in this case, are prisoners of the aberrant version of transmission, an unfathomable magma of information about bonds and betrayals of others or of one's own vocation, as a complement of a domestic system in which adult language is but a redundancy of contradicting orders or mandates, while children employ it in stories of horror, loss and despair.

Until we reach the death of a child. Actually, the film as a whole advances based on the premonition of that death, even though the children themselves are the ones who make that death evident when toying with that enigma. They are the only ones who can portray corpses in a game, the only ones who 'play dead', who refuse to breathe, who attempt those paradoxical poetics of survival or simply an imaginary disintegration which assumes death as if it was real: they are always hovering near the risk of standing in the way of a bullet, of getting lost, of drowning in the stagnant water of a pool (these plot foreshadowing devices are what make that death plausible, turning its almost arbitrary cruelty into a dramatic 'necessity'). Until a child effectively dies, an aspect which this fiction portrays as unavoidable in the troubled novel of the family.

The boy dies in silence, without language. There are no images or sound for his death: only a temporal gap in the flow of everyday repetitions, a fracture which remains off-screen (Martel's chaining of shots works through an operation of subtraction: the interval between the action in a shot and the next makes any reaction impossible, or that reaction rebounds further into the plot, as in the short feature *Dead King/Rey Muerto*, 1995), and abruptly interrupts that repetition, perhaps to begin a new one, but set in the general decline of all belief and certainty.

Pessimism and the cancellation of the idea of future is a recurring topic in contemporary Argentine cinema – and in global cinema, it could be said – produced, like *The Swamp*, during the turning point between centuries or to open a new one. However, I have tried so far to highlight Martel's narrative choices, who even taking the family as a vantage point to analyse society, eludes the trap of psychologism and moral crisis so frequent in that trend, and proposes instead an approach which can be construed as an anthropological document: ages and generations, customs and attitudes of men, women, children, revealing heterogeneous modalities of time and of its rhythms (present, past and future, detention, repetition, speeds) as the formal key of a poetics and cipher of the private reproduction of collective trauma, with its indefinable dose of comedy and tragedy.

Translated by Juan Ignacio García Fahler

NOTES

* This text was originally published in Spanish ('Velocidades, generaciones y utopías: A propósito de *La ciénaga*, de Lucrecia Martel') in Yoel, G. (ed.) (2004), *Pensar el cine 2*, Buenos Aires: Manantial, pp. 187–97.
 1. Deleuze, G. (1987), *La imagen-tiempo: Estudios sobre cine 2*, Barcelona: Paidós.
 2. Didi-Huberman, G. (2000), *Devant le temps*, Paris: Les Éditions de Minuit.
 3. Weil, S. (1994), *La gravedad y la gracia*, Madrid: Trotta, p. 55.
 4. Benjamin, W. (1987), *Dirección única*, Madrid: Alfaguara, p. 56.
 5. Virilio, P. (1997), *La velocidad de liberación*, Buenos Aires: Manantial, p. 159.

CHAPTER 3

Sounding Class, Race and Gender in *The Swamp*

Dianna C. Niebylski

'No aspect of music is capable of being understood independently of the wider gamut of social and cultural processes ... Yet, because of this, it is possible that there are aspects of social and cultural processes which are revealed uniquely through their musical articulation.'

John Shepherd and Peter Wicke[1]

Interviewed for the Argentine film journal *Lumière* in 2009 after the release of *The Headless Woman/La mujer sin cabeza* (2008), Lucrecia Martel observed that film audiences respond differently to (non-musical) sound than they do to music:

[music] is like a net where the spectator rests, and [s]he remains there in some way, contained, prodded, scared, [yet] always supported by something. Instead, when the film works with sound, the spectator has to be mentally attuned in order to make sense of it all.[2]

In an earlier interview with Jason Wood for *Talking Movies: Contemporary Directors in Interview*, Martel noted her objections to conventional film music on the grounds that it 'leads the viewer to anticipate and even prejudge what's next', whereas sound 'only allows one to face what one is seeing at the moment'.[3] Film music scholars agree. Theorising the effects of the 'core musical lexicon' most commonly heard in films intended for wide audiences, in her 1987 *Unheard Melodies: Narrative Film Music*, Claudia Gorbman observed that 'music [. . .] anchors the image in meaning, throws a net around the floating visual signifier, [and] assures the viewer of a safely channelled signified'.[4] More recently, in *Dreams of Difference, Songs of the Same: The Musical Moment in Film*, Amy Herzog states that non-diegetic music 'stabilises the image and secures meaning while remaining as unobtrusive as possible'.[5]

Martel's refusal to use conventional film scoring puts her in a category of filmmakers that practise what Danijela Kulezik-Wilson calls an 'aesthetics of reticence', one defined by 'restraint and a certain level of ambiguity [as] the basic conditions for allowing individuated responses to film'.[6] Partly because of Martel's comments on the subject of film music, partly because the music that is heard in her films is unrecognisable to most audiences, scholars have largely ignored, or dismissed as irrelevant, the music that forms a small but not insignificant part of her films' soundtracks. This lack of interest in the musical content of the director's sound design is especially noticeable in publications that address Martel's greatly admired approach to sound design in the three films that have come to be known as the director's 'Salta Trilogy' (*The Swamp/La ciénaga* [2001], *The Holy Girl/La niña santa* [2004] and *The Headless Woman*).[7]

To address this deaf spot in the considerable literature on Martel's sound work, this chapter examines the pre-existent diegetic music in *The Swamp*, the much acclaimed first film in the trilogy. Added together and including the music heard in the final credits, the musical fragments account for only twelve minutes and thirty-seven seconds of the hour and forty minute film. Yet close attention to the five cumbias recorded for the film by two local Salta bands and the folk song sung by the famous folk singer Jorge Cafrune reveals that every aspect of the music – including but not limited to the choice of genres, song lyrics and rhythmic patterns – has been carefully conceived to add one or more layers of signification both to the particular scenes in which the music is heard and to the film's narrative(s) in general.[8] Locating my analysis at the crossroads of film music studies, musical semiotics and socio- and ethno- musicology, I propose to show that even some the shortest snippets of music fissure the image with sociocultural and/or political footnotes through which the wider issues of social conflict and political memory are articulated.[9] At the same time, the frequent use of irony in these musical fragments ensures that music does nothing to reduce the film's commitment to reticence and ambiguity. What the source music does *not* do, with one brief exception, is to tell the audience how to interpret the images or characters on the screen. In fact, Martel's use of music is in many ways a primer for subverting mainstream cinema's exploitation of the musical soundtrack for affect without dispensing with music altogether.

Although *The Swamp* will be familiar to most readers of this book, a brief summary is in order. The film unfolds through a succession of loosely bound scenes that revolve primarily around the figures of two unhappy women and their troubled domestic situation. What little action there is takes place in a provincial town in northern Argentina during carnival season, which in these provinces can last long enough time for a young woman who may have lost her virginity midway through the film to find out that she is pregnant. The film dialogue is scarce and discontinuous, yet it is from these fragments that viewers must piece together the characters' relation to each other, the source of their dissatisfaction and bits of their history. Visual clues and snippets of conversation convey the entrenched ethnic prejudices of the provincial middle and upper classes and the ambivalent sexuality of adolescents. Easy to miss among ambient noises and sound effects, the source music heard at various points in the film extends the film's treatment of these themes.

THE CUMBIAS: SOUNDING ETHNIC PREJUDICE AND COMPLICATING GENDER STEREOTYPES

'Estos "indios" con su música, machaca que machaca no dejan dormir a nadie.'

('These "Indians" with their thumping music day and night, they don't let anyone sleep.')

Tali, in *The Swamp*

'To study the cumbia is to bring forth problems of race, gender and ethnicity, possibly in ways that no other cultural product in contemporary Argentina can reveal.'

Pablo Alabarces and Malvina Silba[10]

Almost the entirety of what takes place in *The Swamp* occurs during carnival season, yet this detail is only rarely seen as relevant in discussions of this film.[11] In Argentina as elsewhere, the actual carnival holidays take place the weekend before Lent, but in Salta, as in the neighbouring province of Jujuy, festivities associated with *carnaval* retain much of their pre-Hispanic, pre-Catholic traditions, so that the festivities can start as early as January and extend until the day of the big celebration in late February or March. Luis Guantay, the Salta musician whose band Luis y sus Colombianos performs two of the cumbias in this film, explains that in Salta carnival festivities are inseparable from the outdoor *carpas* (large tents) and the *carpera* tradition exclusive to this province, a tradition that consists of setting up large outdoor tents where the area's local population – and especially those who cannot afford to go to or are not welcome in dance halls – can gather to drink and dance during the extended carnival season. In an unpublished thesis on the *carpas* and origins of cumbia co-authored with Fatima Colombo, Luis's son Javier Guantay observes that *carpera* music and dancing have been inseparable from cumbia since the 1960s.[12] If the syllogism stands, for over half a century, in Salta *carnaval* means cumbia.[13]

Given this background, the cumbias and cumbia fragments heard in the film are as much a part of its sonic realism as the screeching sound of the metal chair legs being dragged around the cement that borders the pool in the film's opening sequence. As diegetic music, sometimes blasting and sometimes barely audible, made to sound as though broadcast over the radio (mostly car, truck or transistor radios), cumbias are the spare musical accompaniment to several of the street scenes and the aural equivalent of the visual signs of carnival in the film (water balloons, little girls in costumes, dancers with painted faces). As such, cumbia sounds remind audiences of the local and cultural background against which the two women protagonists' private lives unravel in slow motion. Aside from the infusion of realism they bring to certain scenes, cumbia beats make audible, and sometimes literally raise the volume on, the class and ethnic rifts that traverse the film.

'[C]umbia is "poor people's music" across Latin America', note Pablo Alabarces and Malvina Silba, echoing what virtually all recent studies of cumbia state at the outset. The authors add that Argentina is no exception, but with a difference. While the association of cumbia with race as well as class is not uncommon in much of Latin America, in Argentina it is unavoidable, and the Argentine middle and upper classes have long perceived cumbia to be *música de negros*. As all Argentine cumbia scholars point out, the racial slur does not link cumbia to Afro-Argentines who might be counted as fans of the musical genre but to the mestizo traits of large segments of the poor, particularly in Argentina's northern provinces. Pablo Vila and Pablo Semán, Héctor Fernández L'Hoeste and Alejandra Cragnolini observe that the racialisation of cumbia in Argentina can be traced both to the influx of migrants from these provinces to Buenos Aires which dates back to the 1940s, and to the influx of external migrant workers from the neighbouring countries of Bolivia and Paraguay – nations with substantial indigenous and mestizo populations.[14] Deborah Pacini Hernández sees Argentina's equation of poverty and race as the rule rather than the exception for Latin American countries, stating that 'contemporary cumbia is the voice of the working class, and particularly the migrant workers – most of whom are mestizos (rather than African)'.[15]

The link between cumbia and the indigenous and mestizo bodies moving in and around the town of La Ciénaga (The Swamp) is in plain sight in this film. With two exceptions (the second one in the final credits), the cumbias are visually linked to the Amerindian or mestizo-looking characters featured in many of the outdoor scenes. Not incidentally, the brown-skinned Perro ('dog', as he is called), his equally brown-skinned friends and Isabel (referred to throughout the film by Mecha as 'esta india') are often the focal point or play a crucial role in these scenes. Cumbia sounds emerge from the truck driven by Perro's friend in the scene where Isabel asks him if they would give Vero and the other white adolescents a ride to the dam, and again when the truck drops them off. A cumbia plays when Isabel visits Perro at a billiard bar, and a cumbia is heard when Isabel and Perro exit the clothing shop where Vero asks Perro to serve as a human torso so she can guess her brother's size. Referring to *The Swamp*, Blake Williams writes that the 'pure inertia' of the upper classes 'is put in competition with the rhythms of the natural world'. Williams appears to be unaware of the music in this film. Had he heard the cumbias, he would have found that the beat by which the ethnic population marks its time also provides a stark contrast to middle- and upper-class immobility.[16]

Tali is the only character in the film who explicitly equates cumbia with the marginalised ethnic population in the scene where she complains about 'these "Indians" with their thumping music [who] don't let anyone sleep', implicitly transposing the degrading *música de negros* into the equally degrading *música de indios*.[17] Yet the association between ethnic prejudice and cumbia music can be heard much earlier in the film, although in a more oblique fashion. Towards the end of the remarkable opening scene, Isabel, the family's domestic servant, tells Momi to bring the family car up to the house so that the wounded Mecha can be taken to the clinic in town. Seconds later, a cumbia is heard, acousmatically at first but soon revealed to be coming from a car radio, as a nervous Momi turns up the volume while trying to turn it off. For a few seconds, the singer's voice overwhelms other noises, competing only with a drunken Mecha's furious 'déjame Isabel' ('leave me alone, Isabel') while the young woman is helping her walk to the car. As Momi proves incapable of working the knobs on the radio, Isabel leans inside the car and quickly turns off the music. The act of turning the radio off could simply be another example of Isabel's competence and practicality. Once we identify the music as a *cumbia*, however, the domestic servant's gesture can be interpreted as an instinctive Bourdieusian response of someone who does not need to have read Bourdieu to know that the cumbia sound will only intensify Mecha's racially fuelled anger.[18] Immediately after Isabel turns off the cumbia, Mecha tells Momi to bring her another dress because 'esta india' would have her go to the clinic in a housedress.[19]

This music lasts only ten seconds, but the lyrics the audience hears when the radio volume is turned up speak of the frustration of a man whose lover has left him and will someday pay for doing so: 'Mala mujer, vas a pagar muy caro / porque en esta vida, todo se paga' ('Cruel woman, you will pay dearly / because in this life everything has a price'). Gustavo Costantini observes that while the lyrics heard in this scene can be interpreted as empathetic because they seem to apply to the characters (Mecha, in this case), the music itself seems anempathetic.[20] Contrasted against the pale, drunken, bloated bodies that can barely manage to walk to their cars to escape the rain, the cumbia rhythm is undoubtedly incongruent. On the other hand, given the likelihood that the car radio will only pick up local stations and that local stations would be broadcasting carnival dance music during carnival season, the cumbia is simply part of the sonic-*verité* of the scene. The raised volume of the car radio, however, draws too much attention to lyrics that can only be referring to Mecha, and thus would be too crude a sign for a director who trades in ambiguities. Ana Forcinito finds that the intrusion of loud and abrupt sounds throughout *The Swamp* 'allow the expression of the repressed'.[21] This is a persuasive point with respect to non-verbal sounds, but assuming that the lyrics are there to voice Isabel's or Momi's silent resentment towards Mecha, they would also be an example of narrative as well as musical redundancy. Instead, I perceive the lyrics in this scene to have a quasi-comic effect, one intended to diffuse what might otherwise be a too (melo)dramatic ending to the opening sequence. Contrary to what one might expect, here the cumbia has the effect of temporarily diminishing the tension shown on-screen. At the same time, it is tempting to think that ramping up the volume on the hyper-allusive lyrics is an ironic gesture on the part of a director who makes no secret of her antipathy for film music that tells the audience what to think of or feel about a character.

Three other cumbias are heard within the film and a fourth one during the credits. In only two instances are the cumbias heard in their entirety, but just once within the film (the second cumbia plays during the final credits). As befits the film's musical realism, the cumbia that is heard from beginning to end is the dominant sonic accompaniment to the carnival dance scene that takes place approximately midway through the film. Martel sets up the contrast in musical taste (and class prejudice) by having the carnival patio or *carpa* scene follow Tali's complaint, in the preceding sequence, about the *indios* with their pounding music. Referring to Martel as well as to other film directors grouped under the New Argentine Cinema, Gonzalo Aguilar claims that scenes involving dancing or festive gatherings 'allowed new directors not only to show the predicament of bodies and tastes [. . .] but also to highlight group and class conflicts'.[22] The abrupt transition between the silence that surrounds Tali standing in her patio after she shuts a wooden window that probably faces the street, and the loud cumbia heard a second before the screen registers a group of mostly young men dancing in the next scene magnifies the sense of social, ethnic and racial divide that hovers over the entire film. The music that Tali deplores is almost certainly the same music that provides the beat for the mostly mestizo bodies seen enjoying themselves on the dance floor in the first two minutes of the sequence. As noted earlier, Pierre Bourdieu's rigid notions regarding the 'infallibility' of musical tastes as a marker of one's class have been partially discredited by more recent studies, but in the conservative, deeply divided atmosphere portrayed in the film they continue to hold sway. It is true that José and his white, upper-class friends are part of the dancing crowd in the carnival scene, but even their dance moves show them as outsiders in this space. If the cumbia divides, it also unites. In the carnival scene, group solidarity and class enmity are on display, and once again Isabel is caught in between.

In *The Sociology of Rock*, Simon Frith claims that it is not in the lyrics but 'in the sound and rhythm' that a genre's ideology is recorded.[23] The rhythmic and tonal organisation of cumbia is simpler and slower than other popular Latin American dance music (such as salsa, mambo or rumba), in large part because of the influence of indigenous Andean music on the subgenre of cumbia heard in the film. Although Perro and his cousin appear to be doing little more than shuffling to the beat when the camera focuses on them in the first seconds of this sequence, shuffling to the beat is all that is expected of cumbia dancers – no complicated steps, no hip gyrations or arm contortions needed. The bodies of most of the dancers in the carnival scene are certainly more animated than the lethargic, largely bedridden bodies in Mecha's household and less anxious than Tali's constant pacing to nowhere. At the same time, the unchanging rhythm that mobilises these bodies reflects and encourages a practice, if not a politics, of resistance. On the dance floor, resistance means expending just enough energy to last through the night. Off the dance floor, the modest pace can become a steady but sustained defiance. Mamina, Mecha's older indigenous servant, has

Figure 3.1 *The Swamp*. © Lita Stantic Producciones

no choice but to attend to Mecha's commands, but she will do so in her own time and at her own pace.

While the camera is focused on Perro and his friends the music is strictly instrumental, with the electric guitar marking the rhythm. Only when the camera captures Isabel as she listens to Perro asking her to go buy a beer does the vocalist begin to sing. Throughout this sequence, the lyrics are perfectly audible. The cumbia, titled 'Salud amigo' (a 1985 hit by the Peruvian musician Julio Carhuajulca Capuñay) features two speakers, both male (sung by the same performer in the version we hear). The first speaker is drinking to forget or to remember the woman who left him: 'Voy a beber, por la que se marchó / ella ha dejado sin motivo mi querer / la amaba tanto / que hoy no sé qué hacer / me ahogo en llanto / por esa mujer' ('I drink to the one who left me for no reason / I loved her so / I don't know what to do / I'm drowning in tears / for that woman'). We hear these lyrics as Isabel walks to the bar to buy Perro's beer. On her way there, she is surprised by José, who embraces her as he continues to move to the beat. For her part, she appears genuinely happy to see him but quickly moves on. At this point the first speaker in the cumbia is still drowning in his tears. As Isabel continues to walk towards the bar, she must navigate the attention of other males who reach out to touch her face or her hair, but we do not know if Perro sees any of this or if he is bothered by it. As she nears the bar the second speaker in the cumbia tells the jilted lover to stop drinking (over a woman) and pledges to take care of him ('No bebas más / amigo más que amigo / eres mi hermano y te tengo que cuidar' ['Stop drinking, my friend / You are my brother and I'll take care of you']). The words of the second speaker soon reveal that the show of friendship is simply an overture for mounting a diatribe against all women. While Isabel waits for the beer, the friend tells the despondent lover that 'there is nothing more to say about women' ('de las mujeres, no hay nada más que hablar'): 'Las hay muy malas / y las buenas son igual' ('Some are really cruel / and the good ones are no better'). Beer in hand, Isabel turns to walk back, still defending herself against another man's efforts to touch her or stop her. As she walks by José and his friends, a half-drunken José makes half-hearted efforts to stall her while his (male) friends shower him with attention, almost as if competing with Isabel for his affection. This time her face registers irritation, and she quickly disentangles herself, walking back to where Perro, his cousin and other friends are standing. As the singer repeats the refrain about women making men suffer and cry, Isabel is shown speaking to a sullen-looking Perro, and her expression as she talks to him can only mean that she is telling him to ignore José. Ignoring Isabel, Perro listens to his cousin, who apparently goads him into to picking a fight. At this point the singer stops and the acoustic guitar takes over, while the timbales, drum and the brass (produced by an electric synthesiser) mark the beat long enough to give Perro time to move through the dance floor and headbutt an unsuspecting José. The latter loses consciousness and has to be carried out by his friends.[24]

There are two competing stories in this cumbia: in one, a heartbroken man wants to drink himself to oblivion and drown in his own tears over the woman who has left him; in the other, a second male vents his frustrations against all women while promising to take care of his friend. Although we do not hear any of the dialogue in this scene, the images on the screen suggest that neither Perro nor José is especially interested in Isabel throughout the sequence (Perro remembers her only when he needs someone to go buy a beer for him and his friends; José quickly forgets her after glancing in her direction as she walks on). Taking this into account, it would appear that the first speaker's words do not describe either young man's feelings for Isabel. It is the second speaker's promise of male solidarity in the face of faithless women that applies equally well to both sides of the class divide.

Discussing this scene (though generally ignoring the music), several scholars speak of José's sense of entitlement in attempting to seduce his family's maid, thus justifying Perro's quick reaction. I propose that Perro's fury against José cannot be properly understood without taking into account his humiliation, possibly only hours before the carnival scene, at the hands of Vero, José's sister.[25]

In the scene that takes place in a clothing store Vero, accompanied by Momi and Tali's stepdaughter Augustina, is shopping for a t-shirt for her brother José. When she asks her sister if she knows their brother's size, Momi says that Perro is outside. Vero then asks Isabel to call Perro so she can use him as a mannequin to gauge her brother's size by comparison.[26] Another cumbia plays outside, presumably coming from a car radio on the street, but because it can be heard for only seconds when Isabel or Perro opens the shop door, and even then the sound is 'dirty', so the only words that can be heard, with effort, are 'lágrimas heladas' ('frozen tears'). The frozen tears might be Isabel's or Momi's (but not Perro's, or not yet Perro's at this point). I resist the temptation to say more for the simple reason that even these words might be inaudible to most audiences.

Once inside the clothing store, Perro tells Vero that José is bigger than him, but Vero insists that he try on the shirt all the same. As his friends look on from the other side of the glass door, Perro is first ogled by Vero (he is muscular and his sweaty skin gives him a sexy glow in this scene), then summarily dismissed without a 'thank you'. No sooner has he left than Vero smells the item and, making a gesture of disgust, hands the t-shirt to Augustina, who throws the item down on a table. Perro may not see Vero's gesture, but replaying the scene afterwards, after having been teased by his friends, and remembering Isabel witnessing his humiliation, he would feel only rage. Not surprisingly, then, when José's mild flirtation with Isabel presents him with the excuse he needs to take out his anger on Vero and her family, he takes it. Viewed from this angle, the lyrics voiced by the cynical friend in 'Salud amigo' ('Cheers My Friend') may well reflect the resentment of men like Perro, men who are economically powerless, socially marginalised and routinely humiliated on the basis of their skin colour and ethnicity. As does the friend in the cumbia, these men often take out their frustrations on women who are similarly disempowered and are more likely to become the target of these men's frustrations, as also shown in the song's lyrics.

The last cumbia heard before the closing credits is 'Deudas' ('Debts'), performed by Los Varoniles Lirios Salteños. At first the music appears to be non-diegetic, but soon the nasal sound leads one to assume it is being played on a small radio. The music begins as Isabel walks into a billiard bar to find Perro and continues to play while she talks to him. Her words are inaudible, but most viewers will assume that she has come to tell him she is pregnant (a logical assumption, given that it takes place shortly after Perro, over Isabel's repeated 'no(s)', dragged her into the water and, presumably, had sex with her there). With effort, most of the lyrics can be made out. Once again it is a male who tells the woman who left him that she will pay for breaking his heart ('porque tú hiciste sufrir mi corazón / es una deuda que tienes que pagar / como se pagan las deudas de un amor' ['because you made me suffer / there is a debt you will have to pay / since love debts must be paid']).[27] Too preoccupied with the situation they are in, neither Isabel nor Perro is likely to be listening to the music. But audience members attentive enough to the lyrics may want to decide whether the debt is not Perro's rather than Isabel's. Realistically, it will be Isabel who will bear the burden of what we assume is an unplanned pregnancy, as Perro does not seem to have the maturity to take on the responsibility of being a husband and a father.[28] In any event, this is the second cumbia that speaks of a debt to be collected later.[29]

While cumbia rhythm is what marks carnival time and makes group solidarity possible for the ethnic population that identifies with the genre, there is little doubt that the cumbias heard in the film were also chosen for their lyrics. If the cumbia genre and rhythm extend the film's narrative on class and ethnic prejudice, the cumbia lyrics both support and complicate the film's attitude towards gender roles and gender relations. On the surface, 'Salud amigo' and 'Deudas' seem to share the same misogynist attitude of the speaker in 'Mala mujer', which is heard once more in the film, but barely and for a few seconds, in the scene where Vero asks Perro and his friends if they are going to the dam ('el dique'). As a popular music genre that is overwhelmingly dominated by male writers and musicians (like tango, rock, hip hop and rap), cumbia is mired in systemic sexism. Yet unlike cumbia *villera*, the urban, in-your-face cumbia style that dominated urban *bailantas* in the 1990s and continues to be the subject of cumbia studies in Argentina because of its aggressively political stance, the cumbia *norteña* (also called cumbia *romántica*) heard in the film is not seriously confrontational. There is neither obscenity nor violence in any of the cumbias included in the film.[30]

Sexism and even misogyny are indeed present in the lyrics, in which men wish women ill and declare them cruel simply because these women have left them. Yet with the exception of 'Mala mujer', the cumbia lyrics that can be heard in the film include at least one male speaker who has been devastated by the loss of the woman he loved. Two of these men drown in tears (liquid or frozen), one tells the woman who has made him suffer that he will not cry, but only because life has taught to him to live in pain ('No, no voy a llorar / porque la vida es una escuela de dolor' [No, I will not cry / because life has schooled me in pain']), and the last one ('Amor divino' ['Amazing/Divine Love']) blames his heart for continuing to pine after the 'divine' woman that once loved him but has only superlatives for the woman. As a band of lonely brothers, these men (at least those who do not put women down or tell them they'll have their comeuppance) are weepy sentimentalists rather than confirmed misogynists. It is unlikely that anyone hearing these lyrics will shed a tear for them, but they sound more pitiable than despicable.

It is in this respect that the cumbia lyrics in the film provide a counterpoint to the images of the stifled and trapped women protagonists and, in so doing, point us back in the direction of the two differently 'abandoned' males in the film. The most abject of the two is Gregorio, Mecha's alcoholic husband. Rather than abandon him, Mecha exiles him from her bedroom, rendering him even more impotent than we imagine he already is at the beginning of the film. It is impossible to know if Gregorio is a disappointment to Mecha because he is a serial adulterer, because he has no head for business, or because he is a drunk who has driven her to drink. Whether Gregorio drinks to forget a lost love (Mercedes? Mecha?), the film's depiction of his fear of ageing and the utter disregard in which his children hold him is more pitiful than comical (although little Mariana's and Luchi's mock horror at the fact that he dyes his hair is very funny). Apparently at the other end of the husband-material scale is Rafael. Hard-working, caring, a hands-on dad, he is the antithesis of Gregorio, yet he too suffers from his wife's disappointment in him. With his stocky, short body and homely face, his humble origins – judging by his accent – and his mixed heritage – judging by his appearance – he must be an unpleasant reminder, for Tali, of the unglamorous life she wants to escape. No doubt he should have been perceptive enough to see Tali's wish to travel to Bolivia (a trip that is Mecha's idea) as a harmless attempt to escape her domestic boredom for a weekend and put his concerns about her safety aside. Even so, Tali's insensitivity towards the forlornness he projects in every scene is at least as regrettable as his obtuseness towards her need to escape the confines of her small middle-class home and his overly paternalistic watch over her.

Writing about *The Swamp*, Julián Gutiérrez-Albilla contends that Martel's film offers 'a representational and critical alternative to an orthodox feminist political project', adding that 'the film cannot be interpreted as a mere condemnatory critique of family, sexual, social, generational or racial miscommunication of hostility, which would lead to total social disintegration'.[31] There are many ways in which *The Swamp* resists condemning any one character or behaviour. The fact that most of the cumbia lyrics balance the implicit hostility towards women with the pathos of men who mourn their absence without ascribing blame to them is another instance of Martel's reluctance see or hear in black and white, opting for nuances over unequivocal pronouncements.[32]

THE FOLK SONG: CHILDREN, ENTRAPMENT AND PREMONITIONS OF DEATH

Nearly halfway into *The Swamp*, Vero, lounging on her mother's bed (around which much of the film's loose narrative revolves), presses the 'on' button on an old tape player, and for the first time in the film the characters respond to the music that the audience also hears. As soon as the first chords of a children's folk song fill the room, José, the only male in the scene, begins to move to the beat, at first mockingly, with movements that are robot-like, but the mockery ends quickly as the other characters in the scene slowly join in the dance. First his sister Vero joins him, and soon all but two of the characters in the cramped, semi-lit bedroom are dancing at the foot of the bed. Mecha, presiding over the scene from the bed, is seen laughing for the first and only time in the film. Tali looks both blissful and wistful as she dances with José. Tali's youngest daughter, eerily serious for her age in most scenes, is heard squealing with delight when José picks her up for a turn. Even Momi, the unhappiest of the adolescent characters, smiles contentedly as she looks on at the dancers. At no other time does the film convey the sense of quasi-choreographed congeniality or uncomplicated pleasure as in this brief scene. In a film in which unfulfilled yet vaguely defined desires trouble many of the characters, the dancing bodies in this bedroom scene appear almost child-like. The soft focus of the images further contributes to casting an aura of unreality over the scene, as if the entire episode were a ghostly projection; a miracle sponsored by the Virgin whose apparitions Tali was recounting before the music started.

The song 'El niño y el canario' ('The Boy and the Canary') dates back to the mid-1950s, when it was first performed on National Radio Belgrano by its composer, Hilario Cuadros and Los Trovadores de Cuyo, but it did not become widely popular until Jorge Cafrune and Leonardo Favio – both important references for Martel – recorded separate and very different versions of it in the early 1970s. Favio's version is a pop arrangement of the song with an electronic musical accompaniment; in Cafrune's arrangement, in the style of simple folk music, the singer relies only on an acoustic guitar.[33] Although there is no strict pairing of the guitar accompaniment with the camera movement in any rigid

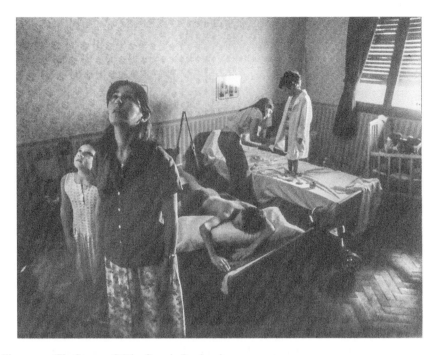

Figure 3.2 *The Swamp.* © Lita Stantic Producciones

way, the rhythm of the guitar accompanies the eye of the camera as the latter travels back and forth from medium shots of the changing dance partners to over the shoulder shots of the characters' wistful or elated faces.

The simple chord progression on the lone acoustic guitar has the rhythmic pattern normally associated with the habanera, the Cuban musical genre that merged the Spanish eighteenth-century 'contradanza' (country music, or rural dance) with Afro-Cuban rhythms to give Latin American music one of its most enduring traits: a non-Western style of syncopation. In turn, the melody, carried only by the singer's voice, registers a complementary rhythm.[34] Still in 4/4 time, the singer's less obvious syncopation makes the melody sound as if written in 6/8 time, the time typical of pre-Columbian music common to the indigenous tribes of Altiplano (the Andean plateau covering north-western Argentina, part of Bolivia and part of Peru). Martel's choice of Cafrune (whose family lived in Salta for decades and whom Martel's own family knew well) will resonate with hispanophone audiences just as much for his singing as for his death, which I discuss shortly. Cafrune has more than one version of this song, but what distinguishes this particular version from others is a guitar accompaniment that sounds like an invitation to dance, for a song that was never intended for dancing.[35] The habanera rhythm, which forms the basis for musical genres that speak of romance and passion (the tango, the milonga and, though less consistently, the bolero) is unusual in Argentine folklore. Discussing the habanera rhythm in the bolero, Frances Aparicio claims that the syncopated rhythm 'prohibit[s] pleasure in the sense of musical closure' and 'suspend[s] any resolution of song and sentiment'.[36] Given that Martel cuts the song and the dancing abruptly after less than two minutes, any sense of suspense the characters or the audience may feel is short-lived, yet it is possible to see reflected in the unresolved tension of the rhythm the same inability to move forward, or to find any kind of resolution, that the characters display throughout the film.

Referring to the lyrics of 'El niño y el canario' in her 2007 interview with David Oubiña, Martel remarks that it is 'a horribly sad song'.[37] The song tells the story of a child who has nothing but his prized canary, whom he dutifully cares for in exchange for the bird's song, and a canary that begs heaven for deliverance. So heaven complies by allowing the bird to die. Heartbroken, the child places the tiny dead bird in his pencil box in order to bury it. Audiences will hear only the first two stanzas of the song, but many Argentine viewers would recognise it, even if vaguely. Since the song playing on the cassette is apparently a home-made recording, viewers must assume that both the adults and the adolescents know the lyrics. Like the multiple visual clues that, in retrospect, anticipate Luciano's death, the music rings a premonitory note, but the characters who seem magically revived by the song do not seem to hear the words. It is impossible not to detect some irony in the director's choice of a song about a poor child's first tragic loss as the music that compels even the adolescents to get up and dance. But the song's lyrics have a haunting property, and in fact will haunt one particular character with devastating consequences.

Martel credits her producer Lita Stantic with suggesting this same song as the music that distracts Tali while Luciano decides to climb the ladder to see if the dog next door might be an African rat like the one in Vero's tall tale. In this later scene, the song is not likely to be audible to someone who does not recognise it from before, both because it is extremely hard to hear it and because the sounds come in and out of range. It is impossible to know if Tali recognises the song as the music to which she danced in Mecha's bedroom, but the way in which she stands there straining to hear it and asking Luciano to be quiet signals, at the very least, a subconscious memory of that happier scene. Her expression, as she looks up at the ceiling waiting to hear the music that Mariana has spotted first, reveals both expectation and longing. Absurdly, tragically, Tali's distraction, combined with little Luciano's obsession with the African rat-dog, results in the child's death.

Writing about popular music in Hollywood film, Anahid Kassabian states that popular songs 'bring the immediate threat of history' to bear on a film.[38] Although the song 'El niño y el canario' may not be familiar to younger Argentine or Latin American audiences, the singer's voice, still easily recognisable for many, will indeed 'bring the immediate threat of history' to those who remember the circumstances of the singer's death. Known and admired for using his voice as an instrument for social justice, Cafrune was hated and feared by the extreme right-wing forces that ruled Argentina in the 1970s. His death in 1978, officially declared an accident, is believed by many to have been orchestrated by high-ranking military officers, at least in part as a response to Cafrune's rather blatant disregard for the Junta's efforts to censor cultural symbols of freedom and hope.[39] In this way, the choice of Cafrune as the performer of a song that speaks of the death of innocents and the end of innocence provides a semantic line to the brutalities of the Argentine dictatorship, and in this sense anticipates the more pointed use of contrasting musical genres as historical markers and political critique in *The Headless Woman*.[40]

CODA

Viewers who sit through the final credits will hear one more cumbia. Titled 'Amor divino' and composed by the founding musicians and long-time leaders of Los Varoniles Lirios Salteños, the cumbia title and refrain is unlikely to provoke any confusion when heard at a carnival *carpa* or some other dancing venue. 'Divino' as an adjective is commonly used to mean 'beautiful', 'amazing', 'fantastic' or some other expression of high praise for a thing or a person in Argentina. The 'amor divino' of the song is the woman for whom the singer pines. On the other hand, a literal translation of the words 'amor divino' is 'love divine' (where love is a noun). What suggests that the double-entendre is intentional is its placement in the film. The cumbia, which plays when the credits begin to mention the team responsible for the music and sound recording, is the first music heard after the desolate last scene in which Momi, who has gone to see the water tank where the Virgin supposedly appeared to others, tells a comatose Vero who is lounging by the pool that she 'saw nothing' ('No vi nada'). Since the cumbia lyrics come in and out of hearing range, the intention behind this musical choice is difficult to pin down. If one hears only the words 'divine love' but misses the cumbia rhythm, one might be justified in thinking that the words, sung to cumbia rhythm, are an ironic commentary on G/god abandoning his children. If one hears and understands the lyrics as the love song it in fact is, is the distant love object the dead child? Or is it Isabel, for whom Momi still pines? Or is the music just a cumbia about another man pining for a woman playing on the radio of the family car that is bringing José back to La Ciénaga for Luciano's burial?[41] Heard merely as music to dance to, this final cumbia could be another confirmation of the film's refusal to provide any sense of closure, much less catharsis. Like the final cumbia, the music heard throughout the film opens up vectors for reflecting further on the tensions that inform the film, but at no point does it offer any solutions to these conflicts. In the end, Martel's minimalist but inspired musical choices confirm the aesthetics of reticence for which she is admired.

NOTES

* My deepest gratitude to the following friends, colleagues and experts in the fields of musicology and ethnomusicology for their encouragement and input at various stages of what has resulted in this chapter: Sherry Velasco, for giving me the opportunity to present my earliest thoughts on this subject at the University of Southern California and for our many conversations on music and culture; Julián Gutiérrez-Albilla (USC), for his insightful comments on early draft; Patrick O'Connor (Oberlin), for asking for more information; Carla Marina Díaz (Instituto de Investigación en Etnomusicología) and Fernando Elías Llanos (Fundação das Artes de São Caetano do Sul), for helping me become a better listener of some of the cumbias and the folk song in *The Swamp*; Luis Guantay – whose band, Luis y sus Colombianos, performs two of the cumbias discussed – for answering my questions about cumbia subgenres and emphasising the link between cumbia, the *carpera* tradition and *carnaval* in Salta; Javier Guantay, for putting me in touch with his father Luis and sharing his co-authored essay on the origins and evolution of cumbia in Salta; Susana Rodríguez (Universidad Nacional de Salta), Irene López, Natalia Christofoletti Barrenha, Silvia Niebylski, Silvia Casini and M. Josefina Gil, for facilitating the initial contacts with the musicologists mentioned here.

 1. Shepherd, J. and P. Wicke (1997), *Music and Cultural Theory*, Cambridge: Polity Press.
 2. In Martel's words, 'es como una red donde el espectador se apoya, y está allí como de alguna forma, contenido, empujado, asustado, o estando siempre como sobre algo. En cambio, cuando lo que hay es un trabajo de sonido, el espectador tiene que estar atento con su cabeza, asimilando todo eso.' From passages cited in this paragraph, it is obvious that when referencing sound Martel refers to those aspects of her films' sound design for which she has been justly acclaimed: her manipulation of ambient sounds and sound effects, among which is her use of speaking voices for pure acoustic effect. See Algarín Navarro, F., M. Granda and M. El Kharbachi (2009), 'Entrevista con Lucrecia Martel', *Lumière*, 1, pp. 87–91 (p. 88), <http://www.elumiere.net/numeros_pdf/Lumiere_num1.pdf> (last accessed 27 April 2021).
 3. Wood, J. (2006), *Talking Movies: Contemporary World Filmmakers in Interview*, London: Wallflower Press, p. 171.
 4. Gorbman, C. (1987), *Unheard Melodies: Narrative Film Music*, Bloomington: Indiana University Press, p. 58.
 5. Herzog, A. (2010), *Dreams of Difference, Songs of the Same: The Musical Moment in Film*, Minneapolis: University of Minnesota Press, p. 6.
 6. Kulezic-Wilson, D. (2019), *Sound Design Is the New Score: Theory, Aesthetics, and Erotics of the Integrated Soundtrack*, Oxford: Oxford University Press, p. 61.
 7. For an extensive study of Martel's sound work in the films that compose the trilogy, see Christofoletti Barrenha, N. (2014), *A experiência do cinema de Lucrecia Martel: Resíduos do tempo e sons à beira da piscina*, São Paulo: Alameda Casa Editorial. See also Beck, J. (2013), 'Acoustic Auteurs and Transnational Cinema', in C. Vernallis, A. Herzog and J. Richardson (eds), *The Oxford Handbook of Sound and Image in Digital Media*, Oxford and New York: Oxford University Press, pp. 732–49; Greene, L. (2012), 'Swamped in Sound: The Sound Image in Lucrecia Martel's *La ciénaga/The Swamp*', *Printed Project*, 15, pp. 52–60, <http://www.lizgreenesound.com/wp-content/uploads/2018/05/LG-Swamped-in-Sound-Printed-Project.pdf> (last accessed 16 April 2021); Monteagudo, L. (2002), 'Whispers at Siesta Time', in H. Bernades, D. Lerer and S. Wolf (eds), *New Argentine Cinema: Themes, Auteurs and Trends of Innovation*, Buenos Aires: Ediciones Tatanka and FIPRESCI, pp. 69–78; Rapan, E. and G. Costantini (2016), 'Sonido e inmersión en la trilogía salteña

de Lucrecia Martel', *Imagofagia*, 13, pp. 1–22, <http://www.asaeca.org/imagofagia/index.php/imagofagia/article/view/935> (last accessed 16 April 2021); Russell, D. (2008), 'Lucrecia Martel: A Decidedly Polyphonic Cinema', *Jump Cut*, 50, <https://www.ejumpcut.org/archive/jc50.2008/LMartelAudio/> (last accessed 16 April 2021).

8. Martel has worked with sound designer and sound mixer Guido Berenblum on all her films. Emmanuel Croset, Hervé Guyader and Adrián de Michele were part of the sound-production team for *The Swamp*. The team won the Award for Best Sound at the Havana Film Festival in 2001.

9. In *The Headless Woman* the pop or europop music has more overt political notes and Martel has noted that Argentines of her generation or older will associate this music with the dictatorship. As discussed in this chapter, references to the dictatorship are less obvious, although, as I remark later in the chapter, the choice of Cafrune makes the connection quite explicit.

10. 'El estudio de la cumbia pone en juego a la vez problemas de clase, género y etnicidad, posiblemente como ningún otro producto cultural en la Argentina contemporánea.' Alabarces, P. and M. Silba (2014), '"Las manos de todos los negros, arriba": Género, etnia y clase en la cumbia argentina', *Cultura y Representaciones Sociales*, 8: 16, <http://www.scielo.org.mx/scielo.php?script=sci_arttext&pid=S2007-81102014000100003> (last accessed 16 April 2021).

11. Wolfgang Bongers and Malena Verardi are among the few scholars to note the importance of carnival in the film. Bongers, W. (2016), *Interferencias del archivo: Cortes estéticos y políticos en cine y literatura*, Frankfurt am Main: Peter Lang; Verardi, M. (2013), '*La ciénaga* (Martel, 2001): El tiempo suspendido', *Imagofagia*, 7, <http://www.asaeca.org/imagofagia/index.php/imagofagia/article/view/393> (last accessed 16 April 2021).

12. All of the musicians in Luis Guantay's band are from Salta. Luis explained that in its first incarnation, the band was called Luis y su Conjunto de Música Colombiana. Originally from Colombia, cumbia is considered to be the most easily adaptable of Afro–Caribbean genres, meaning it can take on musical influences of other particular regions without losing this basic character. Part of what makes it adaptable is its simple quarter-note rhythm with the primary notes on beats two and four. The cumbia recordings by Luis y sus Colombianos and Los Varoniles Lirios Salteños for this film are typical of the cumbia *norteña* popular in Salta and the neighbouring Jujuy and Catamarca, provinces with a large indigenous presence. A distinctive trait of this type of cumbia is the way the rhythm can transition from a 4/4 to the 6/8 rhythm characteristic of the Peruvian huayno and of the Argentine zamba. The strong identification of this cumbia style with the indigenous population of the area applies not only to its fans but also to the musicians of local and regional cumbia bands. YouTube images of the two bands heard in the film reveal that many of the musicians have Amerindian or mestizo features. Nevertheless, both of the bands mentioned are modern cumbia bands and use only electronic instruments, which removes the possibility that audiences – particularly non Latin American audiences – will hear the music as an acoustic rendition of ethnic nostalgia.

13. Los Varoniles Lirios Salteños ('The Manly Salta Singers'), who also call themselves simply 'The Salta Singers', are another local Salta band. The band got its start in the first half of the 1980s – when *carpas* reopened and cumbia returned after having been forbidden and censored by the military dictatorship. In addition to the three cumbias these musicians recorded for *The Swamp*, they wrote and performed the cumbia heard during the final credits of *The Headless Woman*. Despite many attempts at contacting this band, I was unable to reach any members of the group.

14. Semán, P. and P. Vila (2012), 'Cumbia Villera or the Complex Construction of Masculinity and Femininity in Contemporary Argentina', in P. Semán and P. Vila (eds), *Youth Identities*

and Argentine Popular Music, New York: Palgrave Macmillan, pp. 101–23; Fernández L'Hoeste, H. and P. Vila (eds) (2013), *Cumbia! Scenes of a Migrant Latin American Music Genre*, Durham, NC and London: Duke University Press; Cragnolini, A. (2006), 'Articulaciones entre violencia social, significante sonoro y subjetividad: La cumbia "villera" en Buenos Aires', *Trans. Revista Transnacional de Música*, 10, <https://www.sibetrans.com/trans/articulo/147/articulaciones-entre-violencia-social-significante-sonoro-y-subjetividad-la-cumbia-villera-en-buenos-aires> (last accessed 16 April 2021).

15. Pacini Hernández, D. (2010), *Oye Como Va! Hybridity and Identity in Latino Popular Music*, Philadelphia: Temple University Press, p. 139. It is important to note that cumbia's popularity during the 1950s and 1960s was not widespread among all classes, which was in turn reflected in the ethnicity and class of the performers. Los Wawancó, the band that became synonymous with cumbia during these decades, was a multinational band formed by university students of various Latin American countries who had come to La Plata to pursue their professional careers. Almost all of them were middle-class and white. Also notable is the fact that Salta is known as a particularly conservative province in Argentina. The upper classes in Salta never approved of the *carpas* or the crowds these attracted. During the dictatorship, some of the more famous *carpas* were closed (as were *bailantas* – the urban warehouses where the urban migrant population came to dance cumbias). Almost all of these places reopened with the fall of the military government.

16. Williams, B. (2017), 'Those You Call Mutants: The Films of Lucrecia Martel', *Cinema Scope*, 72, <https://cinema-scope.com/features/those-you-call-mutants-the-films-of-lucrecia-martel/> (last accessed 16 April 2021).

17. In general, the characters use the term *indio* to refer to those of indigenous descent, as do most non-academic Latin Americans. Joaquín may be the only character who refers to them by the name of one of the tribes in this part of Argentina when he uses the term *collas* as an insult.

18. Sociomusicologists no longer accept Bourdieu's categorical conclusion that 'nothing more clearly affirms one's "class", [and] nothing more infallibly classifies, than tastes in music'. Nevertheless, all cumbia studies consulted for this chapter insist that the stigma that attaches to cumbia has a very long history and at the same time is very much alive. Bourdieu, P. (1984), *Distinction: A Social Critique of the Judgement of Taste*, Cambridge, MA: Harvard University Press, p. 18.

19. Morita Carrasco writes that the middle and upper classes' hostility towards the indigenous population in Salta became much more intense following the cholera epidemic that devastated this population in the provinces of Salta and Jujuy. According to Carrasco, the upper classes in Salta 'took advantage of this situation to equate the indigenous with poverty, ignorance, savagery and brutality' ('la elite salteña se aprovechó de la situación para resignificar sentidos que asocian lo indígena a la miseria, la incapacidad, el salvajismo y la brutalidad'). Carrasco, M. (2005), 'Política indigenista del Estado democrático salteño entre 1986 y 2004', in C. Briones (ed.), *Cartografías argentinas: Políticas indigenistas y formaciones provinciales de alteridad*, Buenos Aires: Antropofagia, pp. 253–91 (p. 270).

20. Costantini, G. (2007), 'La banda sonora en el nuevo cine argentino', *Cuadernos Hispanoamericanos*, 679, pp. 7–17 (p. 16), <http://www.cervantesvirtual.com/descargaPdf/la-banda-sonora-en-el-nuevo-cine-argentino-939781/> (last accessed 16 April 2021). Costantini is one of very few scholars who state that the musical selections in *The Swamp* are conducted with much rigour, but with the exception of the cited comment he does not engage the music in the film. As defined by Michel Chion, anempathetic music is music that is indifferent or ambivalent in its relation to the film image. Chion, M. (1994), *Audio-Vision: Sound on Screen*, New York: Columbia University Press, p. 8.

21. Forcinito, A. (2013), 'Lo invisible y lo invivible: El nuevo cine argentino de mujeres y sus huellas acústicas', *Chasqui*, 42: 1, pp. 37–53 (p. 37), <https://www.jstor.org/stable/43589510?seq=1#metadata_info_tab_contents> (last accessed 17 April 2021). Forcinito does not refer to music when speaking of sound in the film.

22. Aguilar, G. (2006), *Otros mundos: Un ensayo sobre el nuevo cine argentino*, Buenos Aires: Santiago Arcos, p. 52.

23. Frith, S. (1978), *The Sociology of Rock*, London: Constable, p. 176.

24. There is a visual irony in that with his head thrown backwards and his face bloodied, José's image suggests an ironic take on the famous Pietà, and so in another unexpectedly brilliant connection, Martel links José's wounds to the apparitions of the Virgin in the poorer district on the outskirts of the small city. Except that those who most need divine protection, in the long run, are the underdogs like Perro and other young, frustrated, undervalued and underemployed men like him whose attempts at knocking out one potential enemy or competitor reflect the utter futility of such a move in a society where everything conspires to keep them down.

25. Joanna Page sees Perro's reaction as based on a misunderstanding of José's half-hearted interest in Isabel. Page, J. (2013), 'Folktales and Fabulation in Lucrecia Martel's Films', in G. Kantaris and R. O'Bryen (eds), *Latin American Popular Culture: Politics, Media, Affect*, Woodbridge: Boydell and Brewer, pp. 71–88.

26. Momi's use of the definite article before someone's name is not unusual in colloquial speech, yet using the article with Perro's nickname means that anyone hearing Momi out of context would hear 'the dog is outside'.

27. In this scene, the source of the music is unknown, although it too sounds as though it is played on a radio.

28. Like Isabel, Perro is a victim of a bigoted society that sees any reminders of the country's non-European population as lazy, dishonest and prone to violence, but he is still a male in a culture where sexism and misogyny are alive and well.

29. It is tempting to wonder if there might not be a political footnote dangling from these references to debt. *The Swamp* was released in 2001 and obviously completed before the banking collapse of the same year, but it was conceived, written and filmed during a time when the Argentine economy was in crisis. It has been amply documented that Argentina's economic troubles in the 1990s and early 2000s can be linked to Carlos Menem's neoliberal agenda, which in turn can be directly linked to the military Junta during the 1970s and early 1980s. In both cases, this economic agenda was possible in large part because of the massive increases in the country's foreign debt. By the end of the dictatorship, Argentina's foreign debt had risen from 8 billion to 45 billion US dollars. In 2001, the year *The Swamp* was released, the country defaulted on its external debt.

30. Pablo Semán and Pablo Vila propose that the more sexually explicit lyrics of cumbia *villera* could be interpreted as a feminist display of women affirming their own sexuality. I would find this conclusion more convincing if there were more women composers and performers of cumbia *villera*, but the genre is almost entirely dominated by men. Semán and Vila, 'Cumbia Villera or the Complex Construction of Masculinity and Femininity in Contemporary Argentina'.

31. Gutiérrez-Albilla, J. D. (2013), 'Filming in the Feminine: Subjective Realism, Social Disintegration and Bodily Affection in Lucrecia Martel's La ciénaga (2001)', in P. Nair and J. D. Gutiérrez-Albilla (eds), *Hispanic and Lusophone Women Filmmakers: Theory, Practice and Difference*, Manchester and New York: Manchester University Press, p. 222.

32. It is worth taking a closer look at how Martel ensures that the cumbias will not resonate with audiences except on a conceptual or ideological level. In the first place, neither the cumbias nor the performers are well known outside of their local or regional *carpa* circles. This means the music is unlikely to elicit personal memories even in audiences who hear and understand

the lyrics. Additionally, the vocalist(s) in local cumbia bands in general, and the two bands whose recordings we hear in the film in particular, make no effort to draw attention to their voices. In fact, there seems to be a purposeful flattening of the voices so that they will not stand out. Too much vocal or instrumental artistry and dancers would feel pressured to stop and listen. As noted, the cumbias heard in the film are made to sound as though played on radios of questionable quality or with limited reception. Finally, many of the cumbias are heard for less than two minutes, with some of them taking up only a few seconds.

33. Christofoletti Barrenha adds that, 'for a moment, the scene fills with energy' ('por um instante, se enche de vitalidade'). Christofoletti Barrenha, *A experiência do cinema de Lucrecia Martel*, p. 154.

34. Even listeners unfamiliar with Latin American versions of the habanera are likely to recognise the rhythm as the basis for Georges Bizet's famous 'Habanera' in his equally famous opera *Carmen*. In turn, Martel's fans are likely to connect the guitar accompaniment in this song with the theremin version of Bizet's 'Habanera' in *The Holy Girl*. For an example of this type of syncopation, see Open Sauce Guitar (2016), 'Habanera Rhythm (Tresillo Over 2)', YouTube, 16 June 2016, <https://www.youtube.com/watch?v=zNow1XilNoI> (last accessed 24 April 2021).

35. In turn, Martel fans acquainted with *The Holy Girl*, the second film in the trilogy, might make the connection between Cafrune's habanera-like guitar accompaniment and the theremin rendition of Bizet's piece in this film.

36. Aparicio, F. (1998), *Listening to Salsa: Gender, Latin Popular Music and Puerto Rican Cultures*, Middletown, CT: Wesleyan University Press, p. 127.

37. Oubiña, D. (2007), *Estudio crítico sobre La ciénaga, de Lucrecia Martel*, Buenos Aires: Picnic Editorial, p. 61.

38. Kassabian, A. (2001), *Hearing Film: Tracking Identifications in Contemporary Hollywood Film Music*, New York and London: Routledge, p. 2.

39. In January of 1978, the singer attended the Festival de Cosquín, the biggest folk music festival in Argentina, where he was asked to sing the most iconic song in Argentine folklore, the *Zamba de mi esperanza* ('Zamba of Hope'). Despite its non-political lyrics, this zamba was one of the many songs that performers were forbidden to sing or record. Cafrune said that he knew the song was off limits, but his people wanted him to sing it, so he would. Less than a month later, he announced that he would carry a coffer with soil from the French port city where Argentina's liberator José de San Martín had died in exile, from the national cathedral that houses San Martín's remains to Yapeyú, the hero's birthplace in the province of Corrientes, to commemorate the bicentenary of his birth. As he had done on other commemorative occasions, Cafrune planned to make the journey on horseback. Because the military government had no major plans to commemorate a man who had crossed the Andes and battled the Spanish armies in order to unshackle Argentina from tyrants, his display of patriotism must have rankled the military. What is known by all is that Cafrune was on his way out of Buenos Aires with the coffer and a friend, both on horseback, when a pick-up truck driven by two men who were never charged struck his horse and drove away. The official story was that it was an accident, but many immediately suspected that his death was an assassination sanctioned by the Junta leaders. Many still do.

40. In a paper presented at USC in 2016 and, in revised form, at the Catholic University of Louvain and Radboud University in the Netherlands, I discuss the musical and verbal contrasts that *The Headless Woman* sets up between the europop songs heard near the beginning and the end of the film, the zamba sung by Cafrune midway through the film, and the cumbia during the final credits.

41. The words 'amor divino' serve as a bridge to Martel's next film, *The Holy Girl*, which begins with an acousmatic soprano voice asking God what he wants of her.

CHAPTER 4

Being Unable to See and Being Invisible: Unrecognisable, Inaudible Voices in *Fish*, *New Argirópolis* and *Muta*

Ana Forcinito

In many interviews, Lucrecia Martel has referred to the essential role that sound holds in filmmaking as 'the inevitable in the experience of watching a film'.[1] In this acoustic experience, voices are also a central component, be they in an articulate form, or more unintelligible expressions. Through different intensities, we can hear the modulations of voices very distinctly, and at other times, almost imperceptibly, as relegated to background noise. The function of the different voices and modulations in Martel's films is particularly relevant when thinking about her aesthetics, and even more so when, as I will do in this chapter, focusing on the intersection and disjunction between visual images and different modulations of voices, whispers, sound distortions and echoes. In what follows, I will discuss the use of the voice in three of Martel's short films of the new millennium, *Fish/Pescados* (2010), *New Argirópolis/Nueva Argirópolis* (2010) and *Muta* (2011). Distorted voices in *Fish*, whispers intertwined with translatable and non-translatable languages in *New Argirópolis* and insect-like noises in *Muta* open up new paths for approaching both what remains invisible and our own inability to see. These three short films might be considered experimental attempts to continue the dialogue between sound and image already initiated in Martel's previous films, a dialogue (or tension) that continues in *Zama* (2017). Although the emphasis on the acoustic record does not interfere with the importance assigned to images, the sound might be key to grasping what remains outside the frame (or at least opaque or blurry) and to the questioning of the visual regime. I am not referring to the dominant voice nor a voice clearly articulated (where there is also an acoustic regime), but to those manifestations of the voice that are difficult to hear or understand.

DISTORTIONS, ECHOES AND MEANING

Martel has referred insistently to the centrality that water plays in her understanding of sound. The haptic experience is another sensorial aspect privileged when referring to sound (in particular around water), and it accompanies the visual and acoustic experience. 'Sound reaches us', says Martel referring to the waves and the vibration transmitted as the bodily experience of sound.[2]

The short film *Fish*, presented at the Notodofilmfest, could be considered an experimental exploration of sound, colours, touch and language and of the distortions of the voice underwater and at the surface. *Fish* begins on a highway, with a car driving in the rain; we see the lights of the vehicle driving in front. Then, after a fade to black we start hearing distorted voices. We see fish moving in the water, a tank with fish, swimming and bumping into each other, and talking and singing. One of these voices mentions a highway, and says, 'We all were a car.' Then, we hear different distorted voices. The camera captures the images of fish and experiments with the alteration of sounds. Fish keep swimming and touching each other and making visible the effect of their movements (and sounds) in the water.[3]

What visually frames the scenes in the fish tank is the sequence of the highway, the rain and the car: the highway is seen from the inside of a car with the movement of the windscreens, the sound of tyres rubbing against the highway, and dazzling lights. Then, we see colourful fish in a tank with unrecognisable voices that are unintelligible, although there is text added as a caption. Martel has also referred to voices and conversations that are somehow the background

Figure 4.1 *Fish* brings to the forefront voices that are skilfully blurred and unclear

of some memories, although they can also point to the different voices that shape, invisibly, our culture, and that go unnoticed precisely because they have become normalised and have been incorporated into our daily life. The presence of these voices is recurrent in Martel's films and, in a way, all the sentences in *Fish* could be considered as part of these murmurs that we hear in some of her other films (people talking outside the frame, telling stories, fragments of conversations).[4] However, in this case, the distortion of the voices interferes with the sense of normalisation of the murmurs. The voices become unrecognisable, almost like a parody of the voice as an unintelligible and distorted sound. *Fish* brings sound to the forefront, and not the intelligible voice with an articulate language but voices that are skilfully blurred and unclear, almost in a resonance box, distanced and transformed by the effect of the water.

In playing with sound and resonances, we hear a distorted version of 'No había perros, solo un auto' ('There weren't any dogs, just a car'). And a repetition (with distorted voices) of something that could be 'No lo vi, no lo vi' ('I didn't see it, I didn't see it') until the images of the water and the colours of the fish gradually transform into what could be car lights on a highway at night. The sounds overlap, creating deformed, not completely intelligible voices. There is electronic music that accompanies these distortions. Yet it is possible to think, despite the experiments with sounds and resonances, that there is a connection between *The Headless Woman/La mujer sin cabeza* (2008) and *Fish*. The reference to a dog might be considered as a clear indication that this dialogue is a resonance not only of what is happening on the highway, but also of another film.[5] Martel has drawn connections between her films in general, from the framing of women with no head in *The Swamp/La ciénaga* (2001) and *The Holy Girl/La niña santa* (2004) and the title of *The Headless Woman* to the name of the husband that the protagonist leaves in *Dead King/ Rey Muerto* (1995), Cabeza (Head). These names provide images and sounds that connect all her films. And in *Fish*, Martel seems to be pointing to *The Headless Woman*, not necessarily to solve a puzzle, but to connect the two films in a kaleidoscopic way of looking and naming. The references to what might have happened in *The Headless Woman*, as far as the accident is concerned, do not allay our doubts, but instead give us hints about the same event to which we return through the distortion of the voices in *Fish*. Though the distorted voices might contain the key, we cannot understand the meaning because it is not completely intelligible. The sound also evokes the difficulty of making sense of the acoustic realm. The images of the fish are synchronised with distorted voices while in the fish tank, evoking dogs, rain, a highway and, of course, the difficulty of seeing.

The gaze, as a space in which power relations are explored in Martel's films, is also interrogated here. What is seen and what is not seen are at the forefront from the very first succession of shots on the highway while it is raining. And this tension becomes even more noticeable at the end, when, in the last sequence, the film returns to the highway, but now during night-time. Vision is blurred towards the end, even more so than at the beginning. Martel explores the limitations of the gaze by calling into question the possibility of seeing (and of narrating with images). *The Headless Woman* insists on what is not seen (on what people refuse to see – not just the accident that Vero refuses to look at in the rear-view mirror, but also Vero's condition, which goes largely unnoticed by those around her.[6] Nor is the spectator able to see clearly, with the camera thus posing questions as to the (in)visibility of those same images. In *Fish*, as well, we hear the 'No lo vi' or 'Yo lo vi.' (Is that perhaps what we hear? The caption does not provide that sentence. Is this what we hear because of the resonances of other films?) The difficulty of seeing is clearly not underwater, but on the highway, where rain and dazzling lights seem to interfere with sharp vision.

In contrast, the tank sequence is marked by bright colours. It is still blurry at times, but we can see water and fish and their colours. And this is the space in which sound is explored, in particular through distortion of sounds. Voice and mimicry are also at the centre of this short film, at the intersection of the distortion of voices and the music that seem to encompass some of Martel's obsessions with the exploration of sound and voice in the water.[7]

The emphasis on sound is not only about the transmission of vibrations through the images of water (Martel has compared cinema to a swimming pool on various occasions), but also about the haptic experience of listening, how 'sound touches us',[8] in particular the link between sound and movement that we can see in *Fish*. 'Even if we close our eyes,' Martel explains, 'and this is more noticeable under the water, we can feel the vibration of a presence. We can feel sound.'[9] What I want to emphasise here is this acoustic examination underwater, with distorted sounds detached from their meaning, although not completely. The experience is simultaneously visual, acoustic and haptic. And the visual component here is central. We see fish, and the camera captures them very closely. In this closeness, the haptic experience is set in motion. We see waves in the water, and we see fish touching each other as they swim. We hear their distorted voices, and we see the visual alteration that the water produces in the sharpness of their outlines.

Even if *Fish* can be considered primarily as a playful experiment with water and sound (and the relationship between the two is part of all of Martel films), the bodily experience of sound as vibrations in the fish tank might be interpreted through feminist lenses along the line explored by Mary Ann Doane, who understands sound as a 'sonorous envelope'. Doane is thinking about the pre-symbolic, bodily and maternal language, and therefore pointing simultaneously to a bodily experience and a ghostly presence: the haptic experience of sound and the loss of (articulated) meaning.[10] This loss of meaning takes different forms in Martel's films, but most frequently, it takes the form of murmurs, that is, those surrounding voices that are so constant that we stop listening to them. They lose their meaning although they embody the stories that surround (and perhaps even shape) what remains inside the frame.

Fish also entails an exploration of the many voices that inhabit a voice. In *The Headless Woman* we hear a repetition of the voices of the men putting together an alibi and a new narrative (Vero killed a dog, and not a child), and Vero repeats what they say; in *Fish* there is an echo of this film, and particularly what the voices had enunciated, as resonance. This resonance detaches the voice from its meaning. And in a way, this is a playful experiment, and at the same time, as Adriana Cavarero has suggested in her study about the voice, a tension inhabits echoes. In this 'childish game', Echo repeats Narcissus's words and empties them of semantic content, doing the same thing a baby does when it repeats the mother's sounds but without meaning.[11] The subversive and meaningless repetitions of words through distortions, on the one hand, and of echoes on the other, create an acoustic experience that is somehow unrelated to the images and that has lost not only the words' meaning but also their clarity in the midst of what becomes more and more unintelligible.

THE INVISIBLE AND THE INAUDIBLE

The exploration of the voice in relation to meaning takes another direction in *New Argirópolis*, an eight-minute short film within the context of Argentina's Bicentennial celebrations and the collective project *25 Looks, 200 Minutes/25 miradas, 200 minutos*.[12] Here, Lucrecia Martel offers a look at different repetitions in Argentine history, anchored in the tension between writing and acoustic image, articulated voice and whisper, invisibility and visibility, examining this time the subversive uses of the invisible and the inaudible.[13]

The police arrest a group of five people from the Wichí nations, assuming that they are transporting drugs via the Bermejo River; they are interrogated and subjected to an X-ray that, ultimately, offers no evidence confirming the initial suspicion. Vigilant eyes search for evidence that would prove the police's assumption and the police not only look at them but also construct them as suspicious (as foreigners to the nation). The conflict is first revealed through overlapping voices in Spanish and Wichí. The visual presence of the 'accused' lies precisely in the way they became visible only as suspects.

This short's title is a reference to Domingo Faustino Sarmiento's text, which preceded Argentina's consolidation as a nation and was published in Chile in 1850 with the title *Argirópolis o la Capital de los Estados Confederados del Río de la Plata* (*Argirópolis, or the Capital of the Confederated States of the River Plate*). Sarmiento proposes here a 'solution' for pacifying the Río de la

Plata region (during the final years of the government of Juan Manuel de Rosas in Buenos Aires) and suggests the establishment of the Argentine capital on Martín García Island, an island in the middle of the Río de la Plata estuary that was under French control at the time.[14] In an article written after the release of the short, Martel refers to this island as a fantasy and, at the same time, a symbol. In her reimagining, the islands of the Delta del Tigre are the scenario for the new proposal, instead of 'an island where a sort of nation can be refounded', as Sarmiento had it.[15] The film returns to the text by appropriating Argirópolis from the margins (we hear a woman say 'Argirópolis' in an indigenous language in a video that is circulating on the Internet). Thus, we are able to go back to Sarmiento's images of Argirópolis through the images that Martel offers in the present: the Wichí communities remain 'under suspicion' of a watchful gaze that excludes them from the national project.[16]

Sarmiento and his writings are reflected in a play of mirrors that suggest resonances, bifurcations and appropriations, and at the same time, highlight the dissonances produced in such repetition. The (written) text alluded to in the title of the short is contrasted with an orality marked not only by the dominant voices (the officers attempt to translate into Spanish), but most importantly by voices in the Wichí language that multiply without translation on the Internet, as a new form of 'writing', mainly because it is also marked by the foundational nature of Nueva Argirópolis (and this includes references to Argentina's national anthem).

The short reveals the police's vigilant gaze, which attempts to confirm the theory of drug transport. The camera captures the process of 'investigation', which takes place as much through the visual realm as through sound. Ana Amado suggests the monitoring of the acoustic as 'evidence' of the presence of that suspect otherness, in the short's final line, uttered by the police.[17] The acoustic realm plays an essential role because, alongside what is translated, we also have untranslated passages and whispers. In both cases, the attempt to restore meaning is undermined within the vigilant logic of the nation, where the reference to Sarmiento cannot be separated from the racist practices that culminated in the genocide perpetrated in the so-called Conquest of the Desert.

Language and translation are central to this short. The voices that remain untranslated (and invisible and inaudible) for the gendarmes (and not for the spectator) are precisely those that point to resistance. The tension between dominant and marginal languages is also underscored in this short. For Ana Amado, this interpretive dispute is about the violence perpetrated by the paternal language on the maternal language (Spanish, the law of the nineteenth-century liberal nation represented by Sarmiento) and the annihilation of difference.[18] Yet such difference survives in a pre-Oedipal situation that was never entirely quashed and whose reappearance within the paternal language takes place in untranslatable intermittencies. If translation highlights the imposition of the dominant language (which monitors bodies and the modulation of sound and meaning), the untranslatable evokes both the marginalised and excluded as the subversive. What cannot be assimilated into the norm indicates simultaneously an exclusion, and an existence that has already escaped dominant norms and vigilance.

Martel captures this disparity between languages in a close-up that highlights the importance of what is whispered in contrast to what is said aloud. Whispering in another girl's ear, the girl translates the videos that we see and hear as the translation is taking place. As such, we hear the voice in an indigenous language (we can still recognise the words 'Argentina' and 'Nueva Argirópolis'), the voice of the girl repeating the translation out loud to the authorities, and the weak whisper that translates into Spanish (although the authorities think that the translation is in a different indigenous language). A close-up allows us to enter the space and to hear what the girl is whispering. As the camera approaches the girl in the close-up, we hear her say, 'Indígenas e indigentes, no tengan miedo de moverse. Somos invisibles' ('Indigenous and indigent, do not be afraid to move. We are invisible'); the other little girl doesn't repeat it.

This close-up makes the girls visible and present to simultaneously highlight a juxtaposition of three voices: that of the leader of the community in Wichí language (coming from the video), that of the girl repeating the translation out loud, and that of the girl whispering the Spanish translation into the other girl's ear. The close-up emphasises proximity and allows the spectator

Figure 4.2 *New Argirópolis* emphasises voices that subvert the relationship between image and sound

to hear the translation in Spanish. The shot thus creates complicity with the spectator. This closeness and the possibility it creates to listen to the whispers (and to understand them because they are being translated into the dominant language) invites the spectator to be a witness to the violence in the construction of otherness, and simultaneously to the resistance of two hundred years of violence in Argentine history. Whispers, once again, as in other films, point to the limitations of the gaze, and they record what cannot be completely restored. What is visible in the dominant culture is marked by an interpretive frame that excludes certain groups so that they are visible, as in this case, only as suspects. The voice also registers marginal groups only through partially audible translations, that is, inasmuch as they are translated into the logic of Spanish and its dominance. The whispers in the film reflect not the silences of the community but the silencing to which the community is subjected.

The short emphasises voices that subvert the relationship between image and sound: the whispers of a little girl as she translates the Internet video into Spanish. These whispers contrast with the voices of the doctors who, after looking at the X-rays, say, 'No tienen nada' ('They don't have anything'). They also contrast with the officers' comments, 'Se oyen voces' ('You can hear voices'), on the river. This 'visibility' (they are made visible because they are heard; they are heard because they are suspect) is questioned by the 'We are invisible' claim, highlighting the conflict between a vigilant gaze and the invisibility of social subjects who are seen only to be accused. At the same time, these whispers and what remains silenced give account of practices of resistance, in which articulate and interpretive voices (but very difficult to hear) refer to the protection that being invisible, and remaining untranslatable, provides. Both visual and acoustic control makes audible (and visible) what is marginal and who is marginal. Yet the agency of marginal groups, an agency that is expressed in whispers and silences, not only survives but also plans an organised resistance.

SILENCE, SOUND AND MUTATION

A shot of many insects flying over the Paraná River marks the beginning of *Muta*. This is followed by images of a ship on the river. Then, inside this old cruise liner, eight models are at the centre of the visual field. It is important to start by saying that the short film was commissioned by the fashion firm Miu Miu and belongs to the series *Women's Tales*. Therefore, the images highlight different clothing and accessories. We see the models entering the ship through the hatches. Throughout the six minutes, we see some of them just walking and wearing the featured dresses, others are wearing masks and disinfecting the ship, others are eating paper, while still others are being wrapped in a string of spider silk. Sometimes, the camera captures their dresses without showing their faces or even heads; sometimes, the camera shows their hair and provides close-ups of their eyelashes. We never see their faces.

The short seems to be about a supposedly uneventful situation, and is perhaps even an excuse to show a group of eight faceless models (and most especially their clothing). The sounds suggest, instead, movement and transformation, or more literally, mutation: towards the end, we see their bodies vanishing and their clothing (the fashion being featured in the short film) falling to the floor, as the body leaves the human form to become, possibly, insects and join the numerous insects that we see in the last sequence.

From the beginning, the sound of the insects, repeated at the end, provides a clue about the mutation process, this becoming-insect or these intermittent forms of metamorphoses. Sound also tells us the story of a moment of danger, when we hear the alarm system going off when someone is about to enter the cruise liner, although unsuccessfully. The buzzing or, perhaps better, fluttering sound is the recurrent sound in the short film. Framed by images of insects at the beginning and the end, during the rest of the film (and with a couple of exceptions), these fluttering sounds are synchronised with images of eyelashes and movements of fingers and nails. These sounds might serve as a reminder that we still hear insects, not human beings, despite their human shapes, dresses and bodies. Towards the end, they leave their clothing and accessories on the floor, just as the dragonfly or the firefly leaves the pupa after its mutation. Yet sound also allows us to hear a different synchronisation: the synchronisation of the group, plotting their becoming.

While the first images show many insects in the daylight, the final shots change the focus to the night, and insects are light sources. They shine in the night, and even when they might not be fireflies, the final images emphasise the luminosity of their transformation. We do not have eight models any more, but many insects are flying in the night, irradiating light after their mutation.

The short is described on Miu Miu's website as 'a beautiful and cryptic portrayal of an all-female world of symbolism, hidden meaning and intrigue'.[19] Here, the characters are described as a 'crew of beautiful and exquisitely attired female creatures', who 'emerge insect-like from portals, their faces obscured from view'. The website continues: 'Beneath their tortoiseshell shades, false lashes flutter, and a new private language is revealed, a morse-code of clicks and vibrations. The female chrysalides prepare for their strange metamorphosis.'[20] All these descriptions and explanations (the website also refers to 'a surreal narrative' and a 'mesmerizing personal reflection on the transformative power of femininity at the heart of the Miu Miu obsession') seem to evade some of the possible meanings, first, within the short and, in particular, in relation to a process of empowering that seems to be connected, precisely, with getting rid of the clothing at the end (and the dresses being 'the power of femininity').

Clothing, hair and bodies, now not headless but faceless, are visually the main elements present in the film. The camera captures them from far away or with medium shots and close-ups. Images show the ideal female figures and their long and beautiful hair. They are, after all, non-human, although in a different way, dehumanised by an industry that has transformed women into objects. Extreme close-ups of eyelashes and shiny, silky hair further expose the absence of faces.

On the other hand, silence (silencing?) in terms of dialogue and articulate language is also the central acoustic aspect. Unintelligible sounds or voices point this time not only to non-articulated language but also to non-human sounds or insect-like sounds. In an interview, Martel says about the short: 'I always wanted to make a movie about the insects in the Paraná river.'[21] The models in the film communicate with each other through insect-like sounds that we cannot understand, and that finally will go through a transformation. And this mutation involves precisely leaving behind the clothing that the short is featuring. These models are dehumanised by the fashion and advertising industries while at the same time they are non-human, in the process of becoming (in the precise moment of plotting a metamorphosis). We do not understand the sounds, and we might even think that they are only sounds, until we realise that these eight models are communicating with each other with a common objective: the mutation, and the escape of that particular human form, one that is already dehumanised. They are invisible in their visibility, and as in Martel's short film *New Argirópolis*, they are not scared of moving because they know their own invisibility. Once again, as in *New Argirópolis*, we would need a translation to understand those sounds and languages. And this time, the short leaves us, as spectators, outside the plotting of the becoming. The title also refers to the absence of sound (mute), and perhaps not so much silence but rather the silenced nature of the female voice. The whisper is both a symptom of the silencing of women, and a sound of rebellion since its 'nearly inaudible' nature opens up a space of liberation, of not being under acoustic control. Whispers allow room to find a voice/sound/language that becomes communal or collective.

MUTATION, RESISTANCE AND ESCAPE

When referring to the relationship between image and sound, Martel recognises that she is not interested in sounds that function as affirmations of the image, but instead in sounds that pose questions about images, or that provoke a feeling of distrust of them.[22] Sound allows us to see, with our ears, what remains outside the frame but is now acoustically present. If the gaze creates invisibilities, sound and voices seem to be able to provide alternative ways of looking: one of them is the ear, the possibility of hearing, and even more, sensing with our eyes closed. In Martel's films, dislocations between the visual and acoustic realms lead to questioning the gaze and invite spectators to explore both what remains invisible for them and their inability to see, which also implies a failure to hear.

I return here to what appear to be some recurrent concerns for Martel: being unable to see, and putting the spectator in this position as well. From Luciano's fall in *The Swamp* to the accident in *The Headless Woman*, or the framing of the headless (and the faceless in *Muta*), the visual field seems marked, determined, and framed by the invisible. What are not (clearly) seen (and what the camera does capture but without sharpness) are those hidden zones (and subjects) that Martel brings to the forefront as invisible or blurred. The traces of hands in the car in *The Headless Woman*, for example, point to those beings who are there but unseen. *New Argirópolis* poses the question of invisibility, and of what remains unseen (or distorted) in the dominant visual regime. Yet, it also points to forms of resistance present in those invisible spaces, precisely through the protection of that same invisibility.

Being invisible to others, even when inside the frame, is another concern, present from Martel's first short *Dead King* and pointing to marginal social groups who do not seem to count in the visible (political) world. All the marginal characters in *Zama* resist their invisibility through sounds that prove their oppressed existence. Sound comes to play a central role here and not necessarily to bring these groups, communities or identities to light, but as an ontological mark of their existence, and more specifically of their invisible existence. Be it through gunshots or explosions, or by human voices, sound interferes with the visual images and exposes the tension between the inability to see and being invisible. Yet sound is also subjected to vigilance in the acoustic regime, and Martel underscores this subjection. Many times, articulated voices repeat hegemonic discourses, and create the invisibility of certain groups. The marginal and the invisible only surface in the visible world through languages that further marginalise them. Other instances of the voice, frequently as whispers, or sounds that are difficult to be heard or understood, allow us to think or imagine the existence of marginal or oppressed groups, and our inability to see. These oftentimes almost inaudible voices entail forms of resistance to discourses and norms through the plotting of communal practices.

What is not entirely audible, such as the whispers in *New Argirópolis*, for example, undermines the dominance of sounds associated with power and control, or point, like the murmurs in *Fish*, to echoes and repetitions of sentences and phrases that might have already lost their meaning. Echoes articulate language, and most especially, the taking for granted that articulate language always entails communication, at least in the way we expect it to take place. Murmurs, in Martel's films, seem like backgrounds that we do not hear or do not pay attention to (although they might embody dominant narratives). These voices indeed emphasise sounds that are not always discernible, and reflect the intermittent fracturing of a cinematic representation that must always be coherent or synchronised.

The most subtle and imperceptible voices tell those stories that are not told aloud. Moreover, those whispers can sometimes plot rebellions. Resistance strategies are almost inaudible and invisible. In *The Holy Girl*, whispers account for the subversion of religious discourse and its subversive use to resist and rewrite a scene of abuse in the street (an unwanted sexual touch). Momi's and Amalia's voices, marginal but not completely, shape gestures of disobedience towards the rules of authoritarian patriarchy. Whispers expose, almost silently, what is difficult to hear. With this exposure, they also express a wound caused by violence and oppression. These voices (in whispers) can be contrasted with the more audible voices characterised at times, as in *Fish*, by a chain of repetitions of other voices, to the point that they become distorted and meaningless echoes.

The three shorts examined in this chapter can be understood as a close examination of forms of resistance anchored in voices that successfully escape acoustic control or articulated languages. In these three shorts, whispers, distorted echoes, and non-articulated and intelligible languages (or sounds) escape from the constraints of dominant discourse. *New Argirópolis* highlights the resistance of whispers. Here, an articulated and interpretive (but very difficult to hear) voice refers to the protection that being invisible provides. *Fish* is a playful experiment with the distorted echoes and the haptic experience of sound. What is seen or not seen is opaque and vibrant at the same time (we see the fish and their colours, but the highway is blurry because of the rain). Water (images of the water) seems to be an invitation to feel the voice's vibrations in the water and through the bodies. Yet, what is the meaning of those voices? They are audible but not completely intelligible, and they point to what is lost in the chain of repetitions (meaning) to emphasise, instead, the haptic experience of sound. Finally, *Muta* conceptualises unintelligible sounds that become voices and languages when we understand that they can communicate a meaning that is not translated to us until we see the final mutation. Playing with the two meanings of 'muta' as mute and mutation, it also conceptualises the impossibility of silencing transformation and resistance.

Sound, in Martel's films, interferes with the visible and the invisible, and not to provide answers to the challenges posed by the visual and acoustic fields, but instead to open new questions. These three short films examine some of Martel's recurrent concerns about the audible and the visible. However, they are able to escape the recurrent image of the swamp that characterises the rest of Martel's production. In *The Swamp*, *The Holy Girl*, *The Headless Woman* and

Zama, in one way or another, characters are 'trapped', waiting for something that either does not happen or, at least, does not happen for us as spectators, because the ending is open and suspended. Of all her films, *Zama* is probably the film that most fully explores the act of waiting through very different angles, frames and acoustic registers, and serves as an exploration of the experience of waiting for what will never arrive, and the zombie-like existence that character-ises that atmosphere. A process of endless waiting marks the different swamps anchored in tedious scenarios. Even in *The Swamp*, Luciano's death does not indicate the end of that motionless and mind-numbing tone that characterises the entire film. The final sequence with the two sisters talking about what was not seen points to the return to the tedious monotony, constant waiting, and building up of new tensions. We could also think about this tone in *The Headless Woman* and *The Holy Girl*. Either there is no transformation, or if there might be a change (like in *The Holy Girl*), the camera chooses not to include it and, as spectators, we are left with an inconclusive ending, because the conclusion is, after all, precisely to leave characters and spectators waiting for what might not/ will not arrive.

In contrast, the short films I have analysed in this chapter show an intensity marked by movement and transformation. In Martel's first short film, *Dead King*, this change is quite clear in the final sequences with the confrontation with the violent partner and the escape from the relationship. In more appar-ent or subtle ways, the shorts analysed in this chapter take us away from the metaphor of the swamp or the endless wait, to underscore, instead, movement, mutation and nomadism. This is also very clear in *Muta*, and the characters' plotting of ways of escaping (we hear them but do not necessarily understand what they are saying). Also, in *New Argirópolis* there is a possible escape from the vigilant system by practices of resistance as negation (the resistance to providing the translation of certain parts). Towards the end, even when we see the authorities still searching for 'suspects', we might know that there are voices and languages that are not completely captured by visual or acoustic controls, and therefore plot forms of both survival and political resistance. And finally – even if in a more subtle and playful way, but still along the same lines – there is the exploration of subversive languages: *Fish* proposes lines of flight of both meaning and space through the dream or imagination of fish, but more importantly, through escaping from the constraints of language through distorted repetitions that expose the meaningless and transform the meaning of what is repeated. The exploration of what is audible, understandable and visible is no longer confined or trapped within images associated with water like a swamp, but follows a path to escape or transformation. We leave behind dominant discourses and languages, the confinement of gender norms, and the fashion industry. Whispers, insect-like sounds, and echoes serve to explore the possibilities that sound brings to the transformation of images and, more importantly, to our ability to see (and hear). Invisible, inaudible and unintelligible forms of resistance are not relegated to an endless wait or the margins of the visual field, but are still present, plotting transformations and breaking away from oppressive languages and cultures.

NOTES

1. ('lo inevitable en la experiencia de ver una película'.) Casa de América (2011), 'Lucrecia Martel: El sonido en la escritura y la puesta en escena', YouTube, 26 January 2011, <https://www.youtube.com/watch?v=mCKHzMzMlZo> (last accessed 27 April 2021). This lecture was delivered by Martel at the Festival Vivamérica (Madrid), 8 October 2009.
2. Ibid.
3. In many of her films, Martel invites us to a bodily experience, or to put it like Laura Martins suggests, to an experience in which 'we could place ourselves in the body of another' ('podamos ponernos en el cuerpo de otro'). Martins, L. (2011), 'En contra de contar historias: Cuerpos e imágenes hápticas en el cine argentino (Lisandro Alonso y Lucrecia Martel)', *Revista de Crítica Literaria Latinoamericana*, 37: 73, pp. 401–20.
4. In an interview with David Oubiña, Martel says the following about the relationship between voice and image, to the point of suggesting that what we hear frames what we capture with our eyes: 'For me, the beginnings of the narrative are found in orality. And I don't mean orality in the sense that some guy sits down and begins telling a story, but a situation in which something gets told. When your grandmother comes to tell you a story (and you are in bed with your brothers and sisters, all scattered about), perhaps you don't see the person who's talking, and there are your siblings playing around you – but her telling of the story invades the scene and orients your gaze. The sound guides you.' Oubiña, D. (2019), 'The Cinema as Loving Intent: Interview with Lucrecia Martel', in G. Gemünden, *Lucrecia Martel*, Champaign: University of Illinois Press, pp. 135–47.
5. In an interview with Simon Field, Martel refers to an accident she had when she was younger and to the interpretations of the reaction to traumatic accidents as playing an important part in the image of the 'headless woman'. She refers to the indigenous narratives of an illness that follows an accident: *el susto* (the scare); and explains that in this narrative, the soul is ejected from the body during the accident. That ejection can be undone by returning to the scene of the accident, where the soul stayed. International Film Festival Rotterdam (2018), 'Lucrecia Martel (Spanish audio) – Masterclass #1', YouTube, <https://www.youtube.com/watch?v=Z_zdESWSTxw> (last accessed 27 April 2021). What I want to highlight in this interview is the reference to the return (in this case to the scene of the accident), that in some approaches to trauma studies (such as Cathy Caruth) is also a departure, that is the moment of survival.
6. At the end of *The Swamp*, we hear Momi's words: 'No vi nada' ('I didn't see anything'). The fact that *The Swamp* ends with these words has to do with the duality articulated in this search for the female gaze: a search that invites us to explore a plurality of gazes while emphasising the limits of looking. In *The Holy Girl*, too, a gaze is at work that is insufficient because looking also has to do with the meaning attributed to what one sees: seeing a sign from God or not seeing it also means interpreting it, generally according to a discourse of oppression (religion, science, the patriarchy).
7. Juana Molina, in charge of the sound, music and voices, is a songwriter, but, in addition, she became very famous during the early nineties with *Juana y sus hermanas*, a TV

show, in which she imitated different characters (her 'sisters'), all of them with different modulations of the voice, intonations and ways of speaking.

8. Casa de América, 'Lucrecia Martel: El sonido en la escritura y la puesta en escena'.

9. Ibid.

10. Feminist film studies have explored what Mary Ann Doane calls the 'sonorous envelope'. Doane, M. A. (1980), 'The Voice in the Cinema: The Articulation of Body and Space', *Yale French Studies*, 60, pp. 33–50 (p. 45). The presence of the maternal is ghostly. So the sonorous envelope is sound or voice that promises to unite with the mother's body (resonance, the echo of a lost instance), and on the other hand, it is the voice that dismisses the mother in the moment of separation (marked, Doane says, by the intervention of the paternal voice that summons her with his desire). Water allows not only for the exploration of this haptic experience of sound, but also for the exploration of meaning that is lost in a battle marked by patriarchal dominance (and if we interpret *Fish* in relation to *The Headless Woman*, this battle between feminine and masculine becomes more clear, as does the dominance of the patriarchal voice).

11. Cavarero, A. (2005), *For More than One Voice: Toward a Philosophy of Vocal Expression*, Stanford: Stanford University Press, p. 168.

12. The Secretaría de Cultura de la Nación and the Universidad Nacional de Tres de Febrero developed a collective project through which twenty-five filmmakers would each create an eight-minute short. *New Argirópolis* is one of these short films.

13. Forcinito, A. (2018), *Óyeme con los ojos: cine, mujeres, visiones y voces*, La Habana: Casa de las Américas.

14. It also affirms the importance of unrestricted navigation of the rivers to the 'independencia, desarrollo y libertad del Paraguay, el Uruguay y las provincias argentinas del Litoral' ('independence, development and liberty of Paraguay, Uruguay and the provinces of the Argentine littoral'). Sarmiento, D. F. (1938), *Argirópolis*, Rio de Janeiro and Buenos Aires: Editorial Tor.

15. ('una isla donde se pueda refundar una especie de nación'.) Ranzani, O. (2010), 'Un mapa de la diversidad de las imágenes', *Página/12*, 17 June 2010, <https://www.pagina12.com.ar/diario/suplementos/espectaculos/5-18333-2010-06-17.html> (last accessed 30 April 2021).

16. Martín García Island later became a space used by the liberal nation of the so-called Conquest of the Desert (1879) to hold prisoners and captive indigenous people. As such, Argirópolis (despite Sarmiento's emphasis on calling a congress and revising the federal treaties and agreements) represents both the French presence in the national imaginary of writings about Argentina and a space that would be used (twenty years after the text was written) to hold indigenous captives.

17. Amado, A. (2013), 'No son como nosotros: Lenguas aborígenes, género y memoria en el cine argentino', *International Symposium Erasures: Gender Violence and Human Rights*, University of Minnesota, 24 and 25 October 2013.

18. Ibid.

19. Miu Miu (2011), 'Women's Tales #2: *Muta*', <https://www.miumiu.com/us/en/miumiu-club/womens-tales/womens-tales-2.html> (last accessed 27 April 2021).

20. Ibid.

21. 'I thought it was a good idea to mix movie divas with bugs on a ghost ship. I gave this diva component to the bugs, although they might as well be roaches on an abandoned ship. However, these divas worked a bit better in the movie' ('Me pareció una buena idea mezclar divas del cine con insectos en un barco fantasma. Les di este componente de diva a los insectos, aunque bien podrían ser cucarachas en un barco abandonado. Pero las divas funcionaban un poco mejor en la película'). La Capital – Mar del Plata (2012),

'Lucrecia Martel llegó con *Muta* a Venecia', <http://www.lacapitalmdp.com/noticias/Espectaculos/2012/08/31/228225.htm> (last accessed 27 April 2021).

22. Facultad de Filosofía y Humanidades – UNC (2018), 'Entrevista a Lucrecia Martel: "Cuando en un país la realidad se está negando, la lengua sufre mucho"', YouTube, 12 September 2018, <https://www.youtube.com/watch?v=4IFoi-0951Y> (last accessed 27 April 2021).

CHAPTER 5

Muta: Monstrosity and Mutation

Mariana Souto and Mônica Campo

Starting from the short film *Muta* (2011), produced by the clothing brand Miu Miu in the context of the *Women's Tales* project,[1] this chapter discusses the recurring flirtation with the horror genre in Lucrecia Martel's work, while occasionally referencing other films such as *The Swamp/La ciénaga* (2001) and *The Headless Woman/La mujer sin cabeza* (2008). 'Muta' can refer to both speechlessness and mutation: in the fairytale-like enigmatic universe of the film, a ship that floats on the waters of the Paraná River is occupied only by women: a group of slender young models who, at night, appear to metamorphose into dragonflies. Thus, the objective of this chapter is to call into question two central aspects of the short film: the ideas of monstrosity and mutation. We seek, therefore, to observe the way the film navigates different references like Asian horror and the world of fashion.

Horror is represented as a surreptitious and furtive presence in many of Lucrecia Martel's films, though it is more assertively pronounced in *Muta*. We will first approach these more subtle influences in the filmmaker's feature-length films, especially highlighting the 'monsterfied' nature of some characters. After that we will analyse horror in the short film, considering the characters' inhuman characteristics and their dialogue with other monsters in the cinematographic imagination. We will then note the cycles and suggestion of circular time in this film: it shows us insects, then women, then finishes with insects again. Finally, we will address the performance of the female body amid sign-objects, reflecting on how Martel seeks to subvert – or at least camouflage – some intentions of this advertising piece.

HORROR IN MARTEL'S WORK

Though none of this director's films can be fully included in the horror genre, influences and elements of horror loom over all of her works — and in a very particular way in *Muta*. Some of her films have titles that may be confused with films in the horror genre, like *The Headless Woman* and *The Swamp*, conjuring up legendary creatures or gloomy landscapes in the imagination.[2] The choice of horror titles for films that are essentially dramas is meaningful in this nebulous approximation, in playing with appearances, in that which appears to be yet not always is. Horror works as an indirect or underground presence in Martel's work and is represented less as a genre and more as a key that unlocks new readings of the films. Here we propose that horror functions not as a category that corrals and contains the object, but rather as a doorway to feelings, helping us to more clearly identify some runaway perceptions.

A horror reading of some of the elements in *The Headless Woman* would see Vero's character as a zombie or a ghost. In this 2008 film, the protagonist runs over something without knowing if it is human or animal, and she doesn't stop to help; after a while, she hears news of a boy who has disappeared. This event, which happens in the prologue, disturbs her throughout the entire film. Dazed, as if she has been struck by some type of amnesia, she roams through spaces without appearing to remember her past: upon arriving at the clinic where she works as a dentist, she sits in the waiting room instead of going into the office. She doesn't answer when questioned, she doesn't know where her car is, she falls silent when asked about her children. In northern Argentina, Martel's birthplace, it is believed that 'when there is a trauma, the soul leaves the body — the shock must be cured for the soul to return'.[3] This is what appears to happen to the character Vero after the shock of the hit-and-run. For the majority of the film, she roams like a body without a soul, without memory, without speaking, without expression: a *zombie*.

When she tells her husband and brother of the possible murder of the boy, they hurry to erase her tracks. After the accident, Vero had done exams at a hospital and stayed at a hotel — records deleted by the family. Her car is taken to be fixed in a neighbouring city — the blood and the dent are eliminated. The signs of the protagonist's guilt, a rich white woman who may have killed a poor indigenous boy, are erased, as the crimes of the ruling class often are. Natalia Christofoletti Barrenha draws a connection between this cover-up of evidence and 'the mechanism of forgetting and the methods of denial related to the horror promoted by the authoritarian state that occupied power in Argentina between 1976 and 1983'.[4] There is an association between this erasure of evidence and the Argentine dictatorship, then.

If they erase all traces of the crime and Vero's presence after the accident, it is as if she had not existed in that period: a *ghost*. This impression is reinforced in the final scene in which the character is filmed at a party through a thick pane of glass. Her appearance is smudged, her image dematerialised, different from the other characters around her. Vero is a body that cannot be touched or held: the ethereal, ghostly characteristic also refers to the impossibility of her learning from and being held responsible for her crimes.

In the prologue of *The Swamp*, middle-aged men and women are stretched out beside a pool. They get up to move their chairs around, probably in search of the best position in relation to the sun. From the fragmented construction of the scene, we see only parts of their bodies and pieces of the chairs, which produce an annoying sound from their friction on the ground. The characters move slowly, dragging not only the chairs but also their own aged and flaccid bodies. We don't see their faces, just their bodies moving heavily and sluggishly, like zombies. In her first feature-length film, Martel portrays the decadent Argentine middle class as apathetic and worn-out living dead, speaking to the idea of paralysis that the film elaborates on in the following moments – above all in what it says about the adult characters, while the teenagers, in contrast, are shown as active and vivacious.

We are dealing with subtle understandings here. They are ethereal and abstract: it is clear that neither *The Headless Woman* nor *The Swamp* presents characters as true zombies or ghosts. The approximation to horror conventions is what aids us in this interpretation and identification of monstrous creatures. Our hypothesis is that horror is represented as a potential analytical resource to deal with Martel's films. Additionally, the idea of the 'monster' fits with some of her characters, as the filmmaker herself seems to indicate.

In interviews, Martel reveals that she conceives her characters not as men, women, adults or children – thus escaping age, sexual and social indicators – but as monsters.[5] Thinking of the monstrous would be a form of opposition to the method of the psychological profile, an all too common trick used by screenwriters and filmmakers in the creation of fictional characters. In this way, something of the mystery of those beings who cannot be easily categorised or understood is protected. Monsters are strange beings who cannot be completely known and whose actions and reactions are unpredictable. 'You already think that the Alien is a horrible thing, but then it opens its mouth and out comes another mouth. It surprises you by its nature.'[6] In another interview, the filmmaker points out:

> The monster, from an etymological understanding, is that which shows, that which carries the sign of the divine. Our idea of the monster is linked to the deviant, the marginalised, to that which is outside the idea of what is moral or what nature intended. In the classical tradition, instead of being something to eradicate or eliminate, the monster is something that can bring a revelation.[7]

'Monster' comes from the Latin *monstrum*, meaning 'divine premonition' or 'omen'. It is also related to the Latin verbs *monstrare*, 'to show', and *monere*, 'to warn' or 'to alert'.[8] The monster reveals something uncommon, unique, contrary to the natural course of things, and sends out an alert, producing the feeling that something is out of order.

HORROR IN *MUTA*

The monstrous characteristic, while at times is only underground in the films mentioned, becomes more apparent in *Muta*, most notably with the characters' ability to metamorphose into dragonflies. They are in the company of some classic monsters of cinema that can be understood as symbols of transformation: vampires, werewolves and zombies are examples of creatures that temporarily or permanently shift from a human state to the other. The border is a central concept for the construction of the monster in horror films, according to Barbara Creed.[9] Beginning with Julia Kristeva, the author states that which crosses or threatens to cross a threshold is of the abject order. The nature of the border changes in each film, be it between human and non-human, man and beast (*Dr. Jekyll and Mr. Hyde*, Victor Fleming, 1941), natural and supernatural (*Carrie*, Brian De Palma, 1976), good and evil (*The Exorcist*, William Friedkin, 1973), or male and female (*Psycho*, Alfred Hitchcock, 1960).

The characters of *Muta* appear to be oscillating between human and arthropod forms. The first image of the film is of insects flying over the water. At dawn, figures emerge from below deck via a porthole, hands extended and legs stretched, twisting themselves under the sound effects of joint movements and cracking bones. The masks they wear, black with large circles for their eyes, give them an appearance of a fly or similar insect. They eat paper, blinking ultralong eyelashes that flutter like threads or antennae. Their hair covers their faces like in a J-horror film. The movement is not fluid; it has an irregular speed — at times slowed down, at other times sped up — producing an effect of macabre movement. They drag themselves along the ground until they stand up, resuming their humanoid form. Throughout the day they occupy the boat and interact, at times sensually, at times hostilely. One of them entangles the other in a web that she shoots from her wrist, reminding us of both a silkworm or butterfly larva and the figure of the black widow, a species of spider that devours the male after copulation. They drink a greenish drink, a colour suggestive of venom. They converse in an indiscernible language, whispering and emitting animal-like sounds. At dusk, their bodies disappear and we hear the sound of fluttering wings heading off. Empty dresses and shoes are left behind on the ground. The final image of the film completes the cycle with insects flying over the water, this time at night.

The characters in *Muta* are not defined creatures, as if taken from a bestiary of already named monsters, but they do appear to be inspired by some of them, reformulating diverse sources that range from the ghosts of Japanese horror to the vampire mythology of Eastern Europe.[10] Beginning with the latter, it can be said that there is a vampiresque vibe among these nocturnal creatures that transform not into bats, but into bugs. Ambiguous figures that awaken fear and attraction at the same time, vampires are associated with nobility and luxury, but also cruelty. Different from repulsive, dirty and grotesque creatures, they are seductive and elegant monsters, well dressed, with a certain appreciation for style (in some depictions, Count Dracula is a sensual figure, dignified, well groomed, who dresses in formal wear and a long satin cape) – a characteristic not too different from the well-dressed models in high heels, extravagant glasses and expensive Miu Miu handbags. Vampires mix power, death and eroticism. A vampire attack requires close physical contact to foster the meeting of lips with a nude neck. The creatures captivate the victim like in a sexual conquest, in an action that is intimate, violent and treacherous. The figure of the female vampire especially became prominent in cinema in the 1970s in films that suggested lesbian desire among women.[11]

Crewed only by women and surrounded by water on all sides, the boat in *Muta* is like a ship dreamed up by Sappho. An alarm sounds, the women move onto the alert in the face of a threat: masculine hands try to climb onto the decks, but they soon sink again. Among the women, there is a dubious relationship. Here they appear to work together, while at other times they act as rivals. One snatches a piece of paper out of the hands of another. They touch each other at the waist, like in a dance. After a slap, there's a caress. Inconstancy, unpredictability and fluctuation are behaviours that refer to transformation and change, and taken to the extreme are related to instability itself in bodily form: now a human, now an insect.

In the narrative field, Christopher Vogler talks about the ambiguous archetype of the chameleon, a fickle figure, a creator of instability, mystery and doubt in a plot.[12] Archetypes are flexible, like a mask that various characters can wear; in the case of the chameleon, they are common in gender relations. This archetype can be a matrix of the femme fatale, a seductive and destructive woman whose loyalty to men is put under the spotlight. It is an ancient idea – from the Bible stories of Eve, passing on to the unfaithful Jezebel, and Delilah, who cut Samson's hair in order to rob him of his strength – but it spans across time. It appears in noir films, in which slender, snake-like women provoke and intrigue characters and viewers – as in *The Maltese Falcon* (John Huston, 1941) and *The Big Sleep* (Howard Hawks, 1946) – and also in contemporary thrillers. In the film *Fatal Attraction* (Adrian Lyne, 1987), the hero is surprised by the transformation of a chameleon woman who goes from a passionate lover to an insane, murderous harpy.[13] The Miu Miu instalment created by Martel is inspired by the divas of the 1940s, tuning the film's vintage and stylised costumes to femme fatale references: feminine clothing with wide, square shoulders, hem lengths below the knees and plunging necklines at the back are hallmarks of the fashions from this period.

Like the dragonfly (that goes through mutation), the chameleon is also an animal of transformation and disguise, two elements that hover over *Muta*. 'The number you have dialled has been changed', says the recording when one character tries to call another. The phrase echoes through the film a second time, in the middle of a song as if it were a lyric of the chorus, once again activating the idea of change and deception.

The chameleon characters in *Muta* evoke fatale women, both by their beauty and by their mystery.[14] Their faces, a projection of expressions, are always hidden. When they are not filmed from behind or framed indirectly, their faces are out of focus or covered by some object: a mask, binoculars, hands, hair. This cinematographic trick of hiding the face by framing, angle or obstruction reinforces the impossibility of accessing them or reading their actions, intentions and reactions. They are like shop window mannequins, who express themselves only by the clothes they wear and the postures they adopt and whose faces are blank.

The hidden faces and unknown emotions are in addition to cryptic communications from the characters, who speak through sounds and indiscernible whispers, resulting in an opaqueness in relation to the viewer.[15] Methods of communication like the telephone, radio and loudspeaker are used, but the content of the messages is not understood. Besides these technologies, communication among themselves is carried out through gestures, like that of upturned hands with quickly wiggling joined fingers, once again alluding to an insect's antennae, a gesture that seems to invite similar ones to a ritual around the miniature of the ship. This language, however, is not shared with the viewers. Like the girl in white seated in a canoe adjacent to the boat and with her ears blocked, we too are on the margin of the dialogues. The whispers and codes strengthen the impression of something secret or hidden, be it from the viewer or among the girls themselves in their games and disputes. With this, Martel denies meanings and explanations, keeping that conclave of sleek, devious models a secret.

The long-limbed figures in *Muta* appear immense in the reduced spaces and narrow passageways of the boat. As they are so large, it is not an accident that the bodies must be folded and contorted to fit below deck and get out through the miniscule entryway to the cabin. They are further heightened by high heels. The first woman, upon getting up from the ground and standing completely upright, goes beyond the frame's borders, leaving her head outside the composition. Martel films the crew in a way that accentuates their size and makes them bigger, making use of some low-angle shots and reinforcing how disproportionate the bodies are to the spaces. Thus the characteristic of height (plus thinness), at the same time that it strengthens the idea of power, takes on an angle that is also monstrous, almost inhuman.[16]

The relation between the feminine, death and the monstrous, as in the overt reference of long hair covering the face, recalls Japanese horror films that proliferated in the late 1990s.[17] The contemporary reworking of the *kaidan-eida* (ghost movies) genre, in particular, brings together films in which the characters are haunted by women who died in an unjust or violent way. They return to the world of the living, dressed in white (the colour of funeral clothing in Japan), with a desire for vengeance.[18] These characteristics proliferated in a new wave of films like *Ring* (*Ringu*, Hideo Nakata, 1998), *Pulse* (*Kairo*, Kyioshi Kurosawa, 2001), *Ju-On: The Grudge* (*Ju-On*, Takashi Shimizu, 2002) and *Dark Water* (*Honogurai mizu no soko kara*, Hideo Nakata, 2002), among other very popular works, sparking a flood of Hollywood remakes and instilling their iconography in the international imagination.

In *Muta*, the models leave through a porthole in the boat like the monstrous Sadako, from *Ring*, leaves the television screen: with languid hair covering their faces, their slithering bodies dislocated until reaching a vertical position. In another scene, we see from behind a young red-haired girl crumple a piece of paper ('emergency exit') at the same time that her head, neck and shoulders twist in a fragmented movement, punctuated by a cracking sound effect. The stooped walk in Japanese horror, emulated by the girls in Martel's short, is inspired by traditional kabuki theatre, which is also populated by spectral images and marked by performances in which the actors freeze in picturesque poses. The practice known as *mie* consists of flexing the fingers and arms and dramatic pauses. In cinema, this takes on a new form with the editing, which produces movements of altered speed that at times freezes and other times speeds up, resulting in atypical and interrupted movement. The harsh, dry sound effects help to construct this cracking movement, perhaps due to the hybrid human–insect bodies. It feels like a costly movement, produced by joints and bones rigid from a long period of inactivity — whether it be a type of 'hibernation' of the bodies during the night, or death.

Laura Cánepa and Rogério Ferraraz argue that horror is an attraction in Japanese cinema because of its spectacular nature.[19] The phantasmagorical apparitions and shocking and stylised visual performances develop a certain independence from the plot, and create a shock in the viewer who becomes simultaneously fascinated and scared by the images themselves. It is interesting to notice that in *Ring*, the girl Sadako does not kill by some type of assault or blow to the victim's body, but by her appearance itself: 'The moral power of the spirit resides in its performance.'[20] The performative nature of the characters in *Muta* is not so different: in the scene where the male hands try to enter the boat but don't survive, they drown in the water without any action from the models aside from their simple (and powerful) presence and gaze. They also kill by their performance.

CYCLES AND MUTATIONS

In the prologue of *Muta*, little dragonflies float over the waters of the Paraná River; dawn breaks. The plot of this short film is marked by the journey of light, in which we see female bodies roaming about a boat from dawn to dusk. The day is not defined by faithfulness to the clock, but instead by a narrative suggestion of the cycle of life: a temporal synthesis reduced to a few minutes. The ship sails like a capsule in the river, and we follow it during this period.

This film production does not reference historical time, but rather it constructs an allegorical fable of life, from dragonflies to female bodies (marked by their outfits and jewellery) and again to winged insects. The vessel is dominated by slender bodies in elegant clothing, draped in sophisticated accessories that are shown off on a disguised runway. We can think of the clothes and accessories as silk cocoons the dragonflies emerge from; the pieces, like the bodies, act as a wrapping in the middle of the formation cycle. The symbology of these phases of life is represented by the dragonflies hovering over the water, to the female bodies on the boat, and once again as the insects fly over the river at dusk; the mutation cycles correspond to the different development stages of beings.

Martel took a trip on the Paraná River on a route that could have been done in two and a half hours by plane, or in twelve hours by car, but which took her a month and a half,[21] forming the experience that became the inspiration for *Muta*.[22] This space–time experience contributed to the director raising the question of despatialisation, the way in which today we live in an era full of eras and in which new technologies place us in a process of continuous acceleration. *Muta* is this symbolic voyage where not only time/space, but also the perspective and gaze can be explored in the questioning of the perceptions of the world and humans.

Mixing this biological explanation with symbolic allegory, we might propose exploring the meanings that dragonflies take on in different mythologies. The ship can be viewed as the transitional place for the creatures undergoing transformation. The bodies are feminised by their clothes and accessories, and a hypothesis can be developed that these adornments contribute to the formation of the performance of the feminine.

BODIES AND PERFORMANCE

When we state that the bodies on the runway through the boat are carrying out a performance,[23] we are in conversation with Judith Butler's proposal as we notice the *acted* quality of the bodies. This can be observed in how it is both fed with intentionality and understood in its *performativity*, carrying a dramatic construction that directs the gender meaning.

Shortly after the prologue of *Muta*, the performance of female bodies begins. Inside the ship the lights are turned off, the passenger and captain's cabins are empty. Next, we hear the sound of electricity being turned on and the environment is illuminated; a sign with a woman's silhouette (like those that usually indicate a women's toilet) is lit. In the film, the female bodies start a pretend fashion show on-screen, with prominent props: false lashes, long polished nails, sunglasses, close-ups of sign-objects, which appears to correspond to a performative montage.

For Butler, performativity is understanding this sexuality as a discursive act that is historically and socially constructed. By naming human genitalia, the act unfolds the process of maintaining the heterosexual matrix, that is, the one in which a human being is born with previously categorised genitalia. From this, the subject establishes an expected gender performance (male/female), with their desire (sexual orientation) determined by the corresponding opposite, as heterosexual orientation prescribes. The philosopher explains that 'we are actually in the presence of three contingent dimensions of significant corporeality: anatomical sex, gender identity, and gender performance'.[24] Butler clarifies that the concept of gender is constructed from linguistic-discursive practices. Sexuality is made performative by the regulatory norms of the 'sex' in order to embody sexual difference in function of the preservation of the heterosexual imperative.[25] Butler questions not only the binomial construction of heterosexuality but also that of certain feminist theory, criticised as being loaded with an ontology marked by the naturalist essentialism of sexual places.

The occurrence of the soundtrack, used at specific moments in *Muta*, underscores the observation of the details in the image-concepts. The batting of eyelashes is enhanced by the sound that recalls the beating of insect wings, and throughout the entire film this relation of revealing the sound, at times separating it from the images, works to provoke the viewer's attention, thus accentuating the perception of what is heard and what is seen. In the prologue of the film we hear a wind instrument followed by the sound of insect wings, we see the title of the film and the name of the brand on a background of water with the flight of the dragonflies at dawn. This melding of sounds separated from images, generating sensations of anticipation and intensity, is something that characterises the director's films. The sound design in Martel's films is thought of as a sensorial provocation; the noises and background sounds are concerns inherent in the composition of her language.

The female bodies are very thin and elongated, like models usually are. They are depersonalised bodies, without faces, they carry the sign-objects that mark them; this depersonalisation is the objective of the fashion show because the highlight is the objects and not the models. The pieces are the consumer objects of desire; the models are the coat racks that carry them. However, the runway performance takes on specific meanings in this film, if we notice the

Figure 5.1 In *Muta*, the bodies abandon their garments to fly

imitation of insects that the models adopt in the masks they use, the paper they eat, the strings they release, the sound of their wings beating that are filled out with other strident noises that we hear. The shedding of clothes, objects and accessories in the ship makes sense in the abandonment of this cycle, and perhaps also in the female performance that such signs reinforce.

Dragonflies are carnivorous and predatory insects. They were among the first beings to appear on earth. They live in rivers and lakes until they undergo the mutation process that allows them to live between the earth and the air, thus the idea of transformation and adaptation is projected onto them – the mutation that they undergo makes them resistant to the stages they will face along their life cycle.

The characters in *Muta* are not definable, characterisable, even though their femaleness is perceived through their constructed accessories. Relating this characterisation of the characters to the propagation of the brand Miu Miu in a publicity piece is one of the questions to be considered. The thoughts of philosopher Jean Baudrillard can perhaps contribute to understanding how the director's proposal in *Muta* practises subverting the Italian brand's commission. Baudrillard proposes thinking of life as a simulation and reality as an illusion, as the simulacra of a permanent cycle of life. He was concerned with critiquing what he termed the domination of hyperreality in contemporaneity.

For the philosopher, hyperreality is a constructed reality in which the functional and exchange values of objects were substituted by a sign-value, that is, determined by the symbolic value. Thus, the value of objects as products constitutes the sign-value.[26] The discussion about the sign and consumer society,[27] where objects acquire consumption value in function of the economy, is perceived as the limit of society in hyperreality. In a consumer society, the object does not have value based on use or exchange, but rather on sign; thus the fetish of the product and the object take on in Baudrillard another meaning that is not the same as that ascribed to Hegel or Marx. For Baudrillard, in this new dimension of post-industrial capitalism, the fetishisation of the object carries another meaning, in which human beings no longer reach salvation through work: work fluctuates and remuneration is not equal to the effort of the activity. Thus, what appears to happen in fetishism is the eradication of the body and its substitution by objects/signs.

Muta is a publicity piece from a brand with international prominence, whose objective is explicitly commercial; however, it was created by an independent Latin American filmmaker known for her critical trajectory. Martel reroutes expectations in relation to traditional advertising, bringing the film close to horror, and offering a reading of the well-dressed models' bodies as inhuman, bestial, treacherous creatures. It is significant that the characters' journey ends with their liberation from dresses and shoes. The bodies abandon their garments to fly, as if the clothes were unnecessary after all – an act of nonsense within the true nature of advertising.

Nonetheless, considering the performative nature of *Muta*, in the sense Butler proposes, it is the anamorphosis of the models that functions to call into question the female body, and the cycle of rebirth can mean the break from these cocoons in which our bodies appear to be repressed. For the director, the monstrous apparition appears to be an interesting idea, a phenomenon capable of manifesting an instance of exceptionality. In the end, this is the hope – that art might cause a diversion from the common and discomfort with the conventional.

Martel confesses to having embarked on the project for financial motives and not for having any empathy for 'what fashion or consumption made with women'.[28] She performs, however, a sophisticated gesture that values a language that claws from the inside, which can be seen as *sabotage*. With a nod to Nicole Brenez,[29] Victor Guimarães defines sabotage in cinema – which here can be transposed to the field of advertising – as an insidious gesture, from filmmakers who work at the epicentre of the cinematographic industry grabbing hold of genre codes (like Paul Verhoeven with science fiction in *Starship Troopers*, 1997) and methods to question and implode the system from the inside.[30]

Muta is a hybrid audiovisual work, straddling the border between advertising and cinema and carrying this contradiction within it. Transmitted mainly online, it has a longer runtime than a television commercial yet it is shorter than a cinematographic short film. If, on the one hand, Martel tries to subvert on purpose, on the other, we cannot but think that the subversion is foreseen, assimilated, and even desired by the system itself that she is rebelling against.

With a strong foundation in consumer capitalism, advertising is a machine that incorporates its own criticism, neutralising it. After all, Martel, just like other standout, hyped filmmakers such as Ava DuVernay and Zoe Cassavetes, was invited by the brand, certainly in search of cultural capital, borrowing the intellectual value and aesthetics associated with cinema. If Martel's cinema reroutes advertising, the brand, in a certain way, disarms and domesticates cinema to its own ends. It ends up being a mutual game. The ambiguity and audacity that we are discussing in regards to the chameleon-like characters in *Muta* perhaps are embedded in the very roots of the project, guided by a contract of oblique interests. As some presuppositions are teased out, the film is efficient in creating impact, curiosity and attraction; it sparks surprise, disconcertedness, and by that measure (or maybe for that reason), it seduces us.

The awakening of the monstrous phantasmagoria, the face of what would be the presentation of a fashion collection, challenges whoever watches it. By producing discomfort, hiding the face and refusing speech, the film triggers a release of tension in the viewer. A first reaction to *Muta* orbits the dizzying strangeness, and later migrates to a type of interaction that requires analysis, decodifying and mobilisation of cinematographic references, the elaboration of hypotheses for which there is no confirmation. There is not, however, a passive relation of dazzling the viewer that fashion often produces. This is not a simple seduction – it is critical, and in a way it invites the viewer on a walk through the enigma.

It is significant that precisely with her rare incursion into advertising, an exception in her cinematographic career, the director more openly uses horror and monstrosity. The deadly insect-women stage a hybrid play whose greater purpose appears to be the creation of a strange fascination in which the environment projects the narrative, suggesting more of a cycle than the linearity of a story. Advertising, at the same time that it is a commercial space, also works as a locus of experimentation. Lucrecia Martel takes the opportunity to investigate the limits – both audiovisual and human.

Translated by Alisa Wilhelm

NOTES

1. The *Women's Tales* project was launched in 2011 by Miu Miu, a subsidiary brand of Prada, in partnership with the Venice International Film Festival. It commissions two films per year, always directed by women. The directors have diverse backgrounds and experiences, and they are given carte blanche to create short films, on the one condition that the characters wear the brand in the film.
2. The reference to this type of film is assumed by the filmmaker, who identifies *Carnival of Souls* (Herk Harvey, 1962), an iconic American B-movie, as one of the inspirations for *The Headless Woman*. The 1962 film, against an expressionist background and bizarre

atmosphere, presents a super-blonde protagonist who is also involved in a car accident at the start of the plot. This generates decisive consequences for the story's development. Christofoletti Barrenha, N. (2014), *A experiência do cinema de Lucrecia Martel: Resíduos do tempo e sons à beira da piscina*, São Paulo: Alameda Casa Editorial.

3. Ibid. p. 185.

4. Ibid. p. 187.

5. Among them, Goyeneche, E. (2018). 'Netflix só serve para salvar o matrimônio', *TPM*, 3 April 2018, <https://revistatrip.uol.com.br/tpm/a-cineasta-argentina-lucrecia-martel-nao-quer-saber-de-netflix-so-serve-para-salvar-o-matrimonio> (last accessed 15 April 2021).

6. Ibid.

7. Miranda, M. (2016). 'Entrevista com Lucrecia Martel. Em busca de fissuras', *Cinética*, 25 January 2016, <http://revistacinetica.com.br/home/entrevista-com-lucrecia-martel/> (last accessed 5 April 2021).

8. Messias, A. (2016), *Todos os monstros da terra: Bestiários do cinema e da literatura*, São Paulo: EDUC.

9. Creed, B. (1993), *The Monstrous-Feminine: Film, Feminism, Psychoanalysis*, New York: Routledge.

10. Nazário, L. (1998), *Da natureza dos monstros*, São Paulo: Arte & Ciência.

11. This could be related to the feminist movements that arose in this period and 'that brought a more aggressive expression of female sexuality to public fears'. Ibid. p. 59.

12. Vogler, C. (2006), *A jornada do escritor: Estruturas míticas para escritores*, Rio de Janeiro: Nova Fronteira.

13. Ibid. p. 78.

14. A beauty that follows the standards of contemporary fashion. It should be noted that they are all very young, tall and thin, and none strays even slightly from this inaccessible pattern. They are also almost all white; there is only one black woman among them.

15. Fernanda Alarcón comments on the meaning of mutability in fashion and the way of communicating through clothes and by the denial of the subjectivity of the models who wear them: 'The instability and extravagance of appearances are converted into objects of fascination from a denial of the protagonists' verbal communication' ('La inestabilidad y extravagancia de las apariencias convertidas en objeto de fascinación desde la desarticulación de la comunicación verbal de las protagonistas'). Alarcón, F. (2016), 'Espectros, modelos y mariposas', *Imagofagia*, 13, pp. 1–28 (p. 15), <http://www.asaeca.org/imagofagia/index.php/imagofagia/article/view/993> (last accessed 15 April 2021).

16. In this sense, it is interesting to recall the lyrics of the song 'Terminal Beauté' ('Terminal Beauty'), by the eccentric 1980s French band Les Rita Mitsouko, which comment on the images of models in magazines and describe them as meagre, with an air of death, looking sour and full of pain. See Les Rita Mitsouko (2014), 'Les Rita Mitsouko – Terminal Beauty (feat Serj Tankian) [Audio Officiel]', YouTube, 14 November 2014, <https://www.youtube.com/watch?v=atgKg9ChrGk> (last accessed 27 August 2021).

17. The Twitter account 'Modelos con ciática' gathers images of women in positions that appear to cause them to be suffering, uncomfortable, with dislocated bodies. The description says, 'We are the girl from *The Ring* for your Instagram. Sciatica, spasms, ibuprofen and Amancio are our religion' ('Somos la niña de *The Ring* en su versión de Instagram. La ciática, las contracturas, el ibuprofeno y Amancio son nuestra religión'). <https://twitter.com/mciatica> (last accessed 24 April 2021).

18. Cánepa, L. and R. Ferraraz (2012), 'Espetáculos do medo: O horror como atração no cinema japonês', *Contracampo*, 25, pp. 4–23, <https://periodicos.uff.br/contracampo/article/view/17268/10906> (last accessed 7 September 2021).

19. Referencing concepts by André Gaudreault, Tom Gunning and Diane Arnaud. See Gaudreault, A. (1984), 'Narration et monstration au cinéma', *Hors Cadre*, 2, pp. 87–98; Gunning, T. (2006), 'The Cinema of Attraction[s]: Early Film, Its Spectator and the Avant-Garde', in W. Strauven (ed.), *The Cinema of Attractions Reloaded*, Amsterdam: Amsterdam University Press, pp. 381–8; Arnaud, D. (2010), 'L'attraction fantôme dans le cinema d'horreur japonais contemporain', *Cinémas. Revue d'études cinematographiques*, 20: 2–3, pp. 120–41.

20. Cánepa and Ferraraz, 'Espetáculos do medo', p. 19.

21. Various problems on the route, besides her inexperience, increased the time spent navigating. However, the temporality of the director's trip was not merely restricted to a quantification of space-time, but also included the qualitative experience of the trek, thus much more related to *kairos*.

22. Popfilmes (2012), 'O tempo e o modo | 03. Lucrecia Martel', YouTube, 1 May 2012, <https://www.youtube.com/watch?v=dolsEOTrPF4> (last accessed 24 April 2021). Film at Lincoln Center (2018), '*Zama* Q&A | Lucrecia Martel', YouTube, 25 April 2018, <https://www.youtube.com/watch?v=JtdLaF5tlVs> (last accessed 24 April 2021).

23. Butler, J. (2018), *Problemas de Gênero: Feminismo e subversão da identidade*, Rio de Janeiro: Civilização Brasileira.

24. Butler, J. (1999), 'Corpos que pesam: Sobre os limites discursivos do sexo', in G. Lopes Louro (ed.), *O corpo educado: Pedagogias da sexualidade*, Belo Horizonte: Autêntica, p. 196.

25. Ibid. p. 195.

26. Baudrillard, J. (1991), *Simulação e simulacro*, Lisboa: Relógio d'água.

27. Baudrillard, J. (1970), *A sociedade do consumo*, Lisboa: Edições 70.

28. Brandi, M. A., D. González and G. Vorano (2016), 'Interview with Lucrecia Martel', *Lapso. Revista Anual de la Maestría en Teoría Psicoanalítica Lacaniana*, 1, <http://matpsil.com/revista-lapso/portfolio-items/martel-interview/> (last accessed 24 April 2021).

29. Arthuso, R. and V. Guimarães (2014), 'Entrevista com Nicole Brenez', *Cinética*, 10 February 2014, <http://revistacinetica.com.br/home/entrevista-com-nicole-brenez/> (last accessed 24 April 2021).

30. Guimarães, V. (2016), 'Sabotadores da indústria: Formas da implosão', in V. Guimarães (ed.), *Cadernos do Cineclube Comum #3 – Sabotadores da indústria*, Belo Horizonte: Cineclube Comum, pp. 13–17 (p. 17).

CHAPTER 6

Short Films as Aesthetic Freedom

Emilio Bernini

In the decade of the historical avant-garde (1920–30), when the short film was no longer subject to the strictly physical extension of the celluloid and the technical device of the camera (as was the case with Lumière's and Méliès's shorts), it constituted a whole in itself, independent of other subsequent projects and without being marginalised in the act of exhibition. In its origins, the short film, that is to say the cinema itself, used to be shown as an intermission in a play, or as an accompaniment to another show in the space of an entertainment fair. By contrast the avant-garde short film did not look to be screened as a central part of the show but, on the contrary, did not even include being screened among its main objectives.[1] If we consider the works of filmmakers such as Joris Ivens, Alberto Cavalcanti, Luis Buñuel, Dimitri Kirsanoff, Jean Epstein, René Clair and others, we can notice that what they filmed in the 1920s had a ground that was its very realisation. Later, in the 1930s, the emerging documentary cinema foreclosed that full expression of the avant-garde,[2] which filmed largely short films, for political (European fascist) and institutional (state propaganda) reasons, and thus largely ended short film's autotelism, or apparent aesthetic self-sufficiency.

Throughout the first half of the century of cinema, the short film had other manifestations, although static and well determined: one of its most common destinations was private or state advertising, whose commercial objectives or ideological persuasion made the short film's own short duration adequate, as happened in the United States with the Ford Motor Company's factual shorts,[3] or in Argentina with the series of newsreels *Sucesos Argentinos*, which were shown in theatres before the feature films. In industrial production, linked to the economic logic of industrial studies, the short film was absorbed until non-production, that is, until its very disappearance as an industrial commodity, by the imposition of the standard duration format of the long films (an average of ninety minutes), sustained in the dynamics of the star system.

But this absorption of the short film into the feature film was a question not only of economic order — the feature film was the only profitable commodity for the industry — but also of perceptive order. If the short film found its full expression — its 'pure form', as it were — in the decade of the classic avant-garde, this also meant that it had among its purposes to work with the language of cinema to produce a different perception, emancipated from narrative. The new perception produced by short films was fundamentally contrary to that which took place in feature films — mainly narrative films — but it also constituted a new perception in the field of plastic arts itself, since several of the filmmakers came from there (Man Ray, Fernand Léger, Hans Richter, Marcel Duchamp). This perception-short film, conceived by the historical avant-garde, is in fact what was foreclosed by the institution of the documentary, because the model of the documentary film is the fictional feature film. Its return would not take place until after the whole first half of the century of cinema.

This return of the perception-short film occurs with the great mutation of the image, one of whose modes was configured as what Deleuze called the 'time-image' and that he attributed to historical, political-ideological reasons, and in particular, to the concentration camps.[4] The experimental cinemas of the 1950s, especially in New York, have one of their cinematographic modalities in the short film: it constitutes one of its returns, in properly hallucinatory terms (in the sense of the return of the foreclosed): it is enough to see some of Stan Brakhage's shorts to understand that his idea of vision is of the order of hallucinated perception.[5] The other return is that which is associated with modern cinemas, as alternative cinemas, third-rate cinemas, critical in aesthetic-ideological terms of industrial productions. At first, modern cinemas find in the discursive modality of the short film the very possibility of an unregulated image in terms of perception, narrative and production, precisely because that image had been expelled from the industrial logic of the image.

I consider here, then, the short film, to study it in Lucrecia Martel's cinema, in these terms: as an autotelic filmmaking, emancipated from the commercial and narrative impositions typical of the other formats of cinema, such as the feature films and contemporary television series, which readapted the industrial feature film to a new duration now open to serial extension, and which constitute the contemporary merchandise of the audiovisual corporations. I also consider the short film as a production that can aspire to, or that contains *in nuce*, a type of aesthetic radicalism still possible, in the very era of post-radicality. In this way, I associate the short film with the aesthetic objectives of the historical avant-garde and experimental cinemas, but no longer in the sense of the postulate contrary to the institution of art proper to the avant-garde, nor in the sense of the perceptive hallucination proper to experimentation in cinema. Precisely for this reason

I will not consider Martel's shorts as 'avant-garde' or 'experimental': they are neither, since the historical times of the avant-garde and modern experimentation have already taken place, and since those are not the objectives of her shorts.

I.

In the history of modern Argentine cinema, the short film was the way into the field of cinema. As an essay, or a proof of the formal, stylistic and thematic possibilities of what can, could and would be filmed, the short film, unlike the long film, was full of potential, holding the promise of the future. This conception of the short film as offering the potential for expression was contemplated in the promotion of the experimental that took place in the institutional space of learning itself, that is, in the state educational institution ENERC (instituted by law in 1957), in the mid-sixties. In fact, in the very name of the state film school (Escuela Nacional de *Experimentación* y Realización Cinematográfica), the self-same institution where Lucrecia Martel studied in the late-1980s, this idea was already included as a potential form of testing, rehearsal, promise of innovation and aesthetic transformation.

The cinematographic training provided by the Argentine state in the mid-twentieth century had experimentation as its pedagogical objective. But it must be said that ENERC's idea of experimentation was based on the cinema of the historical avant-garde (expressionism, impressionism, the Soviet school) and not on contemporary New York experimental cinema (Maya Deren, Stan Brakhage, Michael Snow, Jonas Mekas).[6] Even before the creation of the state school, David José Kohon – one of the leading modernist filmmakers whose productions became known as the 'Generation of the 1960s' – made *The Arrow and a Compass/La flecha y un compás* (1950). Kohon called this short film, precisely in the sense of expressive potentialities, 'essay'. In this film, Kohon works with certain forms typical of the classic avant-garde: aberrant framing, generally low-angle and intense high-angle shots, overprinting, discontinuous editing and an iconography of the city that comes, in large part, from the French impressionist school and certain semantic elements of film noir. Each of the parts of this short film, divided by the image of a compass that is tracing with chalk concentric centripetal circles, 'rehearses' formal variations with the same materials – a man in a light coat, a woman, shots of the city, a pianist, a black and white tiled floor, railways – which are configured in different and multiple ways in each of the circles.

This non-narrative and essayistic radicalism of *The Arrow and a Compass* is tamed in Kohon's next short film, *Buenos Aires* (1958), in which, in effect, the aberrance of the previous image is neutralised in a shot that fits the anthropomorphic gaze and in a parallel montage that joins and contrasts two parts of the city:[7] the centre and the *villas miseria*, the urban mass and the individuals who live in the poor ranches, the urban movement and individual work. If this domestication of the aberrant of the discontinuous editing and the contrasting shots of the first short film took place, this allows us to observe that the short film was the way towards narration. In *Buenos Aires*, this tendency towards narration can already be seen, insofar as the parallel editing is a powerful generator of meaning immanent to the film, and it has been one of the central narrative features of industrial cinema since D. W. Griffith imposed it. When Kohon shot his first feature film, *Prisoners of the Night/Prisioneros de la noche* (1960), almost two years after his second short, the image was adapted to industrial narrative standards, even though his thematic and formal, spatial innovations (filming the slum, the poor areas of the city, the night, sexuality) and his alternative modes of production were opposed to the image of the old industry.

Lucrecia Martel's shorts, however, do not seem to have been a way for narration and for entering the field of industrial cinema, precisely because Martel did not oppose that cinema nor narrative, as neither did the cinema of the new line of filmmakers of the New Argentine Cinema or 'Generation of the 1990s'. Towards the end of the 1990s, the status of short films changed. With the foundation of film schools and universities, there was formed what could be called an extension of the field of cinema, so that its limit is no longer industrial study and training is no longer limited to the very experience of filming on its sets and in its workshops. This training has been definitively replaced by schools and universities that are already part of the field of cinema itself. In these new institutions, the short film is part of the learning and teaching, as a curricular exercise, of that very thing that will be made as a feature film and that will have its circulation in the contemporary film market made up of international financing institutions, a vast festival circuit, commercial releases in cinemas or on websites, and specialised critics. The short film of contemporary filmmakers is, then, already a production in the field of cinema and is already, potentially or not, part of the film market. If the short film for modern filmmakers was the possibility of entering the field of cinema whose frontier they had to cross, for contemporary filmmakers it is the very beginning of their activity.

That the short film of contemporary filmmakers is already part of the field and the film market can be noticed in the theatrical release of the series of films gathered under the name of *Short Stories/Historias breves* (1995), the result of the contest promoted by INCAA and composed of 'curricular' works by students of ENERC, the Escuela de Cinematografía de Avellaneda and the Universidad de Buenos Aires. In this film, there are already the works of those who, later on, would produce their feature films with, in some cases, narrative, stylistic and thematic elements that are already in the film: Lucrecia Martel, Adrián Caetano, Bruno Stagnaro, Daniel Burman, Sandra Gugliotta, Paula Hernández, Ulises Rosell. All of them will be part, in different critical configurations, of the New Argentine Cinema or 'cinema of the 1990s'. In this sense, between the short and the long film there is a thread of continuity, a direct line – and no longer the 'essayistic' search, as David J. Kohon called it, of a new image, not ruled by narrative, even if it later tended towards it.

Dead King/Rey Muerto is the short film that Martel presented as part of *Short Stories*. As for the narrative aspect, it follows the type of narration presented in the ENERC 'exercise' *You Won't Get Her, Bastard/No te la llevarás, maldito* (1989). It has all the features of a strongly edited narrative, with shifts between the virtual and the actual in the narrative line: in this case, between the dream of a child jealous of his mother, who imagines how he kills her lover, and the initial situation where the lovers talk on the phone. In the virtual, the lover dies, shot in the head; in the actual, the mother and her lover continue their phone conversation. In *Dead King* we are already looking at a film in which almost all the features of *auteur* films can be recognised, which Lucrecia Martel would shoot from 2001 onwards: not only the presence of actors of local prestige in Argentine cinema (Roly Serrano, in this case) but even a strongly elliptical montage, which produces a narrative with temporal jumps between scenes; frames with bodies piled up or whose locations in space are not precise; and a male chauvinist, patriarchal and provincial violence, which is always intertwined with erotic desire. Eroticism circulates in the violence of

Figure 6.1 *Dead King*: shooting at the oppressive patriarchal gaze

the environment, just as eroticism and violence are linked in all feature films. There is also an alliance of males, quickly and spontaneously formed, who run to warn el Cabeza, the violent husband, that his wife, Juana, is abandoning him, while she runs around the village with her three children and her dog. This alliance of males refers to the tacit alliance — also spontaneous and quick — of the Salta bourgeoisie's family to cover up the crime that Verónica might not even have committed, in *The Headless Woman/La mujer sin cabeza* (2008), as well as being linked to the group of criminals that the governors in *Zama* (2017) are obsessed by, in the figure of Vicuña Porto.

But in *Dead King* there is an instance of feminine freedom that, conversely, is not present in Martel's *auteur* films. Freedom here is an accident: the revolver that Juana bought from a group of men, to defend herself, has no bullets, as one of her sons tells her. However, in the last scene, when she faces el Cabeza she shoots him in the face and right in the eyes, just like the child in *You Won't Get Her, Bastard* shoots his mother's lover in the virtuality of his imagination, which also produces virtual freedom. In feature films, on the other hand, freedom is rather denied, again and again: the swamp of *The Swamp/La ciénaga* (2001) attracts the inhabitants of the house towards their indeterminate drive, keeps them stagnant and does not let them become; and there is no transcendent instance (the vision of the Virgin) that can avoid the entropy of the medium. In *Zama*, the colonial official Don Diego de Zama cannot get the transfer he wants throughout the film to get out of that suffocating and increasingly desolate space; on the contrary, he gradually sinks into the barbarism of the South American colony until he falls prisoner to the Mbayá Indians. *Dead King* and *You Won't Get Her, Bastard*, instead, have the power of a fable in which the conflict is resolved in a way that feature films lack. Freedom is either an accident or it is virtual. Now, in *Dead King*, what allegory is constituted by the shot in the eyes of the oppressive and murderous male (he runs over a cyclist on the road), in a short film in which Juana, the victim of the patriarchy, is observed by the whole town in her escape? *Dead King* is, in fact, made up of plans in which Juana is followed on her journey to freedom by the glance of all the inhabitants of the village. This permanent, inevitable look, and in it also part of the oppression itself, is what articulates the communication of the escape among the inhabitants and what allows the alliance of the males. If the gaze is part of male domination, is not the shot aimed at the very eyes of that patriarchal gaze that includes the entire people?

2.

In 2010, when Lucrecia Martel is already an author, in the sense of the French notion of *auteur* (that is, when we can already recognise in a corpus of films certain stylistic, structural and thematic elements that make up the author), after having filmed three features (*The Swamp, The Holy Girl, The Headless Woman*), she makes, in 2010, a short film to order, *New Argirópolis/Nueva Argirópolis*, for the state-backed series of short films *25 Looks, 200 Minutes/25 miradas, 200 minutos*, as part of the celebration of the Bicentennial of Argentina's independence, financed by the Secretaría Nacional de Cultura y la Universidad Nacional de Tres de Febrero. The film is anything but a celebration of the Bicentennial of the birth of the fatherland, and as a short film, it has a remarkable autotelic power that makes the features of the author's poetics extreme, surpassing them to the point of challenging even narrative.

At first, it takes the title of Domingo Faustino Sarmiento's text, *Argirópolis* (1850), a project of union of the Argentine provinces, Paraguay and Uruguay, which was forgotten after the fall of the governor, Juan Manuel de Rosas, in the Battle of Caseros (1852), because it was written specifically in the context of internal and external wars; once the wars were over, the utopian ideal crumbled. But with that title, Martel does not imagine a bold utopia like Sarmiento's but rather to allude, in *New Argirópolis*, to the great excluded from that same project: the native ethnic groups, repressed and assassinated from the nineteenth to the twenty-first centuries by the liberal and neoliberal state. This repressive violence is what the short film stages, based on two elements: first, central to Sarmiento's liberal political project, the navigability of the rivers; second, the fate of Martín García Island, which Sarmiento's utopia suggested as the capital of Argirópolis, and which after the ethnic genocide of 1879 (the so-called Conquest of the Desert by General Roca) became a place of reclusion for the Indians who survived the massacre.[8] These are then the two semantic elements linked to the Sarmiento project and its future, and at the same time to the present of the Bicentennial: to navigate the rivers and to confine Indians. Thus, *New Argirópolis* seems to point out that the liberal and neoliberal project keeps the policies towards the Indians intact.

The first image in the film is that of a shot in which two gendarmes and a girl see how the gendarmerie boat tows, on the Bermejo River, a raft made of plastic bottles: the short begins like this *in medias res*, when the arrest of a group of native Wichí ('one female and four male' in police jargon) – who wanted to cross the river on a raft of plastic bottles ('camalotes'), allegedly carrying drugs – has already happened, when they are already handcuffed in the police station. What follows is an elliptical narrative of the bureaucratic and banal process, but of a banality that subjects the bodies of the other ethnic groups to an institutional and arbitrary order, ranging from the placing of handcuffs, through the registration of those arrested, the taking of X-rays to verify that they do not carry drugs in their bodies, to their release. This process is interrupted by conversations between natives, adults and children whose pragmatic situation is never revealed. These conversations are shots inserted into that minimal narrative of capture, bureaucratic process and liberation, but these shots are there not as contrast, nor continuity, nor explanation, but on the contrary as scenes of a minority language policy.

Figure 6.2 *New Argirópolis*: the minoritarian politics of the Wichí language undoes neoliberal narration

The minority language policy has in the short an effect of dissemination and disarticulation of the narrative. What is disseminated disturbs the narrative of the police bureaucratic process, deliberately fragments and threatens intelligibility through the ethnic voices that are heard. But it should be noted that this threat of unintelligibility does not occur as a contrast, nor as a confrontation, but as a dissemination. These are small scenes all linked to the Wichí language and the difficulty and (im)possibility of translation. I highlight two senses in the dissemination of the meaning that the short film exerts: on the one hand, the gendarmerie investigates a video of a Wichí woman whose language they do not understand and whose speech mentions 'Argirópolis'; then, in another scene, discontinuous, two girls are made to translate the video, and one of them whispers a phrase that puts the *indigenous* people in phonetic relation with the *indigents* to point out the invisibility of the Indians and the poor, just as in a previous scene, a Wichí man wondered why all the ethnic groups in northern Argentina are poor. On the other hand, a woman explains to children the brown colour of the river water and the formation, by sedimentation, of islands: suddenly, like the whisper of the girl who relates the natives to poverty, a girl here refers to the semantic element of the island: the islands that are formed have no owner, 'they belong to no one'. What does the girl mean, with her low tone, when she says that these islands, which are formed by sedimentation, have no owners? The Wichí language and the speakers of that language thus become an opaque element that resists police investigation, but which enunciates, like an oracle, truths. This same resistance, as a language policy, is exercised in the short against the intelligibility of the story. In the terms of our proposal, this resistance to the intelligibility of the story, and the commitment to a perception that does not depend on the narrative but on the precarious associations that ellipses can produce, belongs to the autotelism of the short film.

3.

This autotelism reaches a notorious degree of culmination in *Muta* (2011), considering that it is a short advertising film that Martel filmed for the Prada brand Miu Miu. At first, the film does not know, or does not fit, the advertising objectives of the sale of the merchandise; on the contrary, the very fine dresses of the women's clothing brand and the women themselves who wear them become here elements of a *mise-en-scène* that withdraw from the bodies what is destined to be seen in advertising: the faces, the movements typical of the fashion show, the grace and beauty objectified by the women.

In *Muta*, the bodies are presented in a strange state of automation: their movements seem mechanical, as if they were non-human or post-human creatures with the bodies of women and brand name dresses, on a luxury cruise liner stopped, alone. After the conventional shots setting the scene, the electricity is activated in the empty ship, a sign with a woman's silhouette is turned on, and a small door opens to the lower part of the cruise liner, out of the field of view, the engine or storeroom. From there they emerge, from that imageless background, activated by that electric movement, those automated bodies, moved by a will that doesn't seem to be their own, crawling until they stand up. This mechanised, electrified movement of the bodies with female forms is accentuated in the strangeness produced by the blinking of the artificial eyelashes (worked in sound terms), in the way they devour paper, as if it were their way of feeding, in their way of walking almost by strides, in the diving suits that some of them wear when they spray another one with some contaminating liquid. They also scream, like a mechanism groans, not with the sound produced by human pain itself; some of them throw from the heel of their hands a white thread, which refers to spiders.

All these features are part of the semantics of genre films: horror, science fiction. The former is of particular interest to Martel, and there are elements of each in her films: the very title of *The Headless Woman* ironically refers to it, but the disorder of her main character, Vero, as well as the hallucinatory perception of the prosecutor Zama, in the eponymous film,[9] also constitute reformulations of this popular genre. In *Muta*, there are *semas* of science fiction that do not exclude horror. The difference with her use of them in feature films lies precisely in the fact that in these films, the semas are subordinated, controlled, and limited to the demand for narrative proper to feature films and authorship. In this short film, the semas (of horror and science fiction) are, so to speak, released. In this elliptical and strange narrative, *Muta* presents a post-human world of women speaking in their own language, and in which there are even living organisms that affect women (the shot of the wallet that contains a body that vibrates and groans) and act in the moments before the disappearance of one of them, who vanishes to take flight in another non-corporeal form, or at least not a visible one (the soundtrack, after the disappearance of the body, is that of a flying bird).

In this representation of a closed, empty space, traversed by bodies that have incorporated into their movements an automation whose causes are not narrated, the short film is sufficient in itself. In other words, the short film allows this representation that is alien to the expectations of the market, to the demands of the author and the specialised critics who, in a certain way, seem to want to confirm, in each author's film, the recurrence of its features. The somewhat adverse reception of *Zama* at the festivals that scorned the film (Cannes, Venice), and its relative success on a commercial level have to do with the fact that it is a feature film that makes autotelic decisions, and in this, fragments, disperses and makes more complex the narrative that tends to become perception. In this sense, Martel's short films are a format of aesthetic freedom, in the most radical sense of the word.

4.

In *Dead King*, in *New Argirópolis* and in *Muta* there is a film policy. In *Dead King*, freedom as a contingency opens up to the future without oppression that begins at the bridge crossing, on the part of Juana and her children, and that allegorically shoots in the eyes of the macho and patriarchal gaze of the entire people. In *New Argirópolis*, the politics is that of the minority language, of the reformulation of the Sarmientine semas characteristic of the liberal state pro-gramme, and of the resistance to the neoliberal narrative, which is the one that predominates today in the networks. In *Muta* there seems to be an allegory for the mutation of women as fashion models, as a consequence of the objectifica-tion of the female body and the alienation of subjectivity in the constitution of a body in the image of merchandise. This alienation and this objectification of the body itself would have produced the mutation represented in the short film: the models are post-human creatures, who have transformed their bodies, their movements, their food and their existence until extinction (or until transforma-tion, a new mutation into another, no longer corporeal, stage).

On the other hand, in *Fish/Pescados* (2010), a short film made for the Notodofilmfest – a short film festival – the allegory, if any, is rather playful. The procedure is simple: there is no assembly of strong ellipses, no people

Figure 6.3 *Fish*: a pure lack of motivation

or characters, no human bodies. There is just a close-up of koi carp in the water, with music by Juana Molina, and an overlay of a road with cars travelling through a dark sunset during a storm. Overprinting also affects the fish, because when they open their mouths to breathe, voices are loudly overprinted. Those voices that 'sing' the fish refer to the cars, which we see intermittently on dark road shots, to the horns, the headlights, the absence of dogs. 'We all were a car', one of the fish says at one point. The short film establishes an unprecedented, unexpected, playful relationship between the cars on the road in the storm and the fish in the water. The indiscernibility of this arbitrary and playful relationship, whose common element cannot be but water (the water that falls and the water in which the fish live), seems to be suggested when one of the fish sings 'Dream, come!', so the images of the shadowy road would be part of the dream of the fish that would be cars.

The collaboration of the experimental artist Juana Molina seems to guide the short film in its decisions: the experimentation here lies in the completely unmotivated link between the route in the rain and the fish; in the imagination, especially sound and musical, which makes the fish sing a dream of a journey, or puts words into their breathing movements. Experimentation, in this sense, does not have a teleology: it is part of a musical and visual inquiry that does not follow a project or a programme, except for the playful practice itself. In the same way, it does not demand and cannot receive an allegorical reading: what do fish that dream of being cars on the road allegorise?

It is the pure act, so to speak, of creation itself. In *Fish* there are no authorial traits, nor is there any politicisation of the image, just as there are no situations of confinement and oppression in a medium that degrades, as happens in long films. In this, the short film, for a prestigious author, with the demands that this imposes, is the format of very short duration, of that freedom of creation. In this way, the short film (non-narrative, which assumes experimentation in the format, which has no formal specificity except the absence of specificity, which finds its end in itself) is one of the paths to aesthetic freedom in the contemporary world of globalised narration.

NOTES

1. Albéra, F. (2009), *La vanguardia en el cine*, Buenos Aires: Manantial, p. 96.
2. Bullot, E. (2013), *Sortir du cinéma: Histoire virtuelle des relations de l'art et du cinéma*, Geneva: Musée d'Art Moderne et Contemporain, p. 86.
3. Chanan, M. (2007), *The Politics of Documentary*, London: British Film Institute, p. 68.
4. Deleuze, G. (1987), *La imagen-tiempo: Estudios sobre cine 2*, Buenos Aires: Paidós.
5. Brakhage, S. (2001), *Essential Brakhage*, New York: Macpherson, pp. 12–13.
6. The North American experimental cinema was not known in Argentina until the years of state terrorism (1976–83) through the diffusion of some of Michael Snow's films, by Narcisa Hirsch, as well as through the making of her own films. Hirsch was one of the promoters of the 'Goethe group'. In Argentina, experimental cinema is promoted by women, unlike what happens in New York. See Denegri, A. (2020), 'El grupo Goethe. Cine experimental, cine militante, underground y clandestino (1974–1982)', Bachelor's thesis, Universidad del Cine.
7. On this notion of 'aberrance', see Deleuze, G. (2018), *Cine III. Verdad y tiempo. Potencias de lo falso*, Buenos Aires: Cactus.
8. Forcinito, A. (2015), 'Los cristales de la memoria, voces y miradas frente a la historia argentina', *Revista Iberoamericana*, 81: 251, pp. 409–33.
9. Bernini, E. (2017), 'El hundimiento. A propósito de *Zama*', *Kilómetro III*, 13 October 2017, <http://kilometroIIIcine.com.ar/el-hundimiento/> (last accessed 29 April 2021).

CHAPTER 7

Masculinity, Desire and Performance in *The Holy Girl*

Gonzalo Aguilar

After finishing their catechism lessons, Amalia and her friends take a walk around the small Salta town they live in. They usually stop by the storefront of a shop in which a musician demonstrates a theremin, a Russian instrument which works through electromagnetic waves. People crowd the pavement before what appears to be a miracle: an instrument which produces sounds not through contact, but through the movements of the player's hands. This scene before the music store happens three times in Lucrecia Martel's *The Holy Girl/La niña santa* (2004). In two of them, we see sexual harassment or what we could call, for lack of an established concept, the *apoyada*.[1] During the first scene, Dr Jano – who is in town to take part in a professional congress – approaches Amalia from behind and presses himself against her. The teenager is frozen, and the aggressor runs away when she turns to look at his face. Amalia, who is just out of her catechism lessons, sees this event as part of a divine plan involving her and this stranger, whom she will later identify as Jano. The second time they meet on the pavement, Amalia takes the initiative and stands before Jano for him to repeat the action. She also tries to touch his hand, and when he pulls it away, scared, she immediately turns to look at him. Jano escapes again. He does not know yet that Amalia is the daughter of Helena, the owner of the hotel he is staying at, whom he is trying to seduce. Jano is also unaware that Amalia believes they are both part of that 'divine plan', which she refers to as 'the calling' after the topic they are covering in her catechism lessons.

Sexual harassment in public spaces is a rather frequent occurrence and has a prominent role in discussions of gender-based violence.[2] It is evident that it bears a significant material and symbolic weight for Lucrecia Martel: the first scene in her first film (the 1995 short feature *Dead King/Rey Muerto*) opens with three characters sitting at a bar table, under a Rambo poster, and watching journalist Silvia Fernández Barrio on TV. Back then, she was on everyone's lips because someone had touched her buttocks during her coverage of the attack on the Israeli embassy in Buenos Aires in 1992.[3] The viewers' remarks (including those of the protagonist, that is, the titular 'dead king') stress the idea of seeing the professional more as a touchable female body than a journalist.[4] The harassment of this woman, which had happened in real life, continues in the media. The huge distance from the televised scene (the show is broadcast from Buenos Aires, but watched in Salta) does not hinder the macho fantasy of the female body as something one has the right to touch.

Carried out in public, against women who are not personally known by the aggressor, who remains invisible, this *apoyada* or 'frottage' – as labelled by a female friend who lives in Europe, where she says the practice is quite frequent as well – defines or confirms the relative places of power of men and women in the public space. Moreover, the actualisation of patriarchal power it suggests also attempts to define a (female) subject and endow it with a psychic inner world comprising fear, guilt and shame. This practice, as a bodily performance, draws a deep difference between inner life (disgust, repulsion, impotence) and the outside world (the inability to denounce this harassment): that difference lets women know about the distance between their idea of a public space and the reality waiting for them. According to that rationale, women are allowed in the public space on the condition that their bodies are touchable and, thus, subordinated to males (upon contact, the male body becomes a phallus; it is the penis itself which becomes a phallus). *The Holy Girl* is a filmic reflection on the power of this ancient practice as reproduced by Jano.

This public act is a variety of sexual harassment, but with specific features. In general, it takes place on public transport, the frontier between private and public spaces, between home life and work life, between trust in others' caring gazes and the indifferent gazes of strangers: it is one in a series of initiation rites which men want to impose on women. The attacker derives something priceless from the means of transport, but also from other types of crowds: the presence of others. Not only does that facilitate the task and make it easier to hide: the indifference of others shows that this act of domination fails to change the relationship between people in this space. It is not that no one wants to help the victim. Rather, what the aggressor wants is for his victim to feel other people are indifferent to her desperation and powerlessness. Fear and paralysis fuel the attacker's arousal, because he is looking not for sexual satisfaction, but for the feeling of domination. The victim's stillness, the rigidity in her body, is central: the victim's body must remain passive (as we know, fear boosts the attacker's adrenaline). What for the victim is knowledge (or realisation) of her place in the public space before the gaze of others, for the attacker is awareness of the power the patriarchy has endowed him with.

This warning (aggression) is, thus, a way to welcome women into the patri-archy. In general, victims are teenagers, not only because they are more helpless, but also because the practice entails a macho pedagogy, a rite of passage: this is your body (which I can touch), this is your owner, this is your future. In the case of a grown woman – for instance, Silvia Fernández Barrio – it appears to have been a very telling way of pointing out a professional shortcoming: you are not a journalist, you are *only* a touchable body. This idea is stressed by the men watching TV in *Dead King*.

Even though the *apoyada* lacks the brutality of outright rape and is perhaps less traumatic than overt workplace harassment, it is also inherent to the male structure of macho desire.[5] Moreover, of all harassment situations, this is the most depersonalised and, thus, the most structural from the point of view of power, the one that expresses power most immediately (inasmuch as bodies convey social mores directly). If 'gender is the discursive and corporal practice in which the subject acquires social intelligibility and political recognition',[6] this action provides bodies with an immediate intelligibility in the public space and in the power relations produced by patriarchal society.

In *The Holy Girl*, harassment scenes play a key role: the protagonist is Amalia (who opens and closes the film), one of the enigmas moving the plot forward is the realisation by Jano that his victim is Helena's daughter, and one of the major themes (i.e. what this 'divine calling' entails) is embodied in this action.[7] In fact, the film's poster shows the moment in which Amalia turns to look her attacker in the eye. We could say that *The Holy Girl* is, among other things, the story of how Amalia gets to know herself, how she discovers, recognises or constructs her

Figure 7.1 *The Holy Girl*. © Lita Stantic Producciones

place in the world. If Amalia sees harassment as the plan God has laid down for her, one has to wonder as well what led Jano, a reputable professional, to harass a teenager. What pleasure does he derive from approaching and pressing himself against her?

This question is hard to answer, because Jano is an opaque character, and its action does not represent a defining trait: it is something he does circumstantially (he does not go there with harassment in mind, but takes advantage of a random situation). That is particularly interesting. Jano is far from being an overbearing pervert (a description which could fit his colleague, Dr Vesalio). Rather, he is a somewhat shy family man (he is married, with three children) and shows himself as proper and kind-natured. What leads him to harass a teenager? What pleasure does he draw from his actions? This is evidently not a quest for sexual pleasure, as it involves but a few seconds of physical contact (even though those few seconds seem centuries to Amalia). Jano's kindness or decency do not necessarily clash with what he did, and it would appear both sides can coexist without conflict. One of the features of domination is precisely that, in order for it to continue over time, it need not be cruel or evil. An ordinary man, shy and respectful, can exercise domination as well (after all, before being ordinary, shy and respectful, he is a man). What is more, the social celebration of the 'lightest' varieties of harassment is part of a society constructed around male desire and approves of – or even encourages – attitudes like Jano's. A very popular scene from Italian Dino Risi's film *Il Sorpasso* (1962), whose conclusion was popular for several years, shows different subtleties of the *apoyada*. At a restaurant's ballroom, Bruno Cortona (Vittorio Gassman) dances a slow dance with the Commendatore's wife (played by Franca Polesello). He hugs her and presses himself against her. When she says 'Oh-la-la', feeling the hardness of his penis, Vittorio Gassman whispers, 'Not to brag, but . . .' ('Modestamente . . .'). It falls short of a textbook sexual harassment situation, but that may be what makes it interesting: the celebration by the audience of Gassman's wit speaks of something deep-rooted. Gassman is a natural-born seducer, and triggers the macho question: what woman would not like being harassed by him? The male sexual fantasy of appropriation of the female body thrives and is reaffirmed in that quip by Gassman. It is as if Jano, only on account of his being a man, without bragging about it, wanted to enjoy the property due to him as a man.

In *The Holy Girl*, there are multiple variations of harassment as well: from the doctor–patient relationship to that between Dr Vesalio and the brands' representatives.[8] However, if Dr Vesalio is what could be defined as a party animal, Jano is emotionally repressed. It is precisely his lack of masculinity, his struggle with masculinity, with what a macho man is supposed to be, that leads him to reaffirm it in a covert, dark and shameful way. As if he were not harassing, but merely channelling the patriarchal power he is supposed to embody. Hence his two-faced nature and his name (a reference to the Roman god Janus). As if the sexual initiative he fails to achieve with Helena (it is she who finally advances and kisses him) could be displayed with a helpless girl (who, in a dark twist of fate, is the daughter of the woman he dare not seduce). When pressing himself against her, Jano not only creates a subdued female subject, but a male subject which represents the ideal he cannot attain. Jano looks for the most vulnerable victim, but finds the strength of the one who has faith and believes in God.

The scenes from *The Holy Girl* analysed here cannot be understood without referring to the construction of shots. Lucrecia Martel does not denounce harassment, but rather reveals its mechanisms through images and sounds. In her narrations, the body receives sound, visual and tactile stimuli which are irreducible relative to each other, leading the viewer to interpret differences, mismatches and coincidences. The theremin is perhaps the best symbol of the allegory of senses in her filmography: it entrances the audience ('a marvel', says one character to describe it), and at the same time causes them to wonder *how it works*. This combination of overwhelming heterogeneous sensations and intellectual enquiry spans Martel's work, from *Dead King* to *Zama* (2017).

Both harassment scenes last approximately the same length of time (about a minute and forty seconds) and can be interpreted in opposition to each other. The difference is that the second time, Amalia takes an active role and attempts to interact with Jano (something which the *apoyada* does not entail), but both scenes' shots have similarities. In the first scene, the theremin plays Bach, which could suggest a mystical atmosphere to Amalia (though the D-minor Concerto BWV 1059 is not a particularly religious work). In the second scene, the music is the famous 'Habanera' from Georges Bizet's *Carmen*, an opera about one of the most notorious cases of gender-based violence.[9] The moment played in the theremin is not the murder of Carmen by Don José, but the moment in which she sings 'L'amour est un oiseau rebelle' ('Love is a rebellious bird'). Carmen's statement coincides with Amalia's, though with more profane intentions: 'L'amour est enfant de bohème, / Il n'a jamais, jamais, connu de loi. / Si tu ne m'aimes pas, je t'aime. / Et si je t'aime, prends garde à toi!'

In her construction of shots, Martel highlights three aspects: first, Jano's arrival from the other side of the street with a depth of field which masculinises space, like an environment appropriated by his body. It is as if the urban social space in which the scene takes place was marked by gender relations before the characters' actions. The second aspect is the fragmentation, typical of Martel's framing, focused on Amalia's and Jano's trousers, in their hands, in the subtle movements of the harassment. The shot's fragmentation leaves the scene devoid of any sexuality: once again, this action has more to do with displaying power than with sexual satisfaction. Finally, in the first scene, the camera focuses for a significant time on Amalia's face. According to Natalia Christofoletti Barrenha, 'The face of the girl — through subtle contortions of alienation, horror, fear, and pleasure — even appears illuminated by a mysterious (divine?) light, creating an epiphany.[10] Amalia expresses all those affections in a subdued fashion, as required by the extortive violence of the *apoyada*. Jano, on the other hand, conveys an absolute impassiveness, as if he were also unable to express the pleasure derived from his domination of her. The action is an internalisation in all its aspects: taking place in a social space, it is – due to its violence – individual, private and silent. They are both vulnerable, but in different ways: Jano, to the power of the patriarchy; Amalia, to the powers of catechesis.

One of the immediate effects of the harassment is that the victim, failing to find help or an anchor point in the gaze of the others, ends up accepting her place, due either to powerlessness or to fear. Exterior supports are fundamental to stand up to abuses of this type, to exercise resistance and put forward a subjectivity different from that which the harassment wants to bring about. Amalia does not have the tools made available by feminist movements or the 'Ni una menos' collective as a counter-pedagogy and as a means to create empowered subjects who say their bodies are not anyone's to touch, their bodies are their own. Amalia does a religious reading of events, but in submitting herself to that power she unexpectedly finds new roads along which she will reaffirm herself as a woman. Amalia's reading is not wrong, but rather self-interested: she reads the act as a message about the Lord's domination and plans for her. During that process, Amalia discovers that her body is hers. Not someone else's property (as Jano would presume) but something she herself owns.[11] The divine plan issuing from heaven ends up becoming an earthly and profane life project.

Amalia's first interpretation must be framed against her catechism lessons and the words of the poem by Saint Teresa of Ávila used to open the film:

> Yours I am, for You I was born,
> What is your will for me?
> Sovereign Majesty,
> Wisdom eternal,
> Kindness pleasing to my soul;
> God, sublime, one Being Good,
> Behold this one so vile
> Signing of her love to you: What do you want of me, Lord?
> [. . .]
> All of me I surrender to you.

Amalia interprets the harassment as something that happens under God's gaze, and her conclusion is not without logic. Her catechism lessons are also a pedagogy aimed at her accepting and constructing her role as a woman subjected to God (and, as God is usually unavailable, a Lord will surely appear); made for God's Sovereign Majesty, ready for his calling and surrendered at his feet. At

Figure 7.2 *The Holy Girl.* © Lita Stantic Producciones

the junction between catechesis and harassment, Amalia looks to Jano's act as a means to justify her existence. Her teenage subjectivity, awakening to sexuality, arises from her interpellation by Jano and by God (the 'calling'). Amalia identifies with her attacker and even imagines him as part of her own divine plan: they will achieve redemption together.

There lies the difference between the two harassment scenes: in the first one, Jano stands behind Amalia; but in the second one, she places herself before him. A scene which appears to depict the confirmation of her submission actually shows the way towards a *new* Amalia. She first *lets* Jano press himself against her, then tries to touch his hand, and finally turns for the Lord to look at her and recognise her as part of a shared plan. Jano, however, runs away. He is but a man, scared of being discovered, and failing to notice that his victim is looking for collusion, and not to denounce him. Even though the recognition of this sovereign gaze is taken from her, Amalia insists with the idea of the plan, but will gradually discover that the plan must surely be different (i.e. that there is no recognition to be found in that sovereign gaze). Amalia and Jano's story ends in the hotel room, when she tries to kiss him, only to be turned away, getting her eye hurt by accident. 'You are good', the teenager tells him twice, but he fails to understand. The misunderstanding is predictable and governs the plot's leaps forward: Jano visits Helena to confess what he did with her daughter, and Helena misreads this and kisses him; Josefina's parents find her in bed with her cousin, and she tells the story of her friend's harassment to cover herself, causing her parents to feel obliged to denounce the doctor at the hotel. The mismatch between images and sounds is replicated between intentions, actions, and their reactions.

However, if Amalia fails to find justification for her existence in Jano's gaze (harassment as a calling), two roads will appear that will enable her to move to a different life. In a scene in her room, Amalia masturbates and gains access to a pleasure Jano will not give her. The same hand she had moved before looking to touch her ally (or attacker) is now a source of comfort and pleasure (i.e. she surrenders herself not to the Lord, but to her own body). However, there is a second way out, one much more important, because it includes the gaze of the other. Throughout the story, Josefina remains Amalia's loyal friend, and she also gives her the kiss Jano refused to accept. With her, the gaze of the Lord disappears. Josefina is so ingrained in Amalia's world that part of her face finds its way into the shot when Jano harasses her friend. Moreover, that scene finishes with a complicit look between Josefina and Amalia, as if the gaze returned by the attacker anchored itself in her friend.

This forking of the story between the divine plan with Jano and friendship with Josefina causes the film to have, in a certain sense, two endings: Jano and Helena's, in the doctor–patient performance which will close the congress; and Amalia and Josefina's, in the swimming pool, pledging their eternal allegiance to each other.

The role-play which was to close the congress ultimately fails to take place. The viewer witnesses only the preamble of what is to be the doctor's public humiliation before his colleagues and family.[12] Before coming on stage, Jano finds out that 'they came to denounce a doctor who touched that girl from the hotel'. His clandestine act will be revealed, and the macho man he once wanted to embody will be his ruin. Meanwhile, in what could be seen as a second ending, Josefina and Amalia swim in the hotel's pool. 'I will always look after you', Josefina tells Amalia. 'You have no sisters. I'm your sister.' When Amalia replies that her father is expecting twins, she stresses the gender. 'I mean *sisters*.' Amalia failed to be the vehicle for a divine plan, but found a friend, an affective relationship which became a blood bond. However, perhaps these are not two endings but one: two ways of telling two events which are part of the same fabric. What has been proved over time is that raising awareness about harassment and sorority are two sides of the same coin: against gender violence, against harassment in public spaces, a new subject emerges to undermine the foundations of the patriarchy.

Translated by Juan Ignacio García Fahler

NOTES

1. There is no specific term to refer to this action in English. What could be the reason for that namelessness? Is it the victims' inability, due to their position of weakness, to name it and thus make the phenomenon more visible and provide it with a social status? Or is it the

performative nature of the act itself, its bodily nature, which bars all discursiveness? Could it be that the action rejects a noun (with the stillness it entails) and requires the fluidness of a verb, seeing as the wording most commonly used to describe the action in Spanish is 'se la apoyó' (translated as 'he pressed it against her'), showing the prominence of the phallus (mentioned with the female pronoun 'la', as is usual in Spanish)? The use of a verb may refer to the need to insert the subject in the action, rather than crystallising it in a noun.

2. Of course, as we are dealing with a clandestine practice, there are no reliable statistics available. However, when in June 2016 the 'Ni una menos' collective encouraged women to speak out on social media about their experiences as victims, there were countless testimonies about harassment in public spaces (particularly on public transport). The 2 January 2019 edition of the magazine *Veintitrés* covers a report by the Development Bank of Latin America and the Fédération Internationale de l'Automobile which analysed the issue in the City of Buenos Aires, the Greater Buenos Aires Area, Santiago de Chile and Quito. See 'El acoso en el transporte público, otro drama cotidiano: 7 de cada 10 mujeres lo sufren', *Veintitrés*, 2 January 2019, <https://www.veintitres.com.ar/politica/El-acoso-en-el-transporte-publico-otro-drama-cotidiano-7-de-cada-10-mujeres-lo-sufren--20190102-0005.html> (last accessed 7 September 2021).

3. In fact, the film opens with an image of the journalist on the TV screen. There are several testimonies about this event available in YouTube, and about how she was criticised for not being professional enough.

4. I use the term *tocable* in Spanish, which, although not commonly used, expresses with its violence on language the type of gender-based attribute bodies have in public spaces.

5. Teresa de Lauretis refers to rape as a 'sado-fetishist' fantasy of the male structure of desire. The expression is applied to the action by which a man presses himself against a woman. See de Lauretis, T. (1992), *Alicia ya no (Feminismo, semiótica, cine)*, Valencia: Cátedra, p. 144.

6. Preciado, P. B. (2014), *Testo yonqui (Sexo, drogas y biopolítica)*, Buenos Aires: Paidós, p. 95. While the words are Paul Beatriz Preciado's, they are a synthesis of Judith Butler's position in several of her books. See, for instance, Butler, J. (2016), *El género en disputa: El feminismo y la subversión de la identidad*, Buenos Aires: Paidós, p. 83.

7. A political-cinematographic reading of the scene is available in Alarcón, F. (2018), 'El miedo cambia de lado', *Latfem*, 18 December 2018, <https://latfem.org/una-apoyada-cine-martel-los-espectros-del-feminismo/> (last accessed 30 July 2020).

8. Of course, there are other relationships of power which do not necessarily involve gender. I present a general analysis of the film in the chapter '*La niña santa* y el cierre de la representación', in my book *Otros mundos: Un ensayo sobre el nuevo cine argentino*, Buenos Aires: Santiago Arcos, 2006. The key thesis of the chapter states that, while Helena is a prisoner of the clear visual relationships of representation, Amalia, instead, dives into a confusing sound labyrinth and resorts to sounds, touch and even smell to catch Jano, the man she is trying to save. She escapes the visual order (which frustrates desire) to move in another, made of sounds, smells and surfaces. An English edition is available: Aguilar, G. (2008), *Other Worlds: New Argentine Film*, New York: Palgrave Macmillan.

9. In fact, in 2018, a feminist version of the opera premiered at the Teatro del Maggio Musicale in Florence, directed by Leo Muscato, with a different ending: rather than being murdered by Don José, Carmen stands up to him and kills him. As expected, the change sparked a lot of controversy.

10. Christofoletti Barrenha, N. (2020), *La experiencia del cine de Lucrecia Martel: Residuos del tiempo y sonidos al borde de la pileta*, Buenos Aires: Prometeo, p. 89.

11. I propose reading 'my body is my own' not as psychological-scientific statement, but as a political-pragmatic one, which aims at expressing not a fact or a piece of knowledge,

but a means for action and affirmation; that is, that 'my own' does not speak of property (following the patriarchal and hierarchical rationale of the lords) but of possession or usufruct (shared use, the right to enjoy something that belongs to someone else in a relationship between equals).

12. In *The Swamp/La ciénaga* (2001), two girls sing before the fan, which warps their voices, the following children's song: 'Doctor Jano, he is a surgeon, / He must operate today / In the operating room / A girl who is his age. / She is twenty-one / And you're older by a year. / Doctor Jano, dear surgeon, / Don't you go falling for her.' According to Diego Lerer, this is a rhyme which children would sing in Spain, inspired in the gorgeous Dr Gannon from the *Medical Center* series, and was not in the original script, but was provided by one of the girls during casting. Lerer, D. (2003), 'Lobo suelto, cordero atado', *Clarín*, 17 July 2003, <https://www.clarin.com/espectaculos/lobo-suelto-cordero-atado_0_HysTleCYg.html/> (last accessed 28 April 2021).

CHAPTER 8

Other Areas: The Bio-communal and Feminine Utopia of *Cornucopia*

Alejandra Laera

MEANINGS OF CORNUCOPIA

Coloured petals unfurl and close in gigantic holograms, flowers, stems and various mushrooms which seem to advance towards us, the audience, from the back and the sides of the stage. Lines and stains which lengthen, expand and escape. Transparencies and mobile filters which reveal or suggest. Flashing lights which intermittently focus on the huge crowd. Everything surrounds us in *Cornucopia*, Icelandic singer Björk's show inspired by her 2018 album *Utopia* and premiered in 2019, which had Lucrecia Martel as theatrical director, who delighted us with the bodies on the stage just as she did from *The Swamp/La ciénaga* (2001) to *Zama* (2017). As in the futuristic fancies of the artist's other albums, as in the sensory and dense realisms of the Argentine director, we feel we step into a different time, with a different speed, and into a different space, with a new gravity.[1]

On stage, Björk drifts with minimal and undulating movements, behind a dazzling mask which surrounds her eyes and in a white dress with tubular sleeves, absolutely retrofuturistic.[2] Before our eyes she is at times almost imperceptible and surprisingly omnipresent; small on the stage, her body and her voice issue forth a force which magnetises space thoroughly. That presence is consistent with her music's sounds, from the constant whisper to the long wail. All the while she sings, in a mantric covenant of sorts, about caring for each other. The affectionate verse echoes in different tones in 'The Gate', the song aptly chosen to open the show. A cast of ethereal power joins Björk on a stage made up of platforms whose organic shapes suggest mushrooms and enable movements with appearances and disappearances. There we see Viibra, the all-female Icelandic seven-flute ensemble, whose members traverse the space lightly and, during one of the show's most intense moments, play a circular flute collectively, as a harmonious ring which moves apart only to come together again. We see a harpist too, whose image speaks of a different world. And we have Austrian percussionist Manu Delago, known from the musical experience born of the 2011 album *Biophilia*, who works miracles on the hang and resorts to natural elements like water and stone for his sound, which become music before our eyes. One of the show's high points is 'Blissing Me', a song sung beautifully with Serpentwithfeet, another experimental musician, with whom Björk really seems to celebrate a state of bliss live: 'falling in love to a song'. If a cornucopia is that horn of plenty which in Classical mythology symbolises fecundity and generous profusion, that is precisely what we get from a *mise-en-scène* in full harmony with the music.[3]

Lucrecia Martel became part of the *Cornucopia* project only in January 2019, when production was quite advanced. It had all started some time before, when Alex Poost, The Shed's artistic director, invited Björk to prepare a special project for the inauguration of the main hall of the new and astonishing New York cultural venue.[4] In fact, during an interview, Martel points out that she would have liked to have been more involved in the '360 experience that show had', for instance, as regards the perception of sounds from different places in the room. Time-constrained (she entered the project with only four months before the premiere), Martel highlights the clear nature of Björk's ideas just as she casts doubts on the importance of her own contributions, and adds, 'Actually, I think she needed to talk to a woman her age [she and those around her laugh]. She wanted to chat with someone who has, more or less, the same problems.'[5] Through that crack, Martel squeezes in a humorous reply which, however, reveals the spirit of the show: female affectivity as the expansive foundation of a bio-community. Björk's view of the Argentine artist goes along the exact same lines:

> When I asked Lucrecia to direct the theatrical aspect of the show, videos were shot, masks were made, and a utopian world was built, and it was challenging for her jump into the project so late, but she found her place and embraced all ideas. I love her. She is a leader who managed to join all of us and build bridges, and she protected my vision, though adding her own touch.[6]

As Martel points out herself, she added 'materiality and physicality' to the musical dimension and also to Björk's visual ideas. If at times she thought that those ideas, about costume design or dramaturgy, for instance, were risky (she got to the point of thinking 'This is a disaster'), in her own material realisation she ended up noticing the effects of all that potential: 'And when I see everything together, it is incredible', she stated back then.[7]

What was that material realisation of Björk's ideas and music? In general, Martel's creative bets can be sorted into two groups, based on interviews with crew members and previews, and, mostly, on the show experience: distribution in space and visual perception. As regards the space supporting the bodies, the stage of mushrooms – designed with artistic designer Chiara Stephenson – harmonises the organic spirit of the rebirth of a world inherent to *Cornucopia*, with the way of distribution and movement on stage. To one side, we also find a reverb chamber requested by the singer, which projects sound through acoustic energy, and into which Björk steps in occasionally, free of all technical equipment. As regards the aerial space, Martel chose unconventional materials for the surface separating the scene from the audience and also for the projection surfaces, aiming in both cases to stress the physical dimension of the production as well as its sensory-perceptual dimension. As a threshold of sorts between the stage and the audience, a long curtain of spaghetti-like ropes provides flexibility to the separation but also to the visual access to the cornucopia. The threshold, then, becomes a mobile way to enter the scene, in which the degrees of visibility shift not only as a result of the rope curtain's own movement, but also because the material reacts to the touch of the bodies. Coherently, the surfaces on which videos are projected are sheer fabrics which create a multi-dimensional effect, diluting the typical high definition of animation in favour of an emphasis on the physical dimension, which in this case gives the impression of enveloping the cornucopia environment. All the unconventional materials chosen, together, create a sort of organic morphology of images, highlighting a tension between the hyper-technological and the natural, which, in the case of Björk, is a fundamental aspect of the way of thinking about a world to come.[8] The visual animations, created by Tobias Gremmler (who was already part of the project when Martel was brought in), assume in this way a warmth and a sensory depth which gives the finishing touches to a particular view of nature. His digital fantasies, which combine wonder with sci-fi, the retro with the futuristic, the world of fairies and the world of super-heroines, flow in the cornucopia and envelop it at the same time, and help show the possible transformations of the environmental threat into a common bio-well-being.

And it is possible, I posit, that everything in *Cornucopia* is about that: about taking care of one another, about protecting the world; an affective bio-care of sorts, naturally powerful, which only female hands can give and only a female voice can sing. Is that not what the song 'Future Forever' shows us?[9]

Somehow, that very materialisation of the environment which provided bottom-up density to the images of *The Swamp* or, from a higher plane, provided weight to the visions in *The Holy Girl/La niña santa* (2004), sheds that weight in the *Cornucopia* production and becomes lighter, making it agile without losing voluptuousness. It could be said that, in this cornucopia, the *mise-en-scène* aims not only at showing family, social, religious and class shrouds, but also at representing materially and physically a natural, matriarchal, sensory and communal utopia for the future. Perhaps, the reverb chamber Björk steps into during various parts of the show is a sort of protective chapel which, in its luminous whiteness, preserves her voice from all artefacts and technologies and is home to the recovery of an origin sound. It is as if from there, from the expansion of that primal sound, all those traits sprang forth, as if that expansion focused the cornucopia matrix laid before us in the scene as a whole. When Björk pronounces from that space the verses of 'Show Me Forgiveness', we understand what makes it possible to leave the past behind, to dissolve the latent threat of the present and for the utopia to grow.[10]

The *mise-en-scène* of *Cornucopia* appears to begin right there, in that white chamber from where the primal singing comes forth, when forgiveness is attained.

On a different level, much of this is foreshadowed in the show's preamble: before all vertical projection surfaces, organised in a couple of rows, the Hamrahlid Choir, comprising fifty Icelandic boys and girls, sing traditional songs from Iceland or a special arrangement of Björk's work.[11]

Always smiling and willing, the youths sing for approximately half an hour, and then the orderly layout of the proscenium gradually comes apart, as they move towards the seats, almost within the audience's reach. That is the first address to the audience of *Cornucopia*: we ask what is expected of us as we wait for Björk to come on stage. To whom that initial scenic resolution is addressed is not that important, as ultimately it all comes together as a whole.

In any event, the idea is to invite us in a special way into the cornucopia. There we see the pure 'Björkenergetic' show: ecological, environmentalist and matriarchal (words used implicitly and explicitly throughout the show), which becomes clear or subtle, which is more or less mediated by the Martelian curtain of ropes which filters images, lights and movements, almost as the camera focus works in film, almost as the graininess can alter perception, almost as the image in a movie can sharpen all senses.

BIO–COMMUNAL ARTISTIC ACTIVISM

And then, when we already feel part of that bio-community full of harmony, we are faced with film, with the document, with a giant close-up of Greta Thunberg, the Swedish teenager famous for her environmental activism against climate crisis.[12] Greta Thunberg stares at us constantly, never stops speaking from the moment she introduces herself or tells us she realised 'you are never too small to make a difference' to the moment when she says that 'our leaders only speak of green eternal economic growth because they are just scared of being unpopular' and that she only cares about 'climate justice and the living planet'. We could not agree more. We also agree when she denounces the sacrifice of the biosphere and warns that 'we are about to sacrifice our civilisation, for the opportunity of a very small number of people to continue making unimaginable amounts of money'.

Most members of the audience probably know Greta Thunberg's face. However, it is possible fewer people can recognise her words. It is the speech she delivered during COP24, the 2018 United Nations Climate Change Conference, which took place in Katowice, Poland.[13] Of course, Greta's self-introduction is different, as she is a year older. But what changes most is the image: not only do we see a gigantic close-up, but the diluted effect of the colours creates a contrast between the luminous sharpness of the face and a darkened and shadowy background. Greta Thunberg's face appears to project out of the screen. This is a close-up which has little to do with Martel's films' close-ups, which with strong and rich colours offer glimpses of parts, fragments of bodies which seem to make up a whole by aggregation, always as intense as they are incomplete. The face here, instead, in its expression, is everything, a visage which in its expressiveness manages to move from intensification to reflection, to borrow Deleuze's concepts, when the bright emerges from the shadows, when the cracks crossing it vertically when projected on the screen can dissipate.[14] As if coming from a beyond in which the diaphanous clashes with the dark, putting the colour of the cornucopia on hold, it establishes a double link between stage and audience, and also between the present and the future. That face which beckons us, which keeps on talking to us, which we feel ever closer, which instils in us ownership of and commitment with the cause, suddenly begins addressing us, even scolding us. An inclusive 'we' turns into a distinctive 'you' which projects into the future:

> The year 2078 I would celebrate my 75th birthday, if I have children maybe they would spend that day with me, maybe they will ask me about you, maybe they would ask why you didn't do anything, while there still was time to act. You say you love your children above all else and yet you're stealing their future in front of their very eyes.

What is that but a provocation? The minutes lengthen and become infinite as Greta's expression grows sterner. The closeness of that face makes us uncomfortable, and the current of empathy which flowed becomes erratic . . . Because, after all, can we who are there be really part of the same community? I wondered precisely that right then: do we all share the bio-communal utopia?

Cornucopia is a pure utopian delivery, a way for us to escape disaster. It is not only a show whose musical sophistication, awe-inspiring digital animations and creative *mise-en-scène* we enjoy and admire. *Cornucopia* is also a deep intervention into the present. I posit that *Cornucopia* can be interpreted as a sort of artistic activism. As a show which is also a concrete action to raise awareness, effect change and propose a way out. The appearance of Greta Thunberg projected on-screen and giving us her speech stresses that activist side of the show, forces us out of our role as mere viewers. Notably, the cinematographic image, the foundation of Lucrecia Martel's trajectory, appears almost as a lost footprint of her films. It is a documentary image; one she did not film but which she did stage and project: a contrasting close-up, with a slightly smaller duplicate set slightly behind, framed by the projection screen's ropes.[15] All spaces, all times, all messages, the activist dimension of the music and the show in its entirety would appear to converge in the staging of that documentary image. Perhaps that is precisely what a cornucopia offers: such prodigality that, in its abundance, the origin of things loses relevance before the arrangement as a whole. That is why I speak of a bio-community, with a female prevalence and a matriarchal power, as a utopia for the future. If we want to attain it, we all must assume the commitment to give something in order to take part in the cornucopia which will transform the world and restore its primal and vital drive.

The spaces in which the show was staged could also be analysed along those lines. *Cornucopia* premiered in an eight-show run in The Shed from 6 May to 1 June 2019, which sold out shortly after made available for sale, after an extraordinary membership-based presale.[16] Then, in August, the show moved to Mexico City, where five concerts were held at Parque Bicentenario, under an enormous white tent for 4,000 people. Lastly, towards the end of the year, an extensive and unconventional European tour took place, with eight concerts in arenas or multi-purpose centres in different countries (Belgium, Luxembourg, England, Scotland, Ireland, Norway, Denmark and Sweden).

I went to see *Cornucopia* in the hyper-modern The Shed cultural centre, designed by the famous firm Diller Scofidio + Renfro, and inaugurated in Manhattan not long before the show. It is a cultural space managed by a non-profit independent organisation, whose largest hall, McCourt, is perfect for large-scale multimedia projects, and housed over a thousand people during the last of the New York shows. This venue, at the end of the High Line, the elevated art and leisure circuit which begins at the Whitney Museum and finishes on 30th Street, almost in Midtown West, faces The Vessel, the city's new and mesmerising architectural structure, located in a field of grass and cement, which is home to a luxurious shopping complex and represents an enormous investment. The Vessel, which evocates Escher's recursive stairways while the coppery circular and vertical shape multiplies our reflections infinitely, fetishises us and amazes us. Could it not be seen as a space which contrasts, opposes and even competes with *Cornucopia*'s sensory envelope? It could almost be said that the world of wealth challenged by Björk's futuristic utopia with the aid of

Lucrecia Martel finds its materialisation in this structure. Could this not be the other horn of plenty? That of accumulation, as opposed to prodigality?

The artistic activism in *Cornucopia*, with its music, its bodies, its images, its staging, its invitation to a matriarchal bio-community, can be activated more than once, for that very reason: it enchants us during the show, addresses us towards the end, and poses again the possibility of neutralising or reactivating it when we leave the venue. To give oneself in to *Cornucopia* is to recharge the utopia to make it possible, to wrap oneself in utopia and launch into the future. Björk says almost as much in the last song in *Utopia*, the penultimate number of *Cornucopia*, 'Future Forever'.

Between perceptive and interpretative reviews of the past (*Zama*) and teenage sensory musings which seek to cross the present (*The Swamp*, *The Holy Girl*), there is in Martel's work a zone which also questions utopia. How else could we interpret her *New Argirópolis/Nueva Argirópolis* (2010), the short feature produced to commemorate the Bicentennial of the first national government, in which she challenges and overhauls the utopia Domingo F. Sarmiento called *Argirópolis*, locating it on an island in the Paraná River as the cornerstone of the Argentine nation? In *New Argirópolis*, Martel shows us fragments of different situations starring men and women, adults and children from indigenous communities, the very same communities who were cast aside in the national project. As if the inclusive and plural utopia of a nation, now shattered, could be reforged starting from a small conspiracy fiction. In Lucrecia Martel's words:

> A conspiracy. Fragments of news about something that could be happening upriver from Buenos Aires. It is fiction, marginally inspired by Sarmiento's *Argirópolis*. In 1850, Sarmiento suggests creating a capital city on Martín García Island for a Confederation comprising Uruguay, Paraguay and Argentina. In that work, he also writes about the importance of navigable rivers. The audacity of that political work always drew my attention. *New Argirópolis* is inspired in that audacity. We liked the pretension of founding a space which represented a new social order. I think the genre would be sci-fi. Faraway islands, unknown languages. Fragments of a foundation movement.[17]

In Martel's imagination, the desired utopia does not imply a retrofuturistic bio-communal future of the matriarchal type, even though she feels that project close. Instead, it proposes a concrete and situated communal indigenous-focused transformation to repair exclusion and injustice in Argentina. There, in the lands shown in *New Argirópolis*, we find no ecological musical instruments crafted from recycled materials, but plastic bottles polluting the rivers; no music with universal lyrics, but misunderstood indigenous languages; no fairy-like or ethereal bodies, but the sick and the dead. There is no place for artistic activism there: all activism becomes conspiracy. There, where it would appear there is no room for spectacle either, Martel delivers a fiction which aims at reinventing her political nature. In this sense, utopias, just like cornucopias, do not lie beyond, but are always situated in a particular time, a precise present from which the future is designed, and also a particular place, be it Iceland, New York, Buenos Aires or Argentina.

Translated by Juan Ignacio García Fahler

NOTES

1. *Cornucopia* is seen as Björk's most ambitious project, both by the press and by the artist herself. *Utopia*, the album that inspired it, whose personnel also took part in the show, was seen as Björk's return 'to optimism, enthusiasm and romantic possibility – her "Tinder album," as she has sometimes jokingly called it. Made in collaboration with the Venezuelan D.J. Arca, it was suffused with birdsong, loose melodies and the female flutists, all Icelandic musicians'. Ryzik, M. (2019), 'How Björk Brought Her Sci-Fi Feminist Fairy Tale to Life', *The New York Times*, 8 May 2019, <https://www.nytimes.com/2019/05/08/arts/music/bjork-cornucopia.html> (last accessed 28 April 2021). Some media outlets chose to focus instead on the project's psychedelic nature: see Hermes, W. (2019), 'Björk's *Cornucopia* Is a Psychedelic Cautionary Tale about the Environment', *Rolling Stone*, 10 May 2019, <https://www.rollingstone.com/music/music-live-reviews/bjork-cornucopia-debut-the-shed-833943/> (last accessed 28 April 2021); and Rockwell, J. (2019), 'Psychedelic Flowers and Singsong Incantations – Björk's Lavish *Utopia* Opens at The Shed, New York', *Financial Times*, 23 May 2019, <https://www.ft.com/content/ed5b5dea-7563-11e9-boec-7dff87b9a4a2> (last accessed 28 April 2021).
2. Costumes were crafted by the haute couture house Pierre Balmain. For an account of the relation of the designers with the show, see Hahn, R. (2019), 'Björk and Balmain's Olivier Rousteing on Their Otherworldly Fashion Collaboration', *Vogue*, 10 May 2019, <https://www.vogue.com/article/bjork-balmain-the-shed-cornucopia-concert-series-performance-olivier-rousteing-collaboration-couture> (last accessed 28 April 2021).
3. Though there are variations, the best-known version of the classical myth of the cornucopia (from the Latin *cornu*, 'horn' and *copia*, 'plenty'), which dates back to the fifth century BC, states that while playing with his lightning as a child, the Greek god Zeus broke off one of the horns of the goat Amalthea, who fed him with her milk, and that, as compensation, he granted the broken horn the power to grant the wishes of those who held it.
4. Strictly speaking, Martel was brought in to replace stage director John Tiffany, of *Harry Potter and the Cursed Child* fame, who, it is said, left the project due to scheduling conflicts. The story of *Cornucopia* began in 2015, as Björk explained to Mexican media before the premiere in that country, when she wrote the phrase 'arisen my senses', which ended up as the title of one of the songs in *Utopia*, and has gone through many stages since then: 'I wrote the songs and the flute arrangements, I produced the tracks, some with (producer) Arca, and based on that I compiled a few references to ask some visual collaborators to contribute.' Santamaría, J. (2019), '"Quiero que laringes mexicanas coloreen mi música": Björk', *Excelsior*, 17 August 2019, <https://www.excelsior.com.mx/funcion/quiero-que-laringes-mexicanas-coloreen-mi-musica-bjork/1330969/> (last accessed 28 April 2021).

5. Cruz, A. (2019), 'Lucrecia Martel: "Polanski es un maestro del cine, pero su película me da pena"', *La Nación*, 14 September 2019, <https://www.lanacion.com.ar/espectaculos/lucrecia-martel-polanski-es-maestro-del-cine-nid2287833/> (last accessed 28 April 2021).

6. Santamaría, '"Quiero que laringes mexicanas coloreen mi música": Björk'.

7. Ryzik, 'How Björk Brought Her Sci-Fi Feminist Fairy Tale to Life'.

8. Designer Chiara Stephenson, who states that her role was mainly to create 'a canvas' for Lucrecia Martel's vision for the show, explains it quite clearly in an interview: 'It's like an exploration of perspective. You know, Björk is totally interested in nature and technology and where those two combine, and how they can combine in the future as we move forward [. . .] We're using kind of unconventional materials to project on. We're not just projecting onto a screen, we're projecting onto layers of a fragile membrane.' Wallace, R. (2019), 'Björk's Set Designer Chiara Stephenson Shares How *Cornucopia* Came to Life at The Shed', *Architectural Digest*, 10 May 2019, <https://www.architecturaldigest.com/story/bjork-set-designer-chiara-stephenson-cornucopia-the-shed> (last accessed 28 April 2021). In a different interview, related to the premiere at The Shed, Stephenson also said, 'If the set design is the plate and Björk is the feast, director Lucrecia Martel has been the chef! Add that with lighting designer Bruno Poet and me as theatre creatives – the show, much like the venue, is a fusion of many things.' Schama, C. (2019), 'Meet the Set Designer Behind Björk's Latest Showstopping Performance', *Vogue*, 10 May 2019, <https://www.vogue.com/article/bjork-cornucopia-chiara-stephenson-set-designer> (last accessed 28 April 2021).

9. See björk (2020), 'Future Forever', YouTube, 30 March 2020, <https://www.youtube.com/watch?v=NOISUWq603c> (last accessed 27 August 2021).

10. See björk (2018), 'Show Me Forgiveness', YouTube, 7 June 2018, <https://www.youtube.com/watch?v=speaooAMIlk> (last accessed 27 August 2021).

11. For the five shows in Mexico, the Icelandic choir was replaced by the Staccato University Choir, from Universidad Nacional Autónoma de México, which performed an opening song and accompanied Björk during different segments of the show. According to the local media, the singer said, 'I want Mexican larynxes to colour my music. I've heard them, and they are amazing.' Santamaría, '"Quiero que laringes mexicanas coloreen mi músicas": Björk'. In terms of its effects on stage, the interesting thing about the replacement, beyond the use of local resources and certain changes to the programme, is that the Mexican choir comprised college-aged people exclusively, unlike its Icelandic counterpart, which had a broader age range (children, teenagers and young adults).

12. Greta Thunberg is a Swedish teenager who has demonstrated since 2018 against global warming, and whose activism has become globally known, eliciting reactions from politicians all over the world, both in favour and against, and also from the press. Her actions, coupled with a powerful environmental discourse, have had an amazing impact, for instance, promoting the organisation of massive student demonstrations against climate change. Moreover, Thunberg has been invited to major international forums and received various awards for her efforts.

13. The 2018 United Nations Climate Change Conference was the 24th conference of the parties to the United Nations Framework Convention on Climate Change, and was held in Katowice, Poland, on 2–15 December 2018.

14. Duplicating the face at a smaller scale, pulling it oddly out of its own contours; the contrast between light and shadow; and the vertical ropes which make up the projection screen: everything in this close-up suggests an expressionist face of sorts, bearing in mind the various cadences and hues imposed by the content of Greta Thunberg's speech. About the relation between close-up, face and affection, see Deleuze, G. (1984), 'La imagen-afección: Rostro y primer plano', *La imagen-movimiento. Estudios sobre cine 1*, Barcelona: Paidós, pp. 131–50.

15. A political documentary by Lucrecia Martel, called *Chocobar*, entered principal photography in 2020. It is about the murder of the leader and activist of the Diaguita people, Javier Chocobar, who was killed while peacefully defending his community's lands in Tucumán (a northern province, bordering Salta, the province in which Martel was born) and the absolution of the defendants after a trial which went on for almost ten years.

16. The full credits of *Cornucopia* and the information on the show are available at The Shed's official site, <https://theshed.org/program/29-bjork-s-cornucopia> (last accessed 7 September 2021).

17. Martel, L. (2010), 'La Confederación de ríos', *Página/12*, 3 October 2010, <https://www.pagina12.com.ar/diario/suplementos/radar/9-6511-2010-10-03.html> (last accessed 2 May 2021). In an intelligent analysis of *New Argirópolis* against the backdrop of the Bicentennial short features, Sandra Contreras refers to Martel's proposal as a 'riparian reimagining of Sarmiento's utopia'. Contreras, S. (2019), 'En torno a 2010: Flujos territoriales y formas de comunidad', Closing Lecture, LASA – Southern Cone Section, 13 July.

CHAPTER 9

Realities Made to Order: On *The Headless Woman*

Malena Verardi

INTRODUCTION: A RETURN AS A BEGINNING

*T*he *Headless Woman/La mujer sin cabeza* (2008) returns to several of the themes and subjects that Lucrecia Martel dealt with in her two previous films — *The Swamp/La ciénaga* (2001) and *The Holy Girl/La niña santa* (2004): the characteristics of relationships in middle-class and upper-middle-class families in the north of the country, and the way the members of such classes relate to those who are considered beneath them. In this case, however, the film focuses on one in particular: the modes through which the gaze is constructed and its implications regarding the configuration of 'reality'. This chapter intends to examine the formal resources and narrative procedures used to shape different notions of 'reality' in the story. It also attempts to analyse the possible correspondence between, on the one hand, the relationships that link the characters — as social subjects — and the environment they belong to and, on the other, the construction of the social scene in contemporary Argentina in terms of its history (the 1976–83 civic-military dictatorship) and of its present at the outset of the twenty-first century.

The opening scenes show a group of children laughing and running along the side of a road. They are followed by a dog. They chase each other, climb over a billboard, and jump into a dry canal that borders the road. In the next scene a group of women and children are saying goodbye to each other after a social gathering. One of the children locks himself in a car. He laughs, bangs on the windows, and refuses to open the door. The car belongs to Vero, the film's main character. She finally manages to make the child get out. 'Don't be a brat', she says, 'Get out or you'll run out of air.' This phrase turns out to be one of the significant markers anticipating the situations that will develop from that moment on. As the woman is driving back, her mobile phone starts ringing. She bends down to answer the call and the car is stopped by a heavy bump. The phone keeps ringing for a few more seconds. The music coming from the car stereo can still be heard. There are traces of a child's hand on the car window. At first, Vero reaches out to the handle, as if to open the car door, and starts looking back to see what has happened. But then, she picks up her sunglasses from the car floor, starts the engine, and drives away. 'I didn't want to get out; I didn't get out', she will say later. In the following shot, as the car keeps driving, the body of a dog lying at the side of the road can be seen through the rear window. After a while, the woman stops the car and gets out. She walks to the front of the car, then to the back, until she leaves the frame. The car is left empty, its door open. There is thunder; the first drops of rain fall on the windscreen. The woman re-enters the visual plane and stands in the rain. The framing places the steering wheel in the forefront and, through the windscreen, the female body from the knees to the neck. After this image − a 'headless' female body − and a cut, the title of the film is shown in white letters on a black background. Thus, the film's first scenes lead to the event that will trigger the conflict at the heart of the story.

SEEING, LOOKING, PERCEIVING

The narrative constructs the event of the crash elliptically, since it does not provide much information on what has happened. Although there are several clues that an animal has been hit − the image of the dog lying at the side of the road, the sign that warns that there are animals on the loose on the stretch of the road where the collision takes place − others suggest a different possibility. The handprints on the car window produce some ambiguity: even though they relate to the scene of the child playing inside the car, they hint at the presence of a body at the scene of the crash (they are marks left by a body). The use of the kind of montage that is presumably alternate, that is, a montage that places the first two scenes of the film consecutively (the children running by the roadside and the group of women at the end of the meeting), produces the same effect, since one might believe that both scenes take place at the same time. Alternate montage shows two situations that take place simultaneously but usually develop in different places. In the language of classical film narrative, this kind of montage usually culminates with a scene where both spaces are reunited into one space (and one time). It is the spectator's prior knowledge of this narrative procedure that operates to construct the idea that the body hit by the car might have been a human body, that of one of the children running by the roadside. In this way, the collision would operate as the point of convergence between two situations that at a certain moment had been developing in different spaces. Alternate montage is an element of the cinematic code very often used by classic film and hegemonic film in general. Martel breaks away from it by eliding part of the image (the entity of what has been hit by the car) at the moment of the — supposed — convergence of both situations, and by using such elision as the trigger for the conflict.

Finally, the insistence and repetition in Vero's discourse (she keeps saying 'I killed someone on the road', 'I think I ran over someone') helps to furnish the episode with a high degree of uncertainty, since its construction alternates between two possible options: she might have hit a child or an animal.

As a result of this event, which is constructed as unclear, the woman falls into a state of confusion, an estrangement that disrupts her relationship with the environment. The veiled image, as if seen through a bluish glass that tinges the scene in which Vero goes to the hospital after the collision, operates as a doorway to the state of confusion that overcomes the protagonist from that moment on. It is as if between the woman's conscience (her head) and the world around her there were an intervening distance that starts giving a new shape to the relationship between both variables.[1] The narrative stages such distancing by means of the framing of the scenes in which the protagonist interacts with her environment after the collision. For instance, in the scene that takes place at the swimming pool, Vero's arm with a glass of wine in her hand is shown in the foreground; in the background, the back of a child who is sitting on the edge of the pool can be seen, and behind that, the image of a woman's torso in the water.

At the other end of the pool, two men are talking after a telephone call has come in. The dialogue between them is in fact the focal point of the scene, because, as will be shown later, it is related to the incident of the collision. In this particular framing, the most significant situation is placed the farthest away in the visual frame, while the foreground is reserved for an irrelevant dialogue. This way of organising image — an internal montage of the frame by means of layers of vision — reveals the filters that separate the gaze from what is being looked at. The distance between both variables, usually conceived as empty, is thus revealed as full of form, and it acquires that 'troubling' effect which, as Maurice Merleau-Ponty points out,[2] the world takes on when the intervals between things are perceived as things.

In this way, the collision seems in principle to have caused in Vero's character some transformations in the area of perception, and it is precisely in the relationship between seeing, looking and perceiving where the conflict that develops in the narrative is centred.

THE GHOST OF CONTEMPORARY MASS CULTURE

The character's state of confusion is revealed immediately after the incident on the road: at the hospital, she fills out a registration card with the wrong name; she cannot remember her telephone number; and the next day, when she arrives at the medical centre where she works as a dentist, she sits in the waiting room until her assistant warns her, 'They [her patients] are waiting for you' (in her office). In this context, the story brings in a number of elements that contribute to build the notion of uncertainty. The relationships between most of the characters remain unclear; the degree of kinship between them is revealed gradually in some cases while in others it is left unsaid. The ambiguity that characterises the family relationships is marked by the presence of a strong eroticism in the way they are established. It is Vero who operates as the object of desire for all the others (her brother, her cousin, her niece). While the relationship with her brother takes on the form of a fraternal bond, the one with her cousin is realised through their love affair. On the other hand, there is a game of seduction with Candita, her niece, where the intensity is regulated by the protagonist.

After the incident on the road, every time Vero hears the tone of her telephone announcing an incoming call, she rejects it openly, as if there were a cut, a breach that cannot be repaired. In Lacanian theory, language is established as a symbolic order that has a defining influence on the constitution of the subject as such, as well as on the relationships between subjects: 'language establishes mediated relationships [. . .] between oneself and others. As a mediator then, it places subjects in their distinct place.'[3] In this respect, one might think that the impossibility of allowing the communication exchange implied in answering the telephone reveals the dislocation the protagonist has been experiencing since the collision. Something in the space that she − as a subject − had occupied until then has changed, and this is shown by the difficulty in connecting both with herself and with others. As Lacan points out, the record of the symbolic is closely linked to the record of the imagined and the real, whereby a movement related to one of these orders implies effects on the others, as will be discussed later.[4] Jacques-Alain Miller uses the term 'suture' to refer to the relationship that the subject establishes with the symbolic order as two instances that are held together.[5] The situation experienced by the character has partly torn this union, creating a sort of breach between her and the surrounding world.

The scene in which Vero finally answers the telephone and speaks with her husband, who is calling her from Tucumán, reveals that the distance that the collision had produced between her (her perception) and her environment has been sutured, since the communication takes place. Vero's overwhelming state of confusion seems to dispel with the acceptance − 'I'm all right now, it was nothing' − of the explanation provided by her husband ('You got scared. You ran over a dog'), and by her cousin: 'You must have been shocked by the noise. It's an awful noise.'[6] Vero's husband reproduces the prior repetition in discourse that she had used before ('I killed someone on the road') but with the opposite intention,[7] that is, to seal off his wife's belief: 'It's a dog. There's the dog. You got scared. It's all right. You got scared. You ran over a dog.' Vero had already installed this idea. When her brother and her sister-in-law remarked, 'You sure dented the car', 'What did you hit?', she responded, 'A dog got in the way.' The comment and the question preclude the existence of a subject in the incident. The first phrase implies that it was the car that was damaged (she 'dented' it badly); in the question, 'what' was damaged shares the characteristics of an object.

At another point in the story, Vero and Josefina go to a football match. During the match, one of the players is hit by a ball and falls. The collision takes place outside the frame, like the one on the road. It refers back to the incident, as does the image of the fallen player (the young man does not move for a few minutes; it is impossible to assess the gravity of the situation). This reveals precisely what Vero has been trying at all costs to avoid seeing: a lying, inert body. The scene upsets her: she locks herself in the sports centre toilets and bursts into tears.

Slavoj Žižek goes back to one of the questions posed by Lacan – why do the dead return? – in order to refer to what he calls 'the fundamental ghost of contemporary mass culture'. His answer claims that such a return takes place within the frame of a disturbance in the symbolic rite implied in a proper funeral rite. That is, the dead 'return' when they have not been properly buried. 'The return of the living dead, then, materializes a certain symbolic debt persisting beyond physical expiration.'[8] In this case, the dead boy 'returns' in the shape of the morally and ethically improper behaviour that starts surrounding the protagonist. This behaviour is presented as twofold: on the one hand, the negligent attitude implied in taking one's eyes off the road in order to answer the telephone; on the other, the outrage of driving away without trying to find out what has happened, and if need be, assisting the victim of

Figure 9.1 *The Headless Woman*

the collision. What went wrong with the obsequies is that they never actually took place: the body disappears until it is found in the canal. Thus, the unpaid symbolic debt is related to the fact that the disappearance is naturalised, normalised, so that the absence of the body, hence the child, can be ignored.

The plant nursery owner's remarks, 'I'm missing a kid. A kid hasn't been showing up', and the image of the firefighters looking for 'something' in the canal pipes install once again the idea that a person has been involved in the impact and cause a sudden change in the way Vero and those around her approach the incident.

THE PLAN

When a body appears in the canal, the confusion and uncertainty related to the moment of the collision give way to a plan to erase what has happened. Whereas until that moment Vero's closest circle (husband, cousin and brother) had refused to acknowledge any explanation other than that of hitting an animal, the news of the child's death — published in the newspaper and quickly spread — makes it clear that such an explanation is becoming less viable. In this line of action, Marcos travels to Tucumán, where his daughters live. The initial purpose of the trip is to visit them, but once there he has the dents in the car repaired. 'Since I was already there, I had a few things fixed', he remarks when he is back. Then Vero goes back to the hospital where she was checked after the collision. She had got X-rays done on that day and she wants to pick up the plates. But she is told, 'There's nothing here. No record of admission, either.' Then she goes to the radiology department to ask about the plates. While she's waiting, she can hear the radiologist telling a patient, 'I'm going to take the shot now. Please, stay very, very still. Don't breathe.' The words 'shot' and 'still' relate to one of the first scenes in the film, where a policewoman is transferring an arrested woman inside the hospital. The idea of the shot and the policewoman's image are linked to the police: the institution that should act if a person had died in the incident on the road. When she hears these phrases, Vero leaves the place without inquiring about the plates. A few seconds later she runs into her brother in the hospital car park. He asks, 'Vero, what are you doing here?' 'I've come for the plates', she answers. 'I have them. There is nothing left. Don't worry. Go home', he says curtly.[9] The brother's presence at the hospital reveals that a whole operation is under way in order to eliminate any traces that might lead back to the incident on the road.[10] This sort of 'erasing' operation which starts after the body is found succeeds in dispelling the ghost of the dead boy's return that had haunted Vero until that moment. It is as if confirming the existence of the — dead — body cancelled the 'unpaid debt' and enabled the return to the usual state of affairs, ignoring how the death took place and the consequences it should bring about. Žižek remarks that the proper funeral rite allows the dead to finally find their place in the 'text of symbolic tradition'. In this respect, the appearance of the child's body (together with the indifference towards the circumstances of this death) means returning those who appear as non-existent in a social order, as shown in the film, to their original place. 'If something had happened, I would know. The police have to inform us', says Juan Manuel – making it clear that no one has reported the child as missing. The dead child's body goes unnoticed once again – it does not exist – as were his body, and he himself, when he was alive. It is the uncertainty in the presence–absence dichotomy that has produced the protagonist's perceptual dislocation. Instead, it is the body's existence (alive or dead) which allows, after certain moves – that is, the erasing operation – a return to the usual state of affairs as if nothing had happened.

The plan to erase all traces of the collision is devised and carried out by Vero's husband, her brother and her lover. She is excluded from the decision, but she is included in these actions and practices through the tacit acceptance granted by her silence.[11] In this scenario and in line with the previous situations, the greatest estrangement takes place when Vero questions the hotel receptionist about the room she and Juan Manuel took on the night after the collision. 'It was empty, nobody checked in', answers the young woman.

Even though it is possible to assume that it was Juan Manuel who eliminated the hotel record, this is not explained in the story. Thus, the 'disappearing' of bodies acquires a supernatural connotation which is also sinister on account of its association with Argentine history. The possible connections point to the theory that where there is no body, there is no evidence of murder, which was one of the premises used by the civic-military dictatorship: 'The missing person has no entity; he is neither dead nor alive, he is missing.'[12]

This produces a lack of correspondence between two discourses involving the existence of a body: Vero talks about having been at the hospital and at the hotel, but the records in both places deny her presence. This incongruity, together with Vero's particular behaviour after the collision and the type of discourse dominated by the repetition of phrases ('I killed someone on the road'), introduces the notion of mental insanity, madness, as an additional element shaping the narrative. The character that the story links directly to the idea of madness is that of Aunt Lala: 'Why is it that there has been such little sanity in our family? Name one who has died in their right mind', says Josefina, talking about her aunt. Aunt Lala never leaves her bed, and from there she sees 'spectres' in the whole house. However, even in her 'madness', she is the only one who detects a change in Vero after the incident on the road: 'That does not sound like your voice', she claims. According to Žižek, madness appears when the boundary that separates reality from the Real (the part of reality that remains unsymbolised and returns in the form of spectral appearances) is broken. For this author, reality is constituted by means of an incomplete symbolisation (there is always an unsymbolised fraction), and spectral appearances emerge in the breach that separates reality from the Real. 'The spectre gives body to that which escapes the symbolically structured reality.'[13] The spectres that inhabit Aunt Lala's life remind us that 'The common everyday reality, the reality of the social universe in which we assume our usual roles of kind-hearted, decent people . . . is nothing but a fragile symbolic tissue that can at any moment be torn aside by the intrusion of the Real.'[14] The ghost in Vero's life is that of the child that has been run over, but it is also her very own, whose presence – as a result of the plan carried out – has 'vanished' phantasmagorically. In the scene where Vero, Josefina and Aunt Lala watch the video of Vero and Marcos's wedding, Aunt Lala mentions a certain Monsignor Pérez, a high-ranking clergyman who served in Salta during the civic-military dictatorship that started in 1976. He was the first one to refer to the Mothers of Plaza de Mayo as 'mad women'. In that phrase, 'madness' was a characterisation used to deny the truthfulness of a discourse (that of the Mothers of Plaza de Mayo). In the context of the film, Aunt Lala puts into words, therefore, an act that all the others are trying to hide and to make disappear. Žižek points out that two of the great traumatic events of the twentieth century (the Holocaust and the Gulag) are paradigmatic examples of the phantasmagorical return of the dead who have not been integrated in our historical memory since they are victims who have not received a proper burial.[15] The spectres that haunt Vero are those that refer back to the mechanism of denial about what happened on the road, but also to the collective attitude that characterised Argentine society during the dictatorship and that is still part of the social dynamics nowadays.[16]

CONTRASTS

When the child's body appears in the canal, the erasing of Vero's body becomes mandatory. The undeniable evidence of the dead body (strengthened by the stench of decomposition: 'Mum, close the window. There's a disgusting smell', says Candita) is what prompts the disappearance of traces that might lead to the woman's presence in the incident (the dents in the car, the X-ray plates and her stay at the hotel). Thus, the fact that the appearance of a body should produce the disappearance of another one reveals the difficulty – or the impossibility – of joining both universes.

The development of the contrast between these two worlds, these two social classes, starts with the alternate montage at the beginning of the film: a group of poor children (their clothes and the language they use identify them as belonging to the working class) and the way they have fun versus a group of women of northern high middle class (the way they dress and speak characterises them as such) and their forms of entertainment. The violent and lethal contact produced by the collision − between the car and what it hits, between two universes − reveals, brings to the foreground, the existence of a social class that the story always places in the background (in the shadows) but at the same time displays as omnipresent. It is as if the everyday life of a social class were sustained by a network of actions carried out by another social group that supports its lifestyle from the margins. Thus, in most of the film's scenes, domestic workers enter and leave the frame (their omnipresence mentioned before) or else remain in the frame but in the background and out of focus.

In this respect, Vero's phrase when she thinks she has recovered after the collision – 'I'm all right. It was *nothing*' – can be connected to the lack of entity of those men, women and children whose existence can only be associated with their condition as servants.[17] Therefore, to the social sector that makes use of their lives, they are *nothing*, or nobody. Out of the great number of domestic workers, gardeners, masseuses and children who perform various tasks throughout the film, only one woman, Zula, is called by her name by her employers, that is, she is given identity. All the others operate as interchangeable pieces whose only function is to keep the mechanism going. They are addressed without being named: 'Will you make me some coffees?', 'Go now, just close the door, please', 'The kid who washes is out there . . .' (meaning the child who washes cars for the characters in the story in exchange for a few coins). There is another character who is called by a nickname, 'Changuila' (a brother of the child who has been found dead), but only by family members or by the owner of the plant nursery that he works for, not by those for whom he performs various tasks. In the scene where some young women bring some plants to Josefina's house, she ironically calls them 'the ladies', while at the same time she stresses the existing distance as she tells her daughter, 'Just get the plants, Candita, don't let them in, all right? Don't have them enter the house, not inside.'

Figure 9.2 *The Headless Woman*

Vero's refusal to see after the collision (even when she finally decides to tell Marcos about the incident, she talks without looking at him, or when they ride in their car to the place of the collision, she tells him, 'Don't stop') is in line with the habit of not seeing those 'others' who surround her in her daily life.

While they are celebrating their new swimming pool, Juan Manuel receives a call. Then he approaches Marcos to tell him something (the spectator cannot hear the dialogue) and they both leave the place. Before leaving, they tell Vero, who has been watching them, 'We are going to have a cup of coffee with a friend.' It is possible to assume that the call and the meeting with the 'friend' are connected to what has happened on the road. A close-up of the back of Vero's head — a take of her profile showing her ear covered by her hair — operates as a prelude to the following scene, where she reads the news about the dead body in the paper. Thus, hinting at the sphere of hearing indicates that it is sound that persists and comes back from an incident from which the gaze has been deliberately withdrawn.

As regards the work done in the field of photography and lighting, the film conveys the idea of contrast clearly by means of the treatment given to interior spaces (Vero's, Josefina's and Aunt Lala's houses, the hotel, the swimming pool) dominated by dark, lightless, earthy shades, as compared with the outside spaces where there is plenty of light (the road, the plant nursery). Thus, the story points to the conventions that rule social life as well as to the hiding of that which must not be revealed. At the same time, the bosses' light skin and hair (especially Vero's platinum blonde) stress most explicitly the contrast with the dark skin and hair of those 'others' who are indistinguishable in the shadows.[18]

In this respect, Vero's change in hair colour (she goes from platinum blonde to brunette), which appears to be the only decision she is competent enough to make by herself, can be interpreted as an attempt to play down the contrast, to lose notoriety in a situation where it is mandatory not to stand out. It can also be seen as a search for a way to 'change her head' and get rid of the issues that have haunted her since the collision on the road. It is the change in hair colour that prompts a remark from Josefina ('How bold you are' — pointing to the fact that she has dyed it herself). The remark, one might assume, is not limited to the decision of dyeing her hair but it reaches other areas that a mandate not to upset the *status quo*, such as her relationship with Juan Manuel, does not allow mentioning. However, Vero's behaviour after the incident has been precisely the opposite of boldness. The decision to keep a certain order of things unchanged is linked to the intention not to upset the characteristics of that world framed and structured to comply with certain rules and social conventions. Thus, the aim is to direct the construction of perception in such a way that the established order will be reproduced.[19]

Vero's refusal to see after the collision is in line with the habit of not seeing those 'others' who surround her in her everyday life.[20] The only one who has a different attitude is Candita, who has started an affectionate and sexual relationship with a young woman who lives in the workers' neighbourhood where the dead boy used to live. Candita is the only one who asks explicitly, 'I want to see the place where the boy who was killed was found' (precisely what Vero and the other members of the family have been trying to avoid). The struggle to look away seems to lose intensity as they drive through the popular neighbourhood where Vero is taken, when she has no alternative but to see the people, the space and, in particular, the situation of the dead boy's family. However, the images that can be seen through the windscreen are out of focus (it is by definition the space of 'others'), that is, the distance and contrast between both universes persists.

In this way, the plan to erase the evidence is designed so that no one will see (Vero's part in the collision), so as to restore the usual state of affairs based, as said above, on the omission of a sector of society that another sector deliberately chooses not to look at, and therefore, to deny. And this plan can be linked to other moments in Argentine history marked by denial, as Martel herself points out, regarding the behaviour of a large part of civil society during the latest dictatorship.

In the story, what in fact deserves to be looked at seems to be banal. 'Mum, come see', says Vero's daughter, referring to a wedding gift she and her father have bought. 'It's an outdoor stove', says Marcos. 'For Tucumán?', asks Vero, surprised, hinting at the warm climate in the region. 'For the winter . . . All right. Useful for two weeks', is the young woman's final remark, revealing how meaningless the purchase has been.

CONCLUSION: THE SPLICING OF THE DISENTANGLEMENT

As a result of the analysis carried out, it is possible to conclude that the transformations in perception that the collision seemed to have caused have been rerouted to fit within the perceptual and cognitive limits that circumscribe the protagonist's world.[21]

In the last scene of the film, Vero goes through a glass door to enter the hotel lounge where − just like at the beginning of the film − a social event is taking place. The camera, placed behind the door, shows the bodies − blurred, out of focus − of several people greeting each other and talking. The murmur of conversations can be heard at the same time as the first bars of a musical piece coming from outside the diegesis.[22] There is a narrow opening between the two door leaves, just a crack that gives access to that space, the space of a familiar world governed by its own predetermined rules. Through the presence of the glass − which does not allow seeing or hearing clearly − the camera distances itself from that space and draws the spectators away; it does not let them in. In this way, the glass and the crack confirm that one is watching a scene from the outside, without participating. Then the camera does enter the place and follows Vero's movements in sequence shot as she walks across the room smiling, like all the other guests. Parts of bodies cross in front of the camera, between the objective and the woman's figure. At some moments there is blurring of the figures' contours, alternating from one of the guests to another. It is as if something had shifted from its place but then returned immediately to its point of origin. In this respect, the procedures used suggest that, even though the glass door has been gone through, there is still a filter between the observer and the observed, revealing the presence of mediations in all relationships and in the construction of every reality. The lack of sharpness, both in image and in sound, points to the features of a world that is unaware of the outside and retreats to the hotel lounge. It is a universe of diffuse shapes, without clear boundaries, that operates autonomously, closed in itself and ruled from the inside.

The last image allows a glimpse of the protagonist beside Marcos and Juan Manuel, her image practically covered by the bodies of the people around her. With the new hair colour, her head no longer stands out. The framing organisation based on layers of vision (bodies that overlap) results here in the hiding of the main character. The erasing operation has been successfully completed.

Translated by Silvia Villegas

NOTES

1. Regarding this, Lucrecia Martel points out that Vero's character was built on the idea that 'What she had lost was the notion of the relationship between her and things around her. We build our environment and our geography like a net with objects. In her case, it is as if that net had been cut. She knows that those things belong to her but she does not know exactly what relates them to each other.' Enríquez, M. (2008), 'La mala memoria', *Página/12*, 17 August 2008, <https://www.pagina12.com.ar/diario/suplementos/radar/9-4766-2008-08-17.html> (last accessed 3 May 2021).
2. Merleau-Ponty, M. (1977), *Sentido y sinsentido*, Barcelona: Península.
3. Rifflet-Lemaires, A. (1992), *Lacan*, Buenos Aires: Sudamericana, p. 106.
4. Lacan, J. (1972/73), *El seminario. Libro 21*: 'Les non dupes errent', unpublished.
5. Miller, J. A. (1973), 'La sutura. Elementos de la lógica del significante', in *Significante y sutura en el psicoanálisis*, Buenos Aires: Siglo XXI. The term 'suture' has been applied to film analysis by Pierre Oudart: 'Suture represents the closure of the cinematic énoncé in line with its relationship with its subject (the filmic subject or rather the cinematic subject), which is recognised and then put in its place as the spectator − thus distinguishing the suture from all other types of cinema, particularly the so-called "subjective" cinema where the suture did exist but undefined theoretically.' Oudart, J. P. (1977), 'Cinema and Suture', *Screen*, 18, December 1977, p. 35.

6. Juan Manuel's comment − 'It's an awful noise' − brings out the importance of sound in relation to the incident: a sound (the ringing of the mobile phone) caused the impact, since Vero bends down to answer the telephone and takes her eyes off the road.

7. Vero insisted on repeating that phrase as a way of installing the subject, of making it visible to her environment.

8. Žižek, S. (1991), *Looking Awry: An Introduction to Jacques Lacan through Popular Culture*, Cambridge, MA: MIT Press, p. 23.

9. On the subject of the police officer, Martel remarks that the film points to the human response when faced with the possibility of having killed someone, rather than to the fact itself: 'If you have not killed anyone but your response is that of a murderer, why are you less of a murderer? Police evidence does not turn you into more or less of a person . . . In my opinion, this has branded itself historically in the Argentine mind: the failure to understand that the culpability condition goes beyond direct action over death.' Solomonoff, J. (2009), 'La realidad es lo que se decide que sea', *La república del cine. Revista de la Academia de las Artes y Ciencias Cinematográficas de la Argentina*, 1, August, p. 82.

10. In this respect, Martel points to 'The way in which people's environment, either due to kindness, love, or affection, creates situations of cover-ups, complicity, and above all, protection for their own class, their social class.' Sabat, C. (2010), 'Lucrecia Martel por Cynthia Sabat', *Liberamedia*, <https://vimeo.com/11196313> (last accessed 3 May 2021).

11. Martel remarks that at a certain point she joins the plan, 'Well yes, she is an accomplice. If you allow others to act for you, you are being an accomplice . . . It is a terrifying mechanism, it is letting others take action for you, it is joining others' convictions. In our discourse, our language is full of denials, of obliterations, of things covered up. And I think this is because society coexists with inequalities that force a daily exercise in denial. An exercise like this requires a great deal of ability, a lot of creativity; it is not something gross, it is a very delicate and sophisticated mechanism.' Enríquez, 'La mala memoria'.

12. Videla, J. R. (1979), *Clarín*, 14 December 1979.

13. Žižek, S. (2003), *Ideología: Un mapa de la cuestión*, Buenos Aires: Fondo de Cultura Económica, p. 31. For Lacan, madness results from the disentangling of any of the three links that form the so-called Borromean knot (the record of the imaginary, the symbolic, and the real). In this respect, it is possible to bring back the state of 'disconnection' that Vero's character experiences after the collision (Martel's idea that what she has lost is the net that links her to the universe around her − see note 2 above) in order to think that the incident on the road has caused some kind of 'disentangling' of one of the records from the others.

14. Žižek, *Looking Awry*, p. 17.

15. Ibid.

16. Martel points out that, 'In the final analysis, this whole film was a personal inquiry into something that I cannot understand in our history regarding the dictatorship, which is denial. How it was possible for those who were not directly involved in activism or in the repressive machinery to deny what was going on . . . For me, the terror felt by the society not involved in activism or in the repressive machinery was the terror of acknowledging that they did know, that they were actually part of the situation, and they let it happen. That is why there is talk of "stirring up things". In order to live with that kind of denial it is necessary to find justifications to such an extent that they change the facts in one's life, one forgets things. But that effort also implies forgetting part of one's own life. Society demands that together with the effort of trying not to be responsible for an event one should forget everything that happened around that event, which also implies forgetting oneself. *The Headless Woman* is a completely personal approach – neither complete nor revealing – to that perverted mechanism we have as a society.' Enríquez, 'La mala memoria'.

17. Emphasis mine.
18. Regarding the actress who plays Vero's role, María Onetto, Martel points out that 'María has the kind of body that was clearly very necessary for the film. A tall, white woman. A visible body in a place where they are trying to make the responsibility for something disappear. I liked the idea that the person who is intended to disappear so perfectly is someone who cannot be hidden, because such a tall blonde woman is not that common in Salta.' Enríquez, 'La mala memoria'.
19. In this respect, Martel points out that 'Taming perception is the way towards political conservatism. Instead, any distortion of perception – this is my sickly illusion – upsets the environment and that allows perhaps, I don't mean always, a different way to conceive reality.' Ibid.
20. Regarding this, Martel speaks of the lack of 'awareness [on the part of employers] of the service provided by the human beings around them. There is some kind of slavery in the personal service given by domestic workers in the northern provinces; clinging to that is out of this world.' Enríquez, 'La mala memoria'. Even the first letters of the protagonist's name (ver = see) hint at what is at stake, while the recurrent appearance of mirrors all along the story brings in the idea of duplication; moreover, of the multiplication of image in a context in which the main characters strive not to see.
21. Martel affirms that 'The experience of an accident shakes perception; there is a derailment that forces one to rearrange things. Or else, leave them as they are, and watch the new relationship between people and things.' Sabat, 'Lucrecia Martel por Cynthia Sabat'.
22. The piece is 'Mamy Blue', composed by Hubert Yves Adrien Giraud and Phil Trim and sung by Demis Roussos. According to Mariana Enríquez, the song became popular in the 1970s in Julio Iglesias's version and nowadays it is still associated with the dictatorship, as if it were a soundtrack of those years. Enríquez, 'La mala memoria'.

CHAPTER 10

Fevers, Frights and Psychophysical Disconnections: Invisible Threats in the Soundtracks of *Zama* and *The Headless Woman*

Damyler Cunha

What are the particularities of the soundtrack in *Zama* (2017)? Is there some type of organisation of sound already present in other films by Lucrecia Martel? We may observe, through an analysis of the soundtracks of both *The Headless Woman/La mujer sin cabeza* (2008) and *Zama*, that some techniques in the use of sound effects and ambient sounds are employed repeatedly. These sounds may be subtle or exaggerated, minimal or dense and loud, distinct sounds or even exaggeratedly rarefied, ethereal.

Just like in *The Headless Woman*, in *Zama* the off-screen sounds build the world as the presence/absence of the other, in addition to showing themselves as non-diegetic sounds: sounds that do not occur in the world of the characters; an invasion that, in previous films, had not yet appeared so prominently. These sounds are the songs sung by Los Indios Tabajaras and a sound effect that appears at specific moments when Don Diego de Zama, the main character and an official of the Spanish Crown, realises his wait is in vain.[1] In addition to these new 'invaders', we can also highlight a process of destabilisation of the narrative as the rarefaction or suspension of ambient sounds used in both films.

Another particularity that is repeatedly employed throughout the director's work is the use of a close-up shot that shows the face, neck and ears, and is nearly always linked to the subjectivity of the framed character, accompanied, at specific moments, by sounds that appear to embody a psychophysical disturbance that affects their bodies. Martel brings us closer to her characters' hearing through the editing of these sounds, creating an atmosphere of continuous and ever-increasing discomfort, which is displayed by the protagonists' inability to recognise the objects and sound events that surround them. In this chapter, we will explore these repetitions and innovations in the use of off-screen sounds.

THE PSYCHOPHYSICAL DISTURBANCES AND CRISES IN *ZAMA*

When watching *Zama*, distinct feelings and impressions affect us. From the start, it is the vastness of the horizon that catches our gaze. The first image of the film reveals the protagonist's silhouette staring at the horizon while on the bank of a broad river. The ochre-orange colour of the cliffs, the muddy river and its milky texture accentuated by the reflection of the sunset light on the water predominate in this shot. In spite of the beautiful image capturing our attention, what opens the film and grants it a unique atmosphere are the strident insect sounds that recall the rattle of venomous snakes. There is something exuberant, seductive and eminently voracious that echoes from the nature depicted in the film.

In the following shots, we accompany Zama crouching behind the cliffs to spy on the bodies of a few women as they bathe and talk close to the river. Given away by a misstep, Zama is chased by one of the women – the house-keeper Malemba, against whom he retaliates with slaps and punches. With the exception of this scene, in the first two-thirds of *Zama*, as in the other films by this director, we see the predominance of mid-shots and close-ups that feature the intimacy of the bodies and the internal environments that the characters inhabit: Zama's rooms at the two inns and his office; the governor's office; the sitting room, bedroom and stables at the house of Luciana Piñares de Luenga. It is only in the final third of the film, preceded by the sequence that introduces Zama's feverish state, that we see open shots of landscapes in the Chaco region – revealed by the cinematography of Rui Poças – making prominent the exuberance and rapacity of the nature featured in the opening of the film. This third large sequence of scenes is marked by the mission undertaken by the protagonist together with other missionaries to hunt down the dangerous outlaw Vicuña Porto – an act that 'authorises' Zama to abandon his wait for a job transfer and go into the wild, marshy landscape in the border region between Paraguay, Brazil and Argentina.

In addition to some recurring aesthetics present in both *The Headless Woman* and *Zama* which we will discuss later, in her fourth feature-length film Martel distances herself from the depiction of the decomposition of family structures to focus on discussing the story of a *criollo* at the end of the eighteenth century, a person who identifies themselves as neither Amerindian nor Spanish. *Zama* was adapted from the eponymous 1956 novel by the Argentine author Antonio Di Benedetto, and its narrative is set between 1790 and 1799, in the aftermath of the change in the colonial system in the region promoted by the Spanish Crown. During this period, a series of new measures was implemented, culminating in the reorganisation of the colony's geographical division with the creation of the Río de la Plata Viceroyalty (1776), in the amendment of the taxation policies and in the redistribution of posts in these territories. Beginning with the creation of this new viceroyalty, we see what can be called the basis of the construction of the Argentine nationality,[2] which in the novel melds with the main character's experiencing an existential crisis.

Di Benedetto's poetic language in *Zama* is constantly considered as a reflection of the gradual process of Don Diego's physical, economic, social and moral decline. As Rafael Arce points out, in addition to the evidence of a transgression of verisimilitude usually adopted by historical novels, in the first part of the book it is noticeable that 'the syntactic complexity and the proliferation of archaisms produce a discreetly baroque verbal resonance, up until the end, where this verbosity is supplanted by the clarity of sentences that are short, laconic, and lightly marked by a few Guaraní words'.[3] In the same article, Arce also argues that Di Benedetto's stylistic process is isomorphic to the story the character experiences. According to Arce, Di Benedetto, with his own pithiness, 'takes on the constitutive lack of language in relation to the real: ellipsis, ambiguity, deliberate poverty, all contribute to an exhaustion of language that brings it closer to silence, that is, to the emptiness of meaning and reference'.[4]

As noted by Tereza Dulci and Libia Castañeda López in 'A recriação da colônia em *Zama*', as with the novel, the existential crisis is also present in Martel's film as a stylistic and contextual element. In the film, Zama, the only American-born man included in the bureaucracy of the Spanish viceroyalty in the region, anxiously awaits to be transferred and, perhaps, recover his former prestige, when he had held the position of chief magistrate. For Dulci and Castañeda López, the identity ambiguity that weighs on the story's protagonist is aggravated the more he realises his transfer is far from his superiors' horizons: 'The harder his transfer becomes, the more Zama questions his own identity.'[5] According to Dulci and Castañeda López, it is only when Zama throws himself into action and decides to enter the jungle on the mission to capture the dangerous outlaw Vicuña Porto that the protagonist begins to recognise himself within that landscape. Zama needs to walk into the Latin American territory to feel his body in that place. When he walks, Zama also stops waiting for his transfer, he acts, he changes the state in which he used to be. However, it must be added that, before realising that he should move himself of his own volition, the protagonist has an episode of bodily illness, afflicted by a state of change between what was and what could be.

At the point we can call the moment of change in the perception of reality experienced by the protagonist, there are scenes that emphasise a collapsed state of the character by the build-up of various events: we follow Zama's impoverishment, his loss of prestige before his superiors with the delay of his transfer request, his feverish body at an inn that appears to be inhabited by ghostly women, and his boss being more invested in trying to hinder his subordinate from writing a book than he is in addressing the issues put forward by Zama.

This seems to confer a tone of strangeness to the film, contributing to the perception of the character's disconnection in relation to the images we see. In the background, we hear and see llamas that come and go without any apparent reason; the gentlemen's servants play chess wearing clothes too pompous for the occasion; women that look like mourning ghosts come and go as figures at the makeshift inn where Zama lives, curing him of an inexplicable fever. In this sequence, Zama is simply unable to react to the acoustic and visual stimuli that affect him; he is, instead, only moved by other people, remaining passive in the situations.

After nearly an hour and twenty minutes of film, the exuberant nature of the tropics is presented as an enigmatic object, unknown, undominated by the men of civilisation. The nomadic indigenous people (in movement, be it temporary or not) that appear in *Zama* understand each other through looks and the moon, they recognise animals and people merely by the width of the footprints left on the earth, camouflage themselves among tree trunks, fear neither wild animals nor the river: all these elements stand out in this third part of the film to better indicate the presence of an enigmatic nature that is itself a character. If, in the first part, we feel Zama's despair at waiting, buried in his earthy, humid office, in this final sequence we are touched by the rays of light and framing that emphasise the silhouettes of palm trees more than the men passing underneath them.

On the depiction of Zama's existential crisis noted by the aforementioned authors, we can see that there is a type of acoustic *mise-en-scène* that Martel

Figure 10.1 Zama discusses his transfer with the Governor. © Rei Cine SRL, Bananeira Filmes Ltda, El Deseo DA SLU, Patagonik Film Group SA

uses – which usually, through the depiction of the experience of the characters' hearing, reveals the strangeness of hearing oneself, or provokes irremediable fears upon hearing the sounds of the world. In *The Swamp/La ciénaga* (2001), Mecha has an accident with wine glasses, and a boy, Luchi, is afraid of the barking of a dog that is never shown within the frame. In *The Holy Girl/La niña santa* (2004), we have a teenager who believes she is hearing divine audible signs while her mother is affected by Ménière's disease, an illness that makes her hear ringing in the ears. In her next feature film, *The Headless Woman*, Verónica hears and senses that she ran over something, but decides not to look.

In these three films, the sounds that denote these accidental situations are kept off-screen for enough time to strengthen an atmosphere of presence, inner feelings, and strangeness in relation to that which is beyond the character's and viewer's sight.[6] In *Zama* we can point out at least three types of invisible threats to the order of the protagonist that appear in the soundtrack, off-screen. They are: the sound effect 'Don Diego de Zama'; the various non-diegetic songs we hear in the film, all recordings by Los Indios Tabajaras; and the sound editing technique of suspending the ambient sounds in the scene so that only silence remains.

To create the sound effect inspired by the Shepard tone,[7] credited as 'Don Diego de Zama', Martel and Guido Berenblum invited the Argentine musician and sound artist Luciano Azzigotti.[8] This sound effect appears in the film in moments when someone comments on Zama's anticipated transfer or when he is lauded for his former fame as a peace-making magistrate. It contributes to maintaining the feeling of an audible perpetuity, an endless fall, but it introduces a variation of textures and sounds each time it is used.

The first time we have this sound effect is when Zama is introduced to The Oriental and the man's child starts reciting a background profile of Zama, praising his qualities from his chief magistrate period. The hand-held camera shows the characters wobbling for the first time and, together with the spiralling sound effect, bolsters a feeling of vertigo. The same effect returns another four times in the film. In a later scene, it appears twice, developing through the manipulated and rarefied sounds of buzzing cicadas, and later, by the reverberation of the sounds of cups overlayed on the dialogue between Luciana and Zama in Luciana's house. When she speaks about Zama's possible transfer, the effect intensifies and takes over the entire ambient sound, with an increase in intensity and density throughout the scene. In its fourth occurrence, the effect reappears when Zama discovers his rival, Ventura Prieto, has been transferred to the region the protagonist himself had requested. Finally, in the scene at the unsanitary inn when Zama is helped by the women and the scribe, who bathe him during his fever, we hear the spiralling sound effect a fifth time.

During the Vicuña Porto manhunt sequence, we are able to notice that the sound effects re-emerge at two distinct times, with much less persistence in the audio illusion caused by the Shepard tones and, consequently, in the perception of a spiralling sound movement. When the first indigenous man, painted in red, appears on the plains, right after Captain Parrilla ironically asks Zama if 'the magistrate could offer some advice', we hear the sound effect with a bit of the continuance of the spiralling movement. And, in the penultimate scene of the film, when Zama's hands are amputated, the only sound we hear is the reverberation of a sharp, ascending sound effect.

Thinking in terms of an anthropology of noise, the 'Don Diego de Zama' sound effect can be considered an expression of the idea of descent, loss of strength, like a fall into an endless abyss. In *Os cantos da voz*, the musician and researcher Heloísa de Araújo Duarte Valente, reflecting on the musicality of voice, recovers the writings of Canadian researcher R. Murray Schafer to remind us that the history of musical aesthetics registers occurrences of methods used symbolically as ornaments.[9] In this case, the movements of descending scales, such as madrigalisms, express an idea of descent, loss of power, contrary to how the ascending movement expresses exaltation, in direct relation to psychological and physical ascents, among others. From this perspective, not only is the auditory perception of the spectator related to the symbolic elements of the things in the world, but their perception is made up of the sum of the symbolic, psychological and physical stimuli experienced by a given individual. As Eleonora Rapan observes, the use of Shepard tones in *Zama* embodies a metaphysical order of waiting experienced by the protagonist, employing a new sense of time in cinema through the use of an auditory illusion.[10]

In two of its uses, the 'Don Diego de Zama' sound effect re-emerges in an ascending version, distinct from the other occurrences when it emphasises the auditory sensation of an endless descending scale. Both scenes address the changes inflicted on the protagonist's body − fever and amputation. The use of sharp sounds in an ascending movement may have been adopted as a strategy to emphasise the situation of extreme discomfort and the threshold of Zama's physical pain, expressing the end of something. After the hand amputation scene, the spiralling form of the acoustic illusion is not employed and we hear only a sharp sound effect, ascending and reverberating, emphasising the character's intense pain; meanwhile, it may still be understood as liberation of energy, for the body to react and continue to live.

DESIRE AND REPULSION IN THE USE OF EXTRADIEGETIC MUSIC IN *ZAMA*

The treatment of the ambient sounds and sound effects in the final part of *Zama* is completely distinct from the first two-thirds of the film. Besides a decrease in the use of sound effects and the processing of ambient sounds, we can perceive an increase in the visual depth of field in auditory terms, which reveals the sounds of a more prominent, ever-closer nature, as if the ambient sounds invaded the space of the foreground soundtrack. During Zama's stay in the city, we hear ambient noise based on isolated, distinct sounds such as horses neighing, whips snapping, llamas braying, wind blowing, brooms sweeping, dogs barking, street vendors, and the crying and whispering of children and adults alike.

However, during the Vicuña Porto manhunt, the textured sounds of water, insects, cicadas, frogs, indigenous people whistling, and other natural sounds is omnipresent. The nondiegetic music, heavily present in the first hour of the film, with six appearances, is rarefied in this last part and appears only in the final scene: when we see Zama disappear with the indigenous people into the lush landscape and the final frame is replaced with the closing credits. In this sequence, another off-screen song is added, reverberating as if it were already playing in the background. This song is heard at a low volume, and Captain Parrilla asks Zama who is playing it.

With the exception of the flute melody in the aforementioned scene, all the songs in the film are recordings played by Los Indios Tabajaras, who use a reverberating vibrato in various songs, offering an extension and an imprecision to the ears also present in the use of the theremin sound in *The Holy Girl*.[11] 'María Elena' (1963), the duo's most famous song, is a Mexican composition by Lorenzo Barcelata (1898–1943) and its guitar sound resembles the lap steel guitar (Hawaiian guitar). The duo's songs in *Zama* provide us with a mixture of styles, predominantly bolero, while also carrying influences of traditional Mexican music and Latin American folklórico, jazz and bossa nova.

The first musical intervention in this film happens during the scene in which Ventura Prieto and Zama question a man who is tied up. Despite his silence in the interrogation, he is freed by Ventura Prieto and oddly remains still; soon after, he bends forward at the waist, runs straight ahead and violently hits into something that is not shown on-screen. We follow the terrified looks of Zama and his colleagues in reaction to the interrogated man's sudden change in behaviour. While the man babbles something about fish and one government employee warns him he is under oath, we hear one of the songs by Los Indios Tabajaras and, afterwards, we see an underwater medium shot of a school of fish swimming in a rollicking river.

In conjunction with these images and the song, we distinctly hear the voice of the prisoner telling a story of fish that try to survive along the banks of a river that is trying to get rid of them. The music here runs through the narrative, breaking its realistic characteristics, and submerges us in a dreamlike, exotic, strange and opaque universe somewhat akin to the muddy waters on the screen and over which the film title appears. In this scene, we distinctly see the resurgence of the book's grand metaphor. Martel subverts the story of the dead monkey that is stuck in the remains of a decrepit wooden dock, its body toing and froing with the river's current, to make us think about fish stuck in the tiniest of movements, similar to the painful and labyrinthine existence Zama is subjected to in the Spanish colony.

The other occurrences of music are used to reinforce the feeling of desire and repulsion experienced by the main character. The boleros by Los Indios Tabajaras emerge in scenes at the stable and at Luciana's house, when she runs her hands along a horse's body, and later when the men admire her beauty, or, again, in Zama's office, when he watches a dog licking the hands of a woman with indigenous features. The fourth song played in the film also serves an exotic scene, in which the governor of the viceroyalty talks to a man with an extravagant moustache while a woman massages his feet. In yet another musical intervention, we see Zama offering to give a bed to the hut of an indigenous woman who he claims is the mother of his youngest son.

The duo's final two songs in the film are not clearly characterised by Zama's desire or repulsion in relation to a female figure, but instead mark the transition between two spaces in the film: the 'city' and the tropical forest. The penultimate musical contribution takes place directly after the scene where Zama discovers it will take another two years for him to get his transfer, while he goes to meet up with the mission that will go in search of the outlaw Vicuña Porto. And, in the final shot, after the indigenous child asks Zama if he wants to live, and then says something in his own language (left untranslated in the subtitles), we hear the last song encroaching on this scene and advancing to the next one, the closing credits.

In the film, we're able to notice a tension between the protagonist and the women that are part of his life. For Zama, women appear to occupy a place of objects of desire and of his sexual and emotional frustration. His wife (represented only in letters), Luciana, the maid Malemba and the indigenous women are shown as distant women or, at times, as objects of the projection of the most obscure aspects of Zama's personality. In relation to gender representation in Martel's films, our approach in this final part of the chapter is only to highlight how sonic materiality is used to depict the subjectivity of the characters, which, consequently, makes us consider the sources of tension surrounding the theme.

As mentioned above, certain scenes in which we hear the songs by Los Indios Tabajaras are distinguished by a clear strategy that underlines the feeling of ironic humour by merging song and narration. In most of these scenes, we notice situations in which the presence of women arouses a look of repulsion or lustful desire in Zama. Another matter we can highlight is the repetitive use of similar melodic themes and motifs present in the songs we hear throughout the film, which also works to emphasise the feeling of labyrinthine circling, just as with the reiterated use of the 'Don Diego de Zama' sound effect.

In her previous films, Martel avoids using music and sounds that are not a part of the diegesis; however, the effect caused by these songs adds to the awkwardness or irony experienced by the characters. If we recall *The Swamp*, the music played after Mecha's accident with the wine glasses is an upbeat Argentine cumbia, with vibrant rhythm and tones, heavily contrasting with the tragedy shown on the screen. In *The Headless Woman*, the music playing in Vero's car at the time of the accident is a cheery pop song, from the post-hippie era of disco, which also carries this irony, underlining the paradox of that traumatic situation. In *The Holy Girl*, the otherworldly melody of the theremin appears in the scene precisely when we witness the sexual harass-ment of Amalia, who, after the situation, starts to feel confused when she recognises the divine signs mentioned in her catechism lesson.

In line with the analysis above, in this final part of the film we can see a dimin-ishing use of music, of distinguished sound effects, of the processing of ambient sounds, and of the dialogues themselves, growing closer, from a certain point of view, to the claims made by Arce, and Dulci and Castañeda López, which were discussed at the start of this chapter. In *Zama*'s third act we see a shift in the treat-ment of sounds and images and, like in Di Benedetto's novel, a decreased use of stylistic tools in order to emphasise the silence, ambiguity, and the psychophysi-cal changes that the human body may experience when entering the wilderness. To indicate the differences and specifications of Martel's auditory *mise-en-scène*, we will make a slight digression to demonstrate an audio technique of rarefying ambient sounds frequently used by Martel, Berenblum and Emmanuel Croset in *The Headless Woman*. This strategy is always used after the sound material in the scene is made denser. The density comes from an increase in the overlapping and processing of ambient sounds in post-production.

LISTENING IN WAIT: AMBIGUITY AND RAREFACTION OF AMBIENT SOUNDS IN THE SOUNDTRACK OF *THE HEADLESS WOMAN*

The characters' disconnection from the perception of their experienced reali-ties is a recurring theme in Lucrecia Martel's work. In the director's other feature-length films, many of her characters are affected by feelings of exhaus-tion, fatigue, or other psychophysical disconnections which alter our perception of reality. Fever as a symptom of a body in a state of change has affected: teenage Amalia, protagonist of *The Holy Girl*; Candita, Verónica's niece in *The Headless Woman*, who also suffered from liver failure; and Luchi, Tali's son, additionally troubled by tooth disease, in *The Swamp*.

In *The Headless Woman*, this disconnection from the perception of what the characters experience is taken to the extreme in the characterisation of the

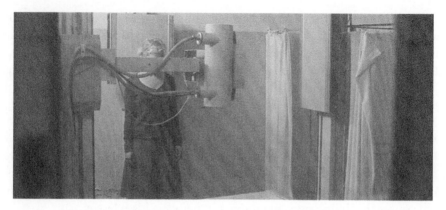

Figure 10.2 Vero in the hospital after the accident, in *The Headless Woman*

protagonist. Vero, after having a car accident in which she decides not to look at what knocked her off the road and caused the accident, starts to act as if a tension in her memory troubles her to the point of affecting her body. We begin to notice constant episodes of her not reacting verbally in conversations; her gestures are slow and silence surrounds her space. Throughout the film, the character is disturbed by sounds that recall the accident, as if her hearing has been put in 'standby mode' ever since her trauma. An external sound that hits her ears becomes internalised and remains in her conscience as the memory of a doubt. The soundtrack was designed in close dialogue with the art direction and scenography crews and was essential for this type of hearing experience to be depicted in cinema.

In the case of *The Headless Woman*, the repetition of ambient sounds with the same material texture of the sounds heard during the car crash creates an atmosphere that appears to spread into various scenes, affecting the character, who begins to feel haunted by the possibility of having accidentally killed a child. The thump from the friction of sand, metal and animal/human body is once more heard by the character in one of the most intriguing scenes of the film: when Vero is working out beside a football pitch and we hear an off-screen thump that scares her. There is a hard cut and, in the next shot, the image shows Vero glancing sideways at the football pitch, where one of the young players has been hit by the ball and is lying in the foetal position. The noise we had just listened to was the ball hitting the wire fence.

We notice in this scene that the sound is constructed from materials (metal, human body, grass field) that are similar, but not identical, to those used in the scene of the accident. The friction of the ball hitting the wire fence at a high speed, and the impact of the human body on the ball and the ground provide an opaque, metallic sound similar to what we heard minutes before in the triggering scene for the film's conflict. The image of the boy falling, in the foetal position, showing no reaction to his teammates' concern, also contributes to our memory of the rear-view mirror shot in Vero's car, just after the accident, in which we are able to see a dog lying in the foetal position in the middle of the road. At the end of the scene, Vero leaves the football pitch and walks up to what appears to be the entrance to a toilet, where she gets nauseous by a sink.

All of the sound editing in this scene, besides favouring what Michel Chion has called 'materialising sound indices',[12] seems to be crafted to amplify this auditory tension that affects the character after her potential memory through the processing and rarefaction of these ambient sounds. As of this moment, Vero admits to her spouse the possibility of having killed someone, and more audible signs begin to appear to the protagonist, challenging her to doubt if she has really killed a dog or a child.[13]

This organisation device of the sounds from the characters' daily life, in which repetition of sound textures that contain the same feeling of materiality as the source, with small variations in their processing, is used in a few other moments in the film. The sounds of our daily life are able to provide us with information on the material (wood, paper, plastic, metal) and on the origin of a sound, whether it is from friction, banging, swinging, or even if the sound has a cyclical rhythm. When left off-screen, these sounds can still be used for their abstract qualities, deprived of reference; this is exactly the type of sound subversion that Martel most uses in *The Headless Woman*. The director uses a 'way of approaching' the character by means of sound editing,[14] using a lack of on-screen reference of objects and sound events that surround the protagonist to create an atmosphere of continuous and increasing discomfort – a strategy of sound organisation reminiscent of horror films, a possible influence on Martel's work, as some critics have remarked.[15] Eliminating the counter-shot which can clarify and grant a visual reference to the origin of an invisible sound within the plot may well be the biggest horror legacy in the film.

Lucrecia Martel's acoustic 'way of approaching' does not solely involve the diegetic and realistic character of the sound. On the contrary, the sounds that appear off-screen exert an energy within the *mise-en-scène* exactly because they wander between not-so-well-defined spaces. In yet another moment in *The Headless Woman*, before the football pitch scene, we see Vero getting out of her cousin's car to rescue her nephew's shoe on the side of the road. During this action, we hear all the ambient sound from the road, in addition to two metallic hisses that stand out for being distinct and very similar to the metallic sounds heard in the opening of the film, when two kids were playing, along with a dog, on the side of the road.

The static, medium shot framing highlights Vero standing with her back to the camera, centred on the background of the image. Upon seeing Vero standing still, one of her nephews gets out of the car and runs to grab the shoe, while she abruptly turns around and gets in the car. In this scene, besides noticing the repetitive use of a somewhat metallic sound effect, the image provides us with indications that the character may have recalled the accident by her abrupt and affected movement as she looks at the canal alongside the road.

The character's abrupt movement is accompanied by a change in the perception of space and time of the scene, beginning with the created ascending sound that accompanies an advancing car driving on the road simultaneously with Vero's action. The processed ambient sounds become harsher and more ethereal, like a cloud of sound dust that echoes through the image of the speeding car on the road. This same sound continues and creeps into the first shots of the next scene, the one by the football pitch described above, in a descending and wide movement, as if it had concluded its cycle only to be interrupted by the sharp, dry sound cut of the ball hitting the wire fence — an ellipsis made from the editing of ambient sounds, but that at the same time maintains its connection between the two spaces and carries on the ethereal atmosphere.

In this scene, we can note that once again the materiality of the car's friction on the sand creates a feeling of suspension, of paralysis of time. The idea of referentiality and of depicting things through sound is lost for a few seconds, as the car passes by. The focus here is perceiving the textures, the ascending movement of airborne dust particles; this minimalistic and banal sound, yet edited in a way that takes over the shot and the theatre. It is exactly due to the density, volume, and material texture of the sounds that the ambiguity in meaning is effected, destabilising the narrative. Does Vero remember the accident by hearing the same metallic hisses, those minimal sounds from when she drove along the road minutes before the accident? Or is it just we, the viewers, who hear these sounds, and the simple act of driving along the same road where the accident occurred was enough to paralyse her reactions? Are the metallic hisses heard at the beginning of the film sound effects produced in post-production and, therefore, non-diegetic, or were they heard by the characters and are thus part of the diegesis?

The sounds created from metallic reverberating hisses appear at various other moments, always after a scene in which Vero comes into contact with signs of the death of the child. They are repeated right after the accident, when we see her standing in the rain from the perspective of the passenger of a car. They appear a third time in the scene where Vero, her cousin Jose, her niece Candita, and her friend go into the dry vegetation beside the road, after going to a plant nursery where the salesperson complains that an employee hasn't come to work. In later scenes, we learn that this employee was the dead child found by the firefighters in the roadside canal. Do these distinct sound motifs influence our involvement with the potential death of the child? Are they intended for this purpose in the film?

The depiction of the subjectivity of the sounds experienced by the protagonists in the two films analysed in this chapter is one of the strategies used to maintain the ambiguity of the narratives. Martel subverts the realistic and diegetic nature of the sounds when she makes them travel through undefined spaces and deprives them of their auditory references for an excessive amount of time, to the point that doubt is introduced. With this type of technique for ambient sound editing, the viewer of *The Headless Woman* and *Zama* comes closer to an auditory experience that has its attention directed towards the enjoyment of the aesthetic and sensorial characteristics of sound, including tone, texture, shape, mass and volume, thus multiplying and expanding their causes and meanings. This sound subversion used by Martel translates into the subversion of the persistence of habits, of perceptive conditions, overlapping the reality of the characters in these films.

With the analysis of *Zama*, we have highlighted three types of invisible sounds that appear in the off-screen space and act to emphasise the existential and psychophysical disturbances of the protagonist: the 'Don Diego de Zama' sound effect, the extradiegetic music played by Los Indios Tabajaras, and the rarefaction or suspension of ambient sounds — this latter method also being used in *The Headless Woman*. Together, these sound elements contribute to the perception of a temporality of waiting in the films.

Unlike the novel, which mentions the time period the protagonist is living in, in *Zama* we can perceive a more accentuated time disconnection related to the absence of temporal milestones. The small perceptions of chronological time that are evident, established by the scenery or the characters' costumes, are not sufficient to exactly pinpoint when and where the story is developing.

In Martel's most recent feature-length film, we can note other temporal perceptions that are not based on the advancing chronological time. First, we have the repetitions of the 'Don Diego de Zama' sound effect. In this case, that is, the use of an auditory illusion based on the Shepard tones sound effect, we have a sonic perception that affects the viewers' ears and Zama's conscience, contributing to the perception of the narrative's cyclical time, perpetual in its unending back-and-forth motion.

The use of extradiegetic music, besides breaking with the concept of a realistic status of the image, also serves to reveal that which escapes Zama's imagination — looks of desire and repulsion that the protagonist directs at the women around him. In these moments in the film, the songs take on the power of an ironic commentary on the objects onto which the most obscure aspects of Zama's personality are projected. The songs by Los Indios Tabajaras that we hear in the film also reinforce a labyrinth-like time perception, with their repetition of themes and melodic motifs. As we have explained in this chapter, the reiterated use of these stylistic sound techniques is concentrated in the first two-thirds of the film and contributes to establishing the moments when the protagonist perceives his useless waiting, exposed to his own shame.

Yet another temporal alteration takes place with the use of the process of rarefaction or suspension of ambient sounds in the scene. The strangeness engendered by this process of decreasing the density or completely removing the ambient sounds, designed in audio post-production processes, makes the viewer doubt the references and temporality of the sound events, thus acting to destabilise the narrative. In *The Headless Woman*, a temporality of waiting is also present in the depiction of the protagonist's hearing who, by listening to certain sounds, is made to recall her hit-and-run accident at the start of the film. Due to this sonic persistence which stresses her memory, Vero undergoes personal changes throughout the film and assumes responsibility for a potential crime.

Vero and Zama experience a condition of numbed hearing, a hearing paralysed by having reached its maximum potential in establishing connections and producing meaning. The sound design in *The Headless Woman* and *Zama* contributes to the spectator perceiving, on an acoustic level, this feeling of depletion and waiting experienced by both the protagonists of these films.

Translated by Alisa Wilhelm and revised by Alessandro Funari

NOTES

1. Los Indios Tabajaras is a musical duo comprised of the brothers Antenor and Natalício Moreira Lima. The two brothers asserted that they belonged to the Tabajara indigenous people from the region of Serra de Ibiapaba, in Ceará, the traditional territory of the Tabajaras in Brazil. They began their career on Brazilian radio in the 1940s and recorded various albums across thirty years, reaching success in Brazil, Argentina, Mexico and the United States. Their biggest success was the song 'María Elena' (1963), which, on its release, reached the top of the charts in US magazine *Billboard*. 'María Elena' (BMG records) is one of the seven songs by the duo that were chosen to make up the soundtrack of *Zama*, in addition to: 'Luces en el puerto' (RCA records), 'A la orilla del lago' (RCA records), 'Siempre en mi corazón' (BMG records), 'Te quiero dijiste' (BMG records), 'Amapola' (RCA records) and 'Marta' (RCA records).

2. Myers, J. (2007), 'A revolução de independência no Rio da Prata e as origens da nacionalidade argentina (1806–1825)', in M. A. Pamplona and M. E. Mader (eds), *Revoluções de independências e nacionalismos nas Américas: Região do Prata e Chile*, São Paulo: Paz e Terra. In this chapter, Myers asserts that the legitimacy crisis of the institutions linked to the viceroyalty of Buenos Aires coincided with the legitimacy crisis of the institutions of the Bourbon monarchy, both mutually strengthening each other, years before the independence of Argentina. In May 1810, the *criollo* elite of Buenos Aires worked to overturn the viceroy Baltasar Hidalgo de Cisneros and take political control of the Río de la Plata Viceroyalty.

3. ('una complejidad sintáctica y la proliferación de arcaísmos producen una resonancia verbal de un discreto barroquismo, hacia el final esa verbosidad se extenúa hasta la limpidez de la frase breve, lacónica y levemente marcada por algunas palabras guaraníes'.) Arce, R. (2016), 'El ejercicio de la espera: Para una lectura de lo grotesco en *Zama*, de Antonio Di Benedetto', *Artelogie*, 8, pp. 1–22 (p. 2).

4. ('asume la falta constitutiva de lenguaje en relación con lo real: la elipsis, la ambigüedad, la deliberada pobreza, contribuyen a una extenuación de la lengua que la acerca al silencio, es decir, al vacío de sentido y de referencia'.) Ibid.

5. ('Quanto mais se torna difícil conseguir deslocamento, mais Zama questiona sua própria identidade.') Dulci, T. M. S. and L. A. Castañeda López (2019), 'A recriação da

colônia em *Zama*: Identidades, gênero e representação do espaço', *Revista Eletrônica da ANPHLAC*, 26, pp. 408–43 (p. 423), <https://revista.anphlac.org.br/anphlac/article/view/3356/2762> (last accessed 7 September 2021).

6. ('Mientras los sonidos tienen que ver con la presencia, lo interior, el recogimiento, la imagen impone la distancia, la exterioridad, la distinción de los elementos. La visualidad impone una relación de poder y dominio diferente de la audición.') Aguilar, G. (2010), *Otros mundos: Un ensayo sobre el nuevo cine argentino*, Buenos Aires: Santiago Arcos, p. 102.

7. Patrício, P. L. M. (2015), *Ilusões sonoras: Um estudo sobre a aplicação da ilusão sonora da escala de Shepard em composição musical digital*, PhD thesis, Universidade Católica Portuguesa. The Shepard tone is named after American cognitive scientist Roger N. Shepard. It is a sound that consists of overlaid sine waves separated by octaves, each wave representing a tone that is double the frequency of the one below it and half the frequency of the one above.

8. Martel usually employs the same sound crew for her films, and in *Zama* she maintains the same sound designer, Guido Berenblum, and sound mixer, Emmanuel Croset, both of whom worked on *The Swamp* and *The Headless Woman*.

9. Valente, H. A. D. (1999), *Os cantos da voz: Entre o ruído e o silêncio*, São Paulo: Annablume, pp. 115–16.

10. Rapan, E. (2018), 'Shepard Tones and Production of Meaning in Recent Films: Lucrecia Martel's *Zama* and Christopher Nolan's *Dunkirk*', *The New Soundtrack*, 8: 2, pp. 135–44, <https://www.euppublishing.com/doi/abs/10.3366/sound.2018.0126> (last accessed 7 September 2021). In this article, Rapan traces the history of the creation and use of Shepard tones and their use in recent cinematographic productions.

11. Note made by the researcher Virginia Flôres, in contribution to this work. Flôres observes that 'in the case of *The Holy Girl* there is the question of the specialists in hearing disorders that are at the hotel for a conference. The eardrum, one of the parts of the ear, vibrates when it identifies pressure variations from the passage of sound, even when these variations are very slight. The hairs inside the cochlea (inner ear) also vibrate when a liquid inside the inner ear propagates sound. These signals are turned into electric signals and sent to the brain; this process is very similar to how sound can be captured by microphones and recorders. In *Zama*, it appears to be more closely linked to something without a defined end.'

12. Chion, M. (2011), *A audiovisão: Som e imagem no cinema*, Lisboa: Edições Texto e Grafia, p. 92.

13. We can also include the song by Jorge Cafrune that plays on the radio in the car at the moment when Vero sees the firefighters trying to get something out of the roadside canal. The melody of Cafrune's song has a dignified character, with a choir that recalls the structure of Catholic religious songs.

14. Mentioned by Berenblum in a talk along with Martel at an event organised by Cátedra Sonido I and Prof. Alejandro Seba, Universidad de Buenos Aires, 12 November 2008. Talk transcribed by Juani Bousquet and kindly provided by Martín Matus.

15. Christofoletti Barrenha, N. (2014), *A experiência do cinema de Lucrecia Martel: Resíduos do tempo e sons à beira da piscina*, São Paulo: Alameda Casa Editorial. Campo, M. B. (2019), 'Lucrecia Martel e Albertina Carri: Narrativas femininas subjetivas no Nuevo Cine Argentino (NCA)', *História: Questões e Debates*, 67: 1, pp. 63–85, <https://revistas.ufpr.br/historia/article/view/63995/37582> (last accessed 3 May 2021).

CHAPTER 11

Martel Variations

Adriana Amante

To Natalia Brizuela

IMPERFECT CINEMA

Lucrecia Martel's cinema is an act of thinking, and I do not mean that cinema is *for* Martel an act of thinking, because I do not know if she considers or would admit that. Even if she does believe so, albeit intermittently, how deliberate and evident a filmmaker finds what he or she does is irrelevant; what is arguably more fascinating is the fact that Martel's cinema is, or becomes in and through its very realisation, an act of thinking.

I also want to stress that I do not say that cinema is for Martel an act of *thought*, because I want to focus on the action, and particularly on the progression, on the drift, on the time which becomes active in the succession. Cinema as an act of thinking – which in its case manifests itself as a narrative or as poetics – which entails, ultimately or primarily, thinking of cinema as writing and of writing as essay-writing. Thus, the essay-like dimension of Martel's cinema manifests itself as materiality and as duration, rather than as a subject, as the deployment of a continuum. Or, perhaps, of an aspect, in the grammatical sense of the word: not making reference to the concrete time in which things happen or happened (that would not be the *aspect*, but the *tense*), but to the actions' internal duration. It does not point out the moment when something happens, but the process of happening. Martel states:

> I don't care at all about telling stories, but I am interested in perceiving a process. When you watch a movie, you don't sit for two hours in front

of a story: you sit before a complex process in which another person tries to reveal his or her perception of an outside.[1]

Thus, aspect does not reveal when something happens, will happen or happened, but how complete that action is, will be or was. And, if there are *perfective* actions, in the sense that they are finished, concluded (regardless of whether that conclusion takes place in the past or in the future), Martel's cinema installs itself (and I choose that verb as long as it is not construed as stillness, but as a way of dwelling, mobile, changing and fluctuating) in *imperfective* actions: the unfinished ones, the durative ones. That consideration of the way aspect works is the source of an aesthetic morality for Martel's cinema, nestled in her search for the imperfect, even — specifically — for the imperfective: for what is clearly unfinished, showing actions or stepping into them *in medias res*, without leading them to a conclusion, because, as the filmmaker says:

> What I don't like about plots [. . .] is that there is an evolution of characters, and I'm still to see in my life an event with a beginning, a middle and an end. In *The Swamp/La ciénaga* (2001), they come together, but it is more procession than plot.[2]

And this is what David Oubiña stresses after quoting her:

> A shot will often not start where something happens, but rather discover or stumble into an event. The camera manages to see it, but suggesting it could have very well missed it. As if unable to control the situation, it enters a flow which exists without it and before it, not knowing what it should capture there.[3]

I posit, then, that Martel's cinema is a deliberate way of analysing an idea which is materialised in certain objects, as is the case in some research essays. The variety of objects deployed (strictly, postulated, but also designed) by her films works as a means to explore something which is (or could be) beyond that which is made visible: fish, dogs, some girls, a river, Silvina Ocampo, *Argirópolis*, a pond, Encarnación Ezcurra, children, some pool, *Zama*. These are not *topoi* understood as topics, but fields on which to experiment with an idea.

This essayistic dimension of her cinema would appear to work, in many cases, through the procedures of the documentary. The documentary? Yes, initially: as a way of recording, as long as it is construed as a note or quick sketch. This will move on from this freehand note, created (seemingly) without instruments, to the materialisation of its re-elaboration, a process which turns what was recorded not necessarily into something different, but into something more. 'Even if you are simply describing something, there is always an extra operation there', as Martel has said.[4] This is a piece of writing, or perhaps a music score, but always — and above all else — a *notation*, articulating image and sound as a purely verbivocovisual composition, as in certain manifestations of concrete poetry. For that reason, in this case I interpret the essayistic not as the study of a subject, but as the search for an idea; and the documentary not as a registry of the real, but as notation for a process in which the real is elaborated. The camera as a *stylo*, but almost literally: cinema as an act of writing.

This is perfectly clear in *Fish/Pescados* (2010). During its four minutes and nineteen seconds, the film is pure notation. The music acquires an almost palpable materiality in the image's surface. Concrete cinema, to borrow a category from music. The short film breaks down the elements to the point of disintegration, paradoxically due to an excess of materialisation. Not an excess of representation, but, on the contrary, of concretion. There are fish (that is, *peces* in Spanish, and not *pescados*, the word used to refer to fish which have been caught; though in this case the aspect of the verb is a trick, or a manner of speaking, quite normal in everyday speech), and the mouth of the fish speak as if writing and put into effect the musical notation of cinema or musical notation *through* cinema: rather than a cine-/kine-matograph, this is a *sono*-matograph. The sounds issuing from the fish's mouths are subtitled. The subtitling of that which — supposedly — the fish say works as a way to fix meaning, just as we try to capture through familiar morphologies the shapeless in a Rorschach test. This is a process of translation: from sound to meaning. Almost all syntagmas of the sounds associated with the fish's mouths are subtitled, and they produce a contagion effect on the sounds which are not, enabling viewers — or, perhaps, condemning them — to infer meanings where perhaps — or surely — there is none. Thus, we hear shapeless sounds (babbling, sibilant fricatives, echolalia) and experience them as sounds with meaning, because we accept that there, in those sounds, there may be meaning.[5]

However, there is more than round-mouthed fish. There is also the rain, cars, a road, a pond, wheels, dreams, dogs, lights. Shown or told, but who could say what difference that makes in this cinema's writing. The light from the cars' headlights explodes against the rain. The lights escape their own boundaries, planting their materiality in the shapeless for another beautiful storm in the pampas of Argentine culture. In spite of the fragmentation and the cut, the fish moving and jabbering under water and the cars driving through the rain are a continuation, with a logic reminiscent of that of poems or, better yet, of surrealist collages. The trucks on the road sweep the water away, and appear to totally disintegrate into fragments which, like the frames in celluloid film, are not the minimum units, but a mere material abstraction.

The mouths and the voices of the fish are rather machine-like (*sound* is quite machine-like). However, that machine-like aspect will adopt a more systematic manner a year later, in *Muta* (2011), the short feature produced for the Italian brand Prada, as a part of the *Women's Tales* series, inaugurated by American filmmaker Zoe Cassavetes. The short film's opening moments confirm that, in Martel's cinema, in the beginning was water (as if, after *Fish* and, of course, *The Swamp* and *The Holy Girl/La niña santa* [2004], we did not know that). This time, bright orange sparkles that buzz over the surface of a calm river, which carries a water hyacinth and a modest vessel adrift. In that boat, a group of female bodies meanders in lines, as if in a dislocated runway show. They wear high and stunning heels, not-too-long nails painted in dark colours, elegant dresses, broad-rimmed glasses of many colours, some handbags, and – above all – long and heavy eyelashes which produce striking flutters.

A woman is in command (the first one to appear, in a grey dress with white embroidered flowers and long blonde hair). Her extremely long legs herald her as she emerges from a compartment into the scene, inside the vessel, with faceted movements, as a makeshift stop-motion segment, and is followed by other women, with a robotic gait, as if those bodies were subjected to the principle of representation of stilled movements, or as if this were one of Anton Giulio Bragaglia's exercises in futurist photodynamism. The shot never captures these women's faces: they are covered by glasses and hands and, at times, gasmasks. And, if we can surmise there are eyes, it is through metonymy, based on the presence of glasses and eyelashes. The flutter of those eyelashes becomes more material when shot to show part of the women's profiles from the back of their heads. If common for a reference plane, in this case, that reference – the profile of the face of the girl showing her back – becomes the central, full object of the plane.

And the rest is not silence, but the opposite: in this short feature for the Miu Miu clothing line, we witness the embodiment of the object through sounds, for in this case sound is not something (a phenomenon, we could say) issuing from things. Rather, things become corporeal through the sounds outlining them, sounds which, incidentally, make fun of the denotative, through excess or because they disrupt the natural (or, better yet, habitual) relation between objects and their function. Once again: it is not that things which exist have sound, but that things exist because sound, as a demiurge, determines their existence. There is a certain echo of *Playtime*'s Jacques Tati in the image's material construction: the objectual dimension of sound in Martel's movies becomes palpable in *Muta*.

A door, eyelashes, fingers which call by stroking, not snapping, as if they were the flutter (yet another) of birds, for a new convention of non-verbal language. Thus does the woman in command summon the rest for a ritual of transformation. We can almost feel the torsion of a spine which creaks when one of the girls begins her metamorphosis and changes (something strange can be glimpsed or emerges from within, just as a few seconds earlier a phone vibrated and contorted in a handbag, alien-like). They are two, but they are all of them. What they no longer are (what no longer is) is shown by what is left: the dress, the glasses, the huge and dense eyeless lashes *on* the bed, and the shoes *at the foot* of the bed. What they have become is shown by the shadow and the fluttering sound which merges with the vibrant sound of fireflies against the black background of the night.[6]

The closing credits give back what was hidden, the poem 'Amigas' ('Girlfriends') by Victoria D'Antonio, which is not spoken, but whose deployment or inclusion can be recovered retrospectively: 'For you, who's really really good at concealing? / The one who forgets', the short film does (not) say. The repercussion of its sign (not understood as meaning, but as direction of movement) is multiplied in the prologue Martel wrote for D'Antonio's *La coleccionista*: 'However, at seven in the afternoon, something begins. I don't know what it is. And things which are barely still go after her in secret rounds. Sometimes she returns with her make-up runny.'[7] The filmmaker-writer chose for this text − almost an illumination or a loving biographeme, another masterful exercise of brief forms − the title 'La naturaleza de las noctilucas' ('The Nature of Sea Sparkles'). Of course, the *Noctiluca*, those fires or phantoms which light up the water for the runway show and the transformation in *Muta*, whatever they may be: chrysalises, *Noctilucae scintillantes*, or curious fireflies in glasses and high heels.

PERHAPS WE DON'T COME TO AN UNDERSTANDING

If the languages in *Muta* (the whisper in a Guaraní of sorts in the helmsman's intercom, or the administrative English from an answering machine amplified by the phone receiver at the ship's bar) work as an articulation of the sound space rather than as a mark of social identity or as a means of communication, in *New Argirópolis/Nueva Argirópolis* (2010), they acquire their full ideological density: 'You're dumb. You're a lazy Indian, an ignorant Indian. What happened? All of us who speak Wichí, Mocoví, Pilagá, Toba, Guaraní . . . all poor. We're all dumb? Ignorant?', asks a character to another and to himself.

This short feature's *incipit* is an inclined plane. A literal one. Of course, I do not refer to a type of shot, but to a surface with a gentle, but evident slope towards the water, where two coastguards and a girl watch as a small motorboat pulls along some water hyacinth (more water hyacinth for Martel's cinema), which we will soon find out it is actually made of plastic bottles, a craft which carries 'one female and four males with no ID' − as the coastguard says in the jargon of *law enforcement* − who are the subjects of the film's first enigma: 'Where do they come from? What are they doing? What do they have?', as they are asked during the interrogation. A different man asks about the meaning of what the woman in the video displayed on the computer screen is saying in a

Figure 11.1 *New Argirópolis*

tongue which is difficult for government representatives to understand, like a mock version of Sarmiento's concept of the clash between knowledge and lack of knowledge, between civilisation and barbarism: 'What does this mean?'[8] However, the involuntary driver of this short feature is not *Facundo*: 'Nueva Argirópolis' comes time and again from the screen, as a *ritornello* or refrain.

The coastguards rule out Qom, Guaraní and other languages, to finally decide to pass on the resolution of this other Argentine enigma to the authorities in Formosa, Chaco, Salta, or some other province. The solution arrives from a girl's lips. 'Why is the little one the only one who knows?', asks a woman who appears to be a public official. 'Because her grandmother raised her', comes the conclusive answer from her two sisters. The translation is murmured: the little one whispers with her mouth close to her sister's ear, multiplying the layers of enunciation and mediation, because one girl tells the other in order for the latter to say what the words of the woman in the video mean (this whispering will be echoed by that of the girls in the room in *Zama* [2017]). 'We should be extinguished, after all the work the nation has done. / Let's climb onto our rafts. / Let's enthrone noble equality. / Indigenous and indigent, do not be afraid to move. We are invisible.'

There is always some eavesdropping (I borrow the concept from David Toop's analysis of Nicolaes Maes's *Eavesdropper* series of paintings, to which I will return later) in Martel's films. Something randomly or intermittently caught is in the diegesis, of course, in a nonchalant fashion, as if *The Swamp* or *The Holy Girl* chose not to take responsibility over what is not understood, enveloping the viewer in a circle in which situations are not always perspicuous, and turning him or her into an auditory spy of sorts. Auditory, rather than visual. Because what is said muffled can be more intriguing than what is half-seen. However, like a gust of wind, what must be understood appears clear and distinct, even if whispered. 'Indigenous and indigent, do not be afraid to move. We are invisible', as the voice of the little translator comes through, spoken into her sister's ear, but which the film shows us without mediation this time around.

The three statements are autonomous, but unfurl under the mindset of the dominated. What in the nineteenth century was applied to the *gaucho*, as illustrated in José Hernández's epic poem *Martín Fierro*'s denunciation of the social injustice perpetrated by the government against the sons of the nation, in Martel's films is said of the indigenous peoples. (This does not mean that the indigenous peoples suffered no injustices in the nineteenth century; rather, they were not even 'part of the world', to paraphrase Juan Bautista Alberdi's *Bases*). In the nineteenth century, the 'lazy and idle' were persecuted and press-ganged to supply armies and forts with men for the fight against the *ab-original*. 'You're a lazy Indian, an ignorant Indian', as someone says in *New Argirópolis*: epithets; or variations in tautology, such as the 'bad gaucho' ('gaucho malo') mentioned by Sarmiento and characterised not only as a barbarian who ignores, but also as one who is outside the law: an outlaw (a word which the author of *Facundo* used in English). However, the procedure is the same in both cases: the noun already possesses, for the person using it, the value which the adjective merely reaffirms through pleonasm: 'bad gaucho', 'lazy Indian', 'ignorant Indian'.

However, in *New Argirópolis*, paradoxically and not very surprisingly, it is Sarmiento's *failed* utopia that Martel turns into a symbol. From the book he published in 1850, already backing Urquiza against his arch enemy Rosas, the proposal is revisited for something which could very well be a dream, but an attainable one, as he argued himself, enunciated as a plan from the very title of the book:

> *Argirópolis or the capital of the Confederate States of the River Plate. A solution for the difficulties undermining the permanent pacification of the River Plate, through the convening of a congress, and the creation of a capital on Martín García Island, on the control of which, currently belonging to France, hinges the free navigation of rivers and the independence, development, and freedom of Paraguay, Uruguay and the coastal Argentine provinces.*[9]

Martel said:

> The audacity of that political work always drew my attention. *New Argirópolis* is inspired in that audacity. We liked the pretension of founding a space which represented a new social order. I think the genre would be sci-fi. Faraway islands, unknown languages. Fragments of a foundation movement.[10]

The short film was produced in the context of a project in which twenty-five filmmakers were invited to submit films on the occasion of the Bicentennial of Argentina's May Revolution:

'Why is the river this colour?', the teacher asks.

'Because it has soil and mud in it', a girl replies.

'And what if it stands still?', the teacher asks.

'The soil settles on the bottle's bottom', a girl replies.

'And that is why the waters come down the hills when it rains. And they take all that soil to the Iruya River, and from there to the Bermejo, the Paraná, and, finally, the River Plate. And, because they slow down there, that soil settles, and islands begin to form', elaborates the teacher, sure that they are paying the utmost attention to her.

Under that didactic explanation, we begin to hear the voice of another girl, repeating as if in a litany, 'They are islands without owners, they are islands without owners.' And then we see, a bit farther away than the rest, the little face matching that voice, which closes, 'They are no one's.'

The way this scene works is interesting, in a mixture of maieutics, which through questions helps the other give birth to knowledge, with the textual syntax of a lay catechism, those question-and-answer books in the manner of the ones used for Christian doctrine on different subjects (mythology, history, biology), prepared for self-directed learning, which Sarmiento used to study when he was a young boy from San Juan, eager to learn everything, and which were available in the editions Englishman Rudolph Ackermann prepared for Hispanic America in the 1820s, such as the following:

Question: What does MYTHOLOGY mean?

Answer: *Mythology* is the explanation of the *Fable*, as evidenced by its name comprising two Greek words which, together, mean: *discourse on the fable*.

Q: Which fable does Mythology explain?

A: What we see as a series of fables were venerable facts for the Egyptians, the Greek, and the Roman, and made up their religious system: this is what is meant by Mythology.[11]

In the short feature *Leagues/Leguas* (2015), learning also takes place through conversation, and refers to rights, properties and encroachments. And, if the main goal is to show that school desertion is higher in areas with an aboriginal population, the situation it shows is both evidence and argument: what we must absolutely know is not necessarily learnt at school. The short film opens with a scene of the wilderness and its sounds, interrupted by a female voice calling the protagonist's name, 'Erick!' Immediately, we hear a roar of motor-cycles, alternating between point of view shots and rodeo shots, chasing cows, and going after a boy and girl to harass them. A more imperative figure, who also rides a motorcycle, catches up to them:

> 'What are you doing here? Whose animals are these?'
> 'The cows are ours', replies Erick.
> 'You know you're not supposed to bring animals here', replies the authoritarian figure.
> 'This land belongs to our community', interrupts the girl.
> 'Don't give me that. We can talk things over and come to an understanding, or perhaps we don't come to an understanding. But you know you have nothing to do here.' [. . .]
> '. . . our rights', we barely hear Erick's voice, drowned by the imperi-ousness of the man on the motorcycle, who is conclusive: 'I'll shoot any fucking cow that sets foot here. I don't want to see you here. Go! Back to the fence! Take them away! I'll shoot any fucking animal that I find between here and the forest. You've been warned.'

Cut. We can hear the off-screen account of the events Erick gives his father, while a close shot shows a boy and girl receiving a lesson which begins with his-tory, about how in 1833 the governor of Tucumán defined by decree how long a *vara*, a unit of measurement, was, and then moves to rigorous calculations of equivalences, and finishes with a lesson which will leave them better prepared to defend and uphold their rights. The problem is presented as a mathematical one, but it soon becomes clear that it is political in nature: 'There was much confusion about how long a *vara* was', says the woman who, in a domestic con-text, deploys an ad hoc pedagogy — one of the most pervasive — which Erick's father approves of and even demands, in order for the boy to understand, in no uncertain terms, who is the real encroacher. From *varas* to leagues, from leagues to hectares: the smiling and focused faces whisper, compute and repeat figures, trying to capture them, writing them down in their notebooks. We always see, in close-up shots, the communal nature of learning and understanding; and the sensitive nature of the scene, in which a woman who explains, two children and two teenagers put their minds to the task of unravelling a problem affecting them as a community and, thus, as individuals:

> 'The neighbour's 1909 deed says that his land measures four square leagues, two to the side. If he respected the law, he should say that it is 7,499 hectares. But he doesn't', says the teenager, and Erick nods as understanding dawns on him.
> 'In the deed, he wrote that his plot is 10,700 hectares, but that's a lie. [. . .] Because he measured what he wanted.'

Figure 11.2 *Leagues*

'Right. He's taking over 3,000 hectares from us', says the man, trying
to make his son understand through any means available (verbal
explanation, sketches, repetitions, emphasis).

After a scene in the actual school, in which an acquiescent headmistress thanks
the 'doctor', a *benefactor*, for the timber he has brought, and they discuss with
concern a 'problem with a pump' which fails to deliver enough water to the
facilities, the short film takes on elements of a daylight gothic, because a girl
recounts a dream she has had: 'I dream of the devil snatching my feet', and
crows appear, signalling the arrival of death. Indeed, Mocha, one of the cows
which are *ours*, has received the promised bullet. The girls cross the fence
deftly and silently. When Erick is about to follow them, he hurries back: the
motorcycle's roar is more fearsome than that of a baited tiger.[12]

THE FIRST MARTEL

Martel tells 'life stories'. That is why the documentary she filmed in 1998
about Encarnación Ezcurra for a series about six Argentine women belongs
with the stories the filmmaker likes to tell. And that medium-length film opens
with another situation related to figures, where we hear a woman's voice part-
way through a litany of costs: '1,275 pesos have been paid for 180 masses. /
2,780 pesos have been spent in mourning fabrics for the ladies and the maids
in the house. / 2,350 pesos for the casket for the body. / That makes, in total,
29,747 pesos.' The woman's voice is scanned and combined with a man's voice,

which provides pieces of information to arrive at the woman in question: Juan Manuel de Rosas's wife. Martel adopts here the aesthetic of silent films: she uses title cards and fragments from *Amalia* (1914), filmed by Enrique García Velloso, the first feature film of Argentine cinema, which works as a palimpsest, when it should have been a counterpoint, since it is based – as it is known – on the anti-Rosas novel José Mármol published in an unfinished edition in 1851 and finished for the 1855 one (this is not the only film quoted, but it provides a matrix). The interesting thing is that *Encarnación Ezcurra* resorts to the structure, the elements and the procedures of silent movies in a production which is utterly talkative, in which everyone speaks: the narrator, the guest researchers, the actress playing Encarnación, or rather, the actress who provides a voice to the font of the calligraphy of this woman who writes to her husband to inform him, warn him and instruct him when he retires from the urban political scene and leaves for the 1833 desert campaign.[13] As I say in the documentary, 'Encarnación works as a file of sorts.'

And Fabio Wasserman quotes a letter from Encarnación: 'The city is like a maze.' That is what I find most interesting in this medium-length feature by Martel: her articulation of the 1833 city which is being rebuilt by textuality (when the Revolution of the Restorers took place), or the one from 20 October 1838 (the date of Encarnación's death), and the present one, always beautiful when shown by night. There is a dominance of russet or reddish hues projected by the city into the shot through the rear windscreen or the window of the car moving across it, taking us who recovered that story in a circuit through the old quarter of Buenos Aires, as if a new blueprint were redrawn over Sourdeaux's. And, besides the streets and buildings, it reveals the contrast with the men on horseback who cross broad expanses in the fragments from the various historic or 'national affairs' Argentine films quoted, while the images shot by Martel discover and follow, full of curiosity, the urban delivery men on motorcycles, modern *chasquis* who often carry and trace correspondence, not only between different places, but also between different stories, matters and circumstances of the city. Even though it is true that Martel's personality is not yet fully-fledged, there are discoveries (the city as a luminous, moving labyrinth) or heralding elements (the direct sounds of the city under the voices of the researchers speaking as they move around).[14]

It becomes evident that Lucrecia Martel responds with variety and creativity to demands, but at the same time designs a recognisable line in her way of writing cinema. And this is clear from a very early stage in *Dead King/Rey Muerto* (1995), of course, with the design of a chorography which outlines her zone (*chorography* is, literally, the description not of a world, but of a region), where actions are articulated between uncertainty and determination; and continues through other means, in a more exploratory fashion, in *The Outbuildings/Las dependencias* (1999, produced for the same cycle to which *Encarnación Ezcurra* belongs). It is between that short film and this documentary that we find a Martel focused on the search for or, rather, the construction (even though both things imply the other) of, a *po(i)etics*: an aesthetic and a making, combined. And if *Dead King* includes fundamental aspects (the rural space, power and submission, or the female figure as an enigma, both strong and fragile), it is *The Outbuildings* which marks the founding of what may be one of Martel's cinema's basic principles: the act of listening.[15]

A phone rings and the camera starts searching for the window of that building in a corner full of trees. Now inside, it pans the room: a rickety chair, potted plants on a white and modest cupboard, the simple grocery trolley leaning against the tiles, an old rust-spotted rectangular sink, a patched gas pipe escaping the wall, the green rubbish bin. The phone is picked up by someone whom we still do not know is Jovita. Her back is to the camera, so it is her voice, high and sharper than quavery, as it would appear initially – not due to fear, but due to nervousness and perhaps because that is the way it naturally sounds – the one which tells someone that 'it'll be a while'. That she's being filmed for a documentary, and that 'she will get the cassette as well'. She is in a corner of an ancient kitchen, reminiscent of old country kitchens, the ones in the *estancias*: pots which betray years of constant use, hanging from the wall; and several kettles, *always ready*, on the gas rings.

From there will emerge the two protagonists of *The Outbuildings*, another medium-length film by Martel. They immediately realise that the object makes the function, and they say so. Then, a cut. And now, there she is. Jovita had everything at hand: the fabric and the old cookie tins with thread and needles. Elena has gone looking for the typewriter to supplement the few papers she had selected that were in a neat pile on the table. The typewriter, for the person who types; needle and thread, for the person who sews. Objects which constitute them by means of metonymy, which provide them with the identity this documentary is looking for, with the truth which the protagonists' freshness will contribute, and the cunning of the procedures of fiction the director will choose to portray them.[16] It is more than evident that the short feature could be part of the series of the masters and favourite servants, which spans *Amalia* and Beatriz Guido, and reaches its zenith in *Don Segundo Sombra*, and which David Viñas did not extend to Silvina Ocampo, perhaps, because he was too focused on her sister, Victoria. More or less consciously, the links operate nevertheless in Argentine culture; and if we bear in mind that Martel received the collaboration, for the purposes of researching and writing the script, of Adriana Mancini and Graciela Speranza, who majored in Literature reading that text by Viñas which identifies and sheds light on one of 'the most significant constants of Argentine literature linked to traditional ruling groups', we cannot speak of chance.[17]

Jovita, in particular, has heard and seen everything. However, her candid account shows that she did not do so by snooping, prying or paying too much attention. However, that may be not only the consequence of her natural discretion, but also of the fact that her mistress, Mistress Silvina, had turned her everyday life into a performance with no secrets from her servant, secrets she did keep from her husband; and that is why Jovita knew (but Bioy was unaware) that when he took longer to return than her fear of losing him could tolerate, Ocampo would sit by the door until she heard with relief the sound of the elevator bringing him, fortunately, back home. That is the limit of this otherwise modest film's indiscretion. Perhaps, the most brazen is what drifts towards a seemingly tangential area, as a series of asides, quips or innocent expressions, such as when Jovita speaks of the 'mutual crush' they felt the first time they met; or the striking way in which she describes her mistress as 'very sexy', as Elena confirms on her own (that is, not when she shares the shot with Jovita, but in a different scene), and even the way in which she dares compare her with Marlene Dietrich, who she says could have felt envy at Silvina's beautiful legs. The servants are more daring than the handsome Bioy, who, in his old age, remembers coyly the 'great charm' his wife had, as well as her intelligence, her blue eyes, and her 'unmistakably Ocampo face', even though how that comment should be interpreted remains unclear.

The other impudence refers to class: Jovita says that Silvina would tell her 'I like watching you work', only for the servant to reply, with raw sensibility and absolutely no contempt, 'Yes, it's nice watching someone else work.' Harmony between social strata which is amplified by the reading of a letter the wealthy Silvina wrote to Elena, in which she tells her of her misery as a traveller who finds everything 'so expensive', who must wash and iron her own clothes and serve herself, closing, conclusively, 'I have never had such a lousy maid. If she ever applies to work for you, I will recommend you not to hire her. Her name is Silvina Ocampo.' A family novel of a neurotic woman which receives from her servants a cheerful conclusion: 'Ah, so funny!'[18]

And a last act of daring, which is more of an indiscretion: the variations of a single scene (that we will get acquainted with later from Bioy's massive diaries): 'Borges dines at home', the matrix which opens the way for the log of their after-dinner dialogues from which (according to Bioy, who is perhaps trying to whitewash himself) Silvina was not barred, even though she used to attend listlessly or asleep on a couch, or simply left to chat with her maid in the kitchen, from where they would listen (furtively or carelessly) as the men 'talked and laughed at silly things', as Jovita remembers, trying to hide her laughter and disregarding the way a writer's public image is constructed. The publication of Bioy's diaries in 2006 multiplies exponentially Jovita's indiscretion, as Jorge Luis Borges says referring to the act of bluffing in the game of *truco*.[19]

EAVESDROPPING

I want to mention something which, though it may seem distant, enables me to think more precisely − I believe − about the *eavesdropping* which is circled in *The Outbuildings* and reaches its culmination in *The Holy Girl* (2004) (I do not mean that it stops thereafter, but that it reaches heights which are hard to surpass). And, thus, I revisit David Toop, whose book *Sinister Resonance: The Mediumship of the Listener* works on that concept based on the work of Nicolaes Maes, a Dutch painter from the seventeenth century who produced a series in which one piece stands out: *The Eavesdropper* (the English word is eloquent in capturing the literal meaning on which the core concept of this habit rests: 'Ear pressed to the wall of a house, the secret listener stands under the eaves, the overhang constructed to protect the walls of a house from rainwater', seeking shelter from the rain drops[20]). It is Julio Schvartzman, building on Toop, who masterfully describes the spatial organisation of the action, which he voluntarily calls '*écouteurisme*' in order to create a sound equivalent to the visual practice of '*voyeurisme*':

> 'Listening housewife', 'Lovers overheard by a woman', 'Eavesdropper and scolding woman', 'The jealous husband'. Reflecting everyday life, but also going beyond thanks to a strange or critical trait, Dutch painting let us glimpse into bourgeois domestic life. And within, as we notice in the various *eavesdroppers* (David Toop suggests taking them as performances of the same work), an inter-class communication is deployed. Verticality speaks volumes. The masters come down and notice that, downstairs, something happens. That is the idea. It would seem that the maid and her lover have violated the rules of this bourgeois home; however, the disturbance comes from the masters. Let us accept that the habitat encourages spies from both sides.[21]

That is, in general, it is the master and the mistress who eavesdrop. However, it is possible that, like in *An Eavesdropper with a Woman Scolding*, the maid is the one snooping, something we should not find surprising after reading Rosas's opponents, who, like Mármol in his novel *Amalia*, make a point of revealing − though in order to denounce it − the espionage carried out by servants, who in general supported Rosas, both in and from the houses of their anti-Rosas masters and even in the neighbours', thanks to the relatively low height of the dividing walls. Domestic architecture, urban persecution and public politics: the way in which information moved, the secrets carried and brought by the letters exchanged by Rosas and his wife Encarnación, are consequences of that system of conspiracies and secrets, espionage and betrayal.[22]

In *Encarnación Ezcurra*, secrets (own secrets and the secrets of others) travel in letters, while rumours, revelations and gossip move from mouth to mouth. However, secrets, when spoken into someone's ear, entail the shortest distance between the reporter's lips to the ear of the listener. So, strictly speaking, they do not move from mouth to mouth, but from mouth to ear. In *The Holy Girl*, such verbal donations (after all, what are secrets but gifts we give to someone worthy of receiving them?) are not infrequently supplemented by a blushing of the girls' cheeks, visible because the shot is close enough to reveal any altera-tion of the skin (and because María Alché and Julieta Zylberberg blush with true candour). Breath, with the delicate lightness of a breeze, carries words as whispers. They mumble, murmur, laugh and fall silent, their lips almost touch-ing the other's ear (the girls touch, yes; or allow themselves to be touched); and at times it is hard to distinguish these whispers and susurrations from prayers, which are said with the same light gesture.[23] We, the viewers, are the main eavesdroppers, even though *The Holy Girl* is an impudent movie about a discreet gaze. Toop points out with great keenness that

> the more serious form of eavesdropping, in which intimate information previously withheld is discovered by stealth and close listening, com-promises the listener with a confusing mixture of self-righteousness, ambivalence and shame. What I want to know, I may not wish to hear.[24]

There is no blushing in *The Outbuildings*, but there are whispers. It is not a secret, but a recitation, which we could consider another form of prayer: 'Anoche en el silencio me abracé a tu caballo. // Anoche en el silencio me abracé a tu caballo. Creyó que era la lluvia, y era yo que lloraba' ('Last night in the silence I hugged your horse. // Last night in the silence I hugged your horse. It thought it was the rain, but they were my tears'), we hear in Silvina's own voice (which makes no distinction between the initial sounds of 'yo' and 'lluvia', a voice perfect for alliteration), a voice which she tried to protect, like her face in pictures. Silvina's acousmatic voice populates (against the grain of her own will?) the movie. The documentary shows through pictures that face which preferred to remain hidden, and lets us hear a voice whose owner considered as a rapping against the throat. Acousmatic. Coming from a place unknown, and, of course, scary. However, the tenebrous (due to its spectral nature) is not in the black and white shots of the house's empty rooms, on which that voice, like scratching a surface, would appear to write (let us not forget that, after all, this is a movie about a dead writer). The tenebrous lies in Silvina's aesthetic project, which in general will take the shape of cruelty or malice; and it could be a good starting point for constructing the ominous in Martel's aesthetic project, which in general will take the shape of decadence and indolence.[25]

Acousmatic. Another adjective used to describe concrete music, where sounds can be unwound, traced autonomously and recombined.[26] In Martel's cinema, perhaps more than in that sound with an unfathomable source, issuing from an unknown place, the acousmatic lies in the fact that sound can come from everywhere, uncontrollably, and operate on the surface of the fabric on which the image unfolds all its proliferation and reverberance. *Everything* in the environment can produce sound: *pan-sound*. However, a person's interior can also be swarmed by sounds, as in the case of Helena, the owner of the hotel in which *The Holy Girl* takes place, and her tinnitus – that ringing or buzzing which resounds in the ear or the head of the person suffering from this condition, and which in a certain way is acousmatic, because its origin is unidentifiable. Helena undergoes a specific study: locked in a soundproof cabin, she must repeat what comes through the headphones. Alternating sounds from without and within the cabin, a list of words is deployed, like a concrete poem which works following a logic similar to that in Luis Alberto Spinetta's 'Por':

Perra
cano
cita
nudo
rizo (does she say *rezo?*)
cola
reto
nave
nulo (she says *rulo*)
asno
misa
nicho
útil
males (she says *madres*)[27]

Words are chained, as are the signifier's phonemes and the prayers of religious girls (the same prayers Helena suggests her daughter should replace by the Spanish *romancero*, another chaining of verses).

And there is something of the tenebrous in *vocation* as well, as the girls are desperate to know from where and how that *calling* from God will come (let us remember that that meaning is part of the word's etymology). That is why one of the girls insists:

But what is the calling like? Is something you notice? I don't know . . . A voice in the night? I get very scared at night, so if I hear a voice calling me, I'll think it's the devil. And what if the voice asks me to kill someone, like it did with Abraham?

It is unrest that confuses them, evidently, and that is why the girls attribute it to 'fear of God', to the chagrin of the young and pretty catechist, who always feels upset.[28]

I think those scenes show the minimal or most representative unit of Martel's po(i)etics: catechism or catechesis scenes, which, based on their etymology, refer to sound within or in a top-down fashion, and include both the idea of *echo* and the idea of *instruction*. Once again: sound. These scenes show, as an *aleph* of Martel's cinema, the way in which dialogue or speech flow, get lost, take shortcuts, and become chained with and to other flows, following deliberately and with artifice the natural disorder of conversation. Almost like the stream of consciousness, not of a character, but of a movie, jumping from the lips of one character to the next, and even, it could be said, poured into the lips of the different characters to be distributed among them. Martel — as she has said herself — does not like it when actors follow the chart of what has been written into the script, because that departs from the complexity of speech (though she is also vigilant of actors straying from the dialogue she has orchestrated meticulously, under the banner of reflecting everyday life and speech). And, surely, that is also what drives her to decide where to place the camera, not before directing the actors to their respective spots in the scene, but during their read-through.[29] *Shot composition with people*, that criterion could be called, if it were a painting. Those customary close shots, crowded, from *The Holy Girl* or *The Swamp*. Because not only beds (always overcrowded, invaded or taken by force by others, as if that were normal) are promiscuous in Martel's cinema, but those tumultuous shots as well. Inhabited shots; or, rather, the shot — in Martel's cinema — as a space to be inhabited: the shot as habitat, where the close-up faces are (further) cropped, as if taking to the extreme the synecdochical nature of all framing.

There, in that type of shot, the syntax of the modes of storytelling in Martel's films installs itself. I like the way she likes these conversations which occurred when her grandmother or other adults would take her or children in general to visit bedridden people whose ailments were unclear to all. Conversations which surely followed the rhythm of one thing leading to another and to another, but which could also be lost, wasted, left unfinished. These summer conversations in which the topic being discussed was always uncertain.[30]

And it is not surprising that the syntax of her writing for her films keeps, in its rationale, some traces of that. The following is the transcription of the synopsis of her first feature film:

> February in the Argentine north-west. Earth-shattering sun and tropical rains. In the forest, some parts of the land get flooded. / These swamps are death traps for heavy animals. / At the same time, they are teeming with happy vermin. This is not a story of swamps, but of the city of La Ciénaga

(The Swamp) and the surrounding area. // 90 km away is the town of Rey Muerto (Dead King), as well as a farm La Mandrágora (The Mandrake). / Mandrake is a plant which was used as a sedative before ether and morphine, when it was necessary for a person to undergo a painful procedure, like an amputation. / In this story, it is the name of a farm where red peppers are harvested, and where Mecha, a 50-year-old mother of four, married to a man who dyes his hair, spends her summers. / However, that is something to forget quickly over a couple of drinks. Even though, as Tali says, alcohol comes in through a door but fails to leave through another. // Tali is Mecha's cousin. / She has four children as well, and a husband who loves his house, hunting, and his children. She lives in La Ciénaga, in a house without a pool. Two accidents will bring these two families together in the countryside, where they will try to survive a summer come straight from hell.[31]

Rather than the movie's subject or plot, this synopsis includes the syntax, not only of *The Swamp*, but of Martel's whole filmography. A syntax which involves or *realises* (i.e. crystallises) her prosody, because it sets the tone or even the key. Because that syntax defines diction, the *tempo* of the rationale or the (dis)order in which the moods of the situations, rather than the facts, become chained: *modalisation*. That is, the *mark*. That writing, like the musical notation of variations, condenses or expands in Lucrecia Martel's films. It is not the movie that she writes in that brief notation, but its projection, as long as we think of projection as an instance of future − or modulation of time, as in music − and not only as the inscription of light.

Translated by Juan Ignacio García Fahler

NOTES

1. Oubiña, D. (2007), 'Entrevista a Lucrecia Martel. El cine como intención amorosa', in *Estudio crítico sobre La ciénaga, de Lucrecia Martel*, Buenos Aires: Picnic Editorial, pp. 68–9.
2. Oubiña, *Estudio crítico sobre La ciénaga*, p. 24.
3. Ibid. p. 24. With the exception of the death of Luciano, the boy, in *The Swamp*, where the opposite dominates, that is, the perfect, also in the grammatical sense of verb aspect: it is what is finished, the completed action, the most conclusive, we could say, but which Martel also interprets in terms of duration or projection, though in the negative, as she states that that death − like all deaths − 'is the absolute loss of a certain dimension of future'. Ibid. p. 59.
4. Ibid. p. 58.
5. In *Fish*, we must add to Lucrecia Martel's direction the music and the voices of Juana Molina, and the audiovisual editing of María Onis. There is something of video art in the short film, of course. And I associate it, even though the works are not related to each

other, with Jorge Macchi's video, *Musical Box/Caja de música* (2003–6), where the cars driving down Figueroa Alcorta avenue, filmed from the pedestrian bridge crossing the avenue and leading to the School of Law of the University of Buenos Aires, work like musical notes distributed along the score outlined by the avenue's lanes (the procedure in *Streamline* [2006], also by Jorge Macchi, but with music by Eduardo Rudnizky, even with differences in terms of sound articulation, is based on the same conceptual matrix).

6. The fact that María Onis was in charge of both the music and the art direction is not random. Guido Berenblum's sound and Alberto Moccia's make-up and hairdressing also carry significance.

7. D'Antonio, V. (2010), *La coleccionista*, Buenos Aires: Bajo la Luna, p. 9.

8. Sarmiento, D. F. (1845), *Civilización i barbarie: Vida de Juan Facundo Quiroga i aspecto físico, costumbres, i ábitos de la República Argentina*, Santiago: Imprenta del Progreso, p. 4. As well known as the misunderstanding scene is, it is always interesting to revisit: Sarmiento is leaving for his exile in Chile from his home province, San Juan, and writes with a piece of charcoal, while passing the 'baños de Zonda', a taunt in French, which is not his native tongue − clearly − but the language of culture: 'On ne tue point les idées.' A 'hieroglyph' impossible to decode for the envoys of the 'barbaric' government Sarmiento despises and from which he flees, fearing for his life. 'What does this mean?', the government officials ask, and they fail to understand even when the Spanish translation is handed to them, as Sarmiento makes a point of stressing through a scenic and dramatic display enshrined in the long silence represented by two long lines of ellipses, as a graphical symbol of the lack of answers.

9. '*Argirópolis o la capital de los estados confederados del Río de la Plata. Solución de las dificultades que embarazan la pacificación permanente del Río de la Plata, por medio de la convocación de un congreso, y la creación de una capital en la isla de Martín García, de cuya posesión (hoy en poder de la Francia) dependen la libre navegación de los ríos y la independencia, desarrollo y libertad del Paraguay, el Uruguay y las provincias argentinas del litoral.*' I have already written about Sarmiento's 'prayer' in *Argirópolis*: 'there are few books in which Sarmiento appears to be as concerned with creating a plausible and realistic proposal as in this one. The exotic idea of making Martín García the capital, the element which has been labelled the most outlandish, will end up being for the writer a minor aspect, compared with the core proposal: to achieve the free navigation of rivers and create a nation to find the way in which it will represent and rule itself.' Amante, A. (2007), 'El letrado y el poder', prologue to D. F. Sarmiento, *Argirópolis*, Buenos Aires: Losada, pp. 9–31 (pp. 15–16).

10. Martel, L. (2010), 'La Confederación de ríos', *Página/12*, 3 October 2010, <https://www.pagina12.com.ar/diario/suplementos/radar/9-6511-2010-10-03.html> (last accessed 2 May 2021).

11. Urcullu, J. de (1826), *Catecismo de mitología*, London: R. Ackermann, p. 1. A preliminary note reads: 'In order to vanquish all scruples the use of the word "catechism" may give rise to, applied in general to religion books, we must warn our reader that this word is not exclusively consecrated to religious subjects, but rather refers indistinctly to any book written in questions and answers. This is the way in which the word is used in all cultured, Catholic countries of Europe.'

12. What Daniel Link correctly says about Martel's first feature film can be applied to her filmography as a whole: '*The Swamp* is a dialectal movie, not only because a linguistic variety different from that of Buenos Aires is spoken, but also because the subject and the way the story is told stray from the urban stories established years ago as the standard of cinematographic "modernity".' Link, D. (2001), 'Tres mujeres', *Página/12*, 18 March 2001, <https://www.pagina12.com.ar/2001/suple/Radar/01-03/01-03-18/nota1.

htm> (last accessed 2 May 2021). A nice idea. And I underscore: it is in the dialectal as alternance that Link sees the eccentric and the valuable of Martel's cinema, referring to certain aspects 'of respect of the way people speak in her region' − the use of the article ('la mamá') and diminutive, the placement of the pronoun before the verb ('le digamos'), the use of the preterite perfect ('ha venido') − which the critic spots keenly. However, I disagree with Link when he speaks of 'all those dialectal varieties that the "civilisation" of Buenos Aires has tended to silence since Sarmiento', not because I fail to understand the overwhelming nature of the civilising drive and agenda, but because I see it as a generalisation, because the dialectal as a way of enunciation of an aesthetic is profoundly Sarmientine: let us not forget that his literary language follows the dialectal customs, still very linked to the Spanish peninsular variety, of his native San Juan, as he informs the linguist Matías Calandrelli in relation to his *Facundo* in 1881; and as is ratified by his early support for the acceptance of the spellings based on the forms of Spanish prosody used in America. Thus, civilisation has silenced dialectical varieties; but not Sarmiento – at least, not in this case.

13. Encarnación's voice: Rita Cortese; narrator: Marcelo Chirino; guest researchers: Jorge Myers, Carlos Canzanero, Fabio Wasserman, Gabriel Di Meglio, Adriana Amante.

14. In this case, the sound technician is Abel Tortorelli.

15. Of course, there is a voice in *Encarnación Ezcurra*: Encarnación's, recreated by Rita Cortese. However, the focus is on the fact that she was Rosas's eyes in the city when he was away. Even though the letters reveal not only what her eyes saw, but also what was whispered, what was said, and what was suspected of being whispered. The filmmaker's work before *The Swamp* represents what we could term *the first Martel*, to paraphrase the concept of *the first Borges*, that is, the work which founds an aesthetic universe which will become something else later on, but precisely based on what was established, built or created in that beginning. The person who saw it with clarity (or clairvoyance, not only as a producer but also as a filmmaker) was Lita Stantic, who in a logical chaining of sorts cast her eye over *Dead King*, commissioned the two TV documentaries from Martel, and believed that Lucrecia should direct the fantastic screenplay she had submitted, which − as we now know − was to become *The Swamp*.

16. Metonymy, as a rhetoric trope of contiguity, includes those cases in which subjects take on the name of the instrument they dominate or use, such as when one speaks of a *pen* to refer to a writer. Even though Jovita's and Elena's names are not replaced by the objects in question, the trope works conceptually in this documentary.

17. Though, of course, the documentary does not make a literal use of the royal *we* (that fake inclusion that, through the pronoun or the verb, reveals the authority of a notable person − a pope, an emperor, or a king − who is the issuer, enunciating an action which will not be executed by him, but by those who serve him), there is a drive which resembles it in the tone of remembrance and the modality in which the interaction between mistress and servants is reconstructed. And it is tempting to imagine an inversion of the gesture which could lead a valet to say 'we', to actually refer to the master or mistress whose body and desire the valet would appear to be an extension of: *we dress*, when the servant does not actually dress herself, but only the one she serves. There are explicit instances of what in Spanish is known as *dativo de interés*, a dative case not required by the verb and used to designate the person affected by the action, an example of which ('y entonces me las comía así') can be seen when Jovita says how she would make Silvina toast with the small loaves Bioy brought (because 'he was an expert in bakeries'), and how she would cut them as thin as altar bread; and how, as if that was not enough, she would take the pips from the strawberry jam her mistress loved so much, because 'the master said they were unhealthy for her', spinning a spoon in a small colander, and how Silvina would eat the toast. Following that line, another link − in this

case, cinematographic – can be established with *The Outbuildings*: the beautiful film *Santiago* (2007), by Brazilian João Moreira Salles, a character who could very well have been the star of some Brazilian novel by Manuel Puig.

18. An interesting aspect is pointed out by Julia Kratje: 'In all feature films [. . .], servants are the only characters which, together with children and teenagers, manage to set into motion the stories adults are swamped in.' Kratje, J. (2020), 'Contagiosas, sinuosas, insinuantes: La naturaleza de las voces insumisas en *Las dependencias* de Lucrecia Martel', *Revista Digital DocuDAC*, 4, <http://revistadocudac.com.ar/es/dossier-la-naturaleza> (last accessed 2 May 2021). And it should be noted that that lapse of sorts ('adults' meaning 'masters') shows that Kratje thinks, correctly, of domestic service as a form of minority, and all of those forms as inflections of subordination.

19. Bioy Casares, A. (2006), *Borges*, Buenos Aires: Destino.

20. Toop, D. (2013), *Resonancia siniestra: El oyente como médium*, Buenos Aires: Caja negra, p. 122. The credit for the syntagma's strength should be shared with – and, perhaps, given to – the translator of the Spanish version: Valeria Meiller. The original English version is Toop, D. (2010), *Sinister Resonance: The Mediumship of the Listener*, New York: Continuum Books, p. 184.

21. Schvartzman, J. (2017), '¡Shhh!', in 'fono/gramas', *Bazar Americano*, November 2017, <https://www.bazaramericano.com/columnas.php?cod=185&pdf=si> (last accessed 3 May 2021).

22. The distribution of functions and classes in Argentine domestic architecture offers at least two models: that of colonial houses, with two or three courtyards, the last of which, in the back, is used as a service area, with the kitchen, the vegetable garden and the livestock, generally with an earthen floor; or that of the post-1880 aristocratic manors, mainly those in Buenos Aires, where the distribution could take place along the vertical axis, and the 'last floor', used as a service area, could be either the topmost floor or the ground floor.

23. Whispering into ears is exacerbated during catechism lessons, as is blushing, indolence and the raw emotions of the girls, whose reactions are unpredictable: they can form alliances, they can clash and they can ignore each other with the same indifference or speed.

24. Toop, *Sinister Resonance*, p. 188/*Resonancia siniestra*, p. 125.

25. Even with the great affinity that is developed between Ocampo's universe and Martel's gaze in *The Outbuildings*, it is in *The Swamp* and *The Holy Girl* where the deepest link is found, even if it is involuntary. However, the actual source of the ominous, in Martel's work, lies in (or is) her own grandmother.

26. For a specific and extensive analysis of sound in Martel's movies, see Christofoletti Barrenha, N. (2014), *A experiência do cinema de Lucrecia Martel: Resíduos do tempo e sons à beira da piscina*, São Paulo: Alameda Casa Editorial. And, as regards the *concrete* forms of sound, Petit de Murat, F. (2020), 'La ciudad del ruido. Antropología de la experiencia sonora en Buenos Aires', PhD thesis, Universidad de Buenos Aires. Both works revisit, though with different purposes, the main theories about sound produced in the twentieth century.

27. However, in 'Por', with the exception of the preposition used in the title and as the last element in the series, the text is only made up of nouns (Pescado Rabioso [Luis Alberto Spinetta] (1973), 'Por', from the album *Artaud*). The words pronounced during the audiometry test are basically functional, and the study focuses on the succession of phonemes, paying attention not to meaning but to sounds, although they are inevitably offered to viewers' interpretation, particularly the words Helena mishears.

28. The theremin, which works as a MacGuffin throughout the film, is also acousmatic. The girls hear it during their catechism meeting, and one asks, 'What is that?', only to receive as an answer not a substance, but a precise, though unspecific, source: 'It comes from the

street.' However, that is not all: the instrument itself disconcerts (and, thus, attracts) the people in the street, who cannot understand how sound can be produced by touching air, and thus wonder where it comes from. In parallel, in that crowd, Dr Jano presses himself against Amalia, and she begins searching for the source of that contact which fills her with erotic curiosity: who is that brushing against her from behind whenever he finds (or they find) an opportunity.

29. Oubiña, 'Entrevista a Lucrecia Martel', pp. 63, 59.

30. Casa de América (2011), 'Lucrecia Martel: El sonido en la escritura y la puesta en escena', YouTube, 26 January 2011, <https://www.youtube.com/watch?v=mCKHzMzMlZo> (last accessed 27 April 2021). This is very clear in *The Headless Woman*, when the cousins visit Aunt Lala, who gathers around her bed the vague ailment, the biting meanness, the potpourri of disconnected topics, the chatting as a random, and even gratuitous act.

31. I transcribe Martel's synopsis from p. 15 of David Oubiña's *Estudio crítico sobre La ciénaga*. That synopsis includes a digression: from La Mandrágora to the mandrake, from the farm to the sedative, that lexical cohesion, rather than uniting, diverts. In the drift of what is being told (and we know that digression is a substantial part of oral communication), the *excursus* is not only a spatial mark but also a (temporal) delay, in order for things not to happen yet or ever; or in order for that which does happen to be precisely that delay in the succession of things.

CHAPTER 12

'They smother you'

Nora Catelli

We owe the highest praise to *Zama* (2017) from the Iberian Peninsula to Serafín Fanjul, an incredible member of the Spanish Royal Academy of History. In the 26 January 2018 Opinion section – a significant detail – of the *ABC* newspaper, he wrote:

> They smother you: the movie starts with Don Diego slapping a native woman after playing the Peeping Tom, followed by a different native ruthlessly bound and harassed by officials [. . .], and dismal brothels, an evil and negligent governor, slaves, the hunting of natives, domestic and personal filth galore, only to finish with a minor arc of the hunter becoming the prey, which not even some shots of beautiful landscapes manage to improve.[1]

In Fanjul's oceanic and also fluvial ignorance, we recognise the most naive aspect of what we may call the Spanish foul mood, almost an obsession with dispelling the Black Legend. Serafín Fanjul accepts that he has not read Antonio Di Benedetto, whom he describes as the author of the 'base novel', or Lucrecia Martel (to whom he clearly ascribes no 'reading skills', to borrow the pedagogical term). That is why he ignores that, as the director herself has pointed out repeatedly, she drew her inspiration from Félix de Azara and his 1801 *Descripción e historia del Paraguay y del Río de la Plata*, and that, when fleshing out Zama, she would think of Azara rather than of Di Benedetto's character. As Martel has said in an interview:

> Actually, that world is the Chaco Gualamba. With the exception of the Amazon, the Chaco is curiously the region which the colonisers took the longest to massacre and penetrate. Take Félix de Azara, who is the

character I focused on to create Zama. He said in the late 1700s that he was alarmed at how clumsily the Chaco trees were being cut down. In 200 years, he said, the region would be completely devoid of trees. That place, which was ultimately destroyed by Creole skill [a note to Fanjul: Martel refers to the voraciousness which did away with the Chaco woods during the era of our republics], is the location I wanted for my film. That place has a very dry area, towards the southern bit of the Chaco region − that is, the Chaco of Salta, Santiago del Estero and the north of Santa Fe − and then we have the super humid Chaco which extends up to the Chiquitanías. The Chiquitanías are also part of the Chaco Gualamba. And all the Jesuit architecture, the architectural details of the Chiquitanías, is what I based the governor's house and the public buildings on.[2]

It so happens, as should be known by Mr Fanjul (whom I sadly recognise as an indisputable member of Spain's university community), that any person from that disobedient shore of the Atlantic we call the Southern Cone interested in understanding their own history has read Azara, just as they have read and appreciated Tulio Halperín Donghi's subtle remarks in his *Historia contemporánea de América Latina*. I assume I need not educate Serafín Fanjul about the biography of this illustrious historian, who was born, alas, not in Spain, but in Buenos Aires. Halperín analysed the continuities and permanence of what he describes as the transition − slow, morose − from the colonial order to the order he terms 'neocolonial'.[3]

What piqued Di Benedetto's interest and fascinated Martel in a sense is the permanent crumbling of the Spanish colony, which persisted in living on well after it should have disappeared. The dying breaths of 1794–9, which coincided with the emergence of our republics (the first one, Haiti, in 1790–1804), continued, agonising but efficient, well into the first half of the nineteenth century. Thus explains Halperín Donghi, whose work I refrain from recommending to Fanjul, as I have decided to assume he is aware of it.

MARTEL'S PLACEMENT

When assuming her figure as an artist, Martel decided against being the emblem of a group, a generation, or a school. As pointed out by Mariano Llinás in relation to *The Swamp/La ciénaga* (2001), she decided to represent only herself.[4] That peculiarity had already been highlighted by David Oubiña in his critical study of the same film.[5]

I do not think that position has shifted as her career progressed. Martel appears to outline an answer to a question asked by Annalisa Mirizio: 'When

Figure 12.1 During the filming of *Zama*. Photo by Valeria Fiorini. © Rei Cine SRL, Bananeira Filmes Ltda, El Deseo DA SLU, Patagonik Film Group SA

does a return to the classic become possible? Which are the circumstances which enable, in the case of filmmaking, turning the past into heritage?'[6] It happens when realism is, as in her case, a boundary between the flow of time, sound and image, in takes in which, following André Bazin, there is a real time of things which insinuates itself insidiously in the *mise-en-scène*.

Perhaps that is why, as Emilio Bernini says, there is a rejection of narrative linearity and causality. However, I believe the narrative thread is not hard to follow in 'the scenes which appear to be temporal blocks (blocks made up of fixed, still takes)'.[7] In *Zama*, causality is political: the successive (even the succession of positions and destinations) depends on power. The static, in turn, emerges in the rotten, decomposing parts of the colony, which lies in the late eighteenth century between life and death.

According to Bernini, *Zama* takes to an extreme Martel's project of creating a cinema of perception. Precisely, those elements or aspects which 'smother' in Martel's film are the perceptual transitions: between image and sound, skin and rot, greed and cruelty, aloofness and abandonment, mail and smuggling, masochistic delirium and the accelerated ambition towards any type of triumph the news of which could reach the metropolis. That is why I deem Fanjul's accidental laudatory outburst ('They smother you'), which also includes an unnerving plural ('They'), so telling. Who does the smothering? Is it the characters, those who made the film, the sequences, or the complex whisper, at times incomprehensible and never homogeneous, of voices, creaks and cracks?

To say that a work smothers is one of the highest accolades any aesthetic artefact may receive at this stage of the twenty-first century. It proves the continued relevance of a trait attributed to true art: the ability to instil a feeling of unrest, of alienation, a discomfort, which Fanjul clearly felt to an almost superlative degree.

ACCENTS

The 1790–1800 linguistic customs of the inhabitants of these 'shores of delirium', as Juan José Saer called the gullies of the river which work as the setting for his novel *The Witness/El entenado*,[8] must necessarily be a whim – a speculation – just like Martel's decision to dress some characters with dishevelled wigs which may have come from the Viceroyalty of Peru, which, unlike its River Plate counterpart, had a court.

How would the Creole (that is, those born in America to Spanish parents) speak? How would the Spaniards mumble their annoyance, those that, like the governor, went from enclave to enclave in that River Plate Viceroyalty created during the last throes of the empire? How would that newly arrived Spanish woman express herself, probably affecting an exaggerated peninsular accent? Why is it jarring that actors from Buenos Aires speak like people from Buenos Aires, if Martel did not attempt to reconstruct the imagined speech of that city in 1799?

Aware of her choice, Martel points out the following:

> In that sense, going to the past is similar to moving away from narrative centres. The decision was to move to the provinces and reap there. The intonation, for instance, is taken from the provinces of Santiago, Formosa. There's a sprinkle of Cuyo as well . . . I also used the neutral Spanish the Venezuelans invented for their *telenovelas*. I once had to do some work about Encarnación Ezcurra. What to do with language if I had the chance of making a period piece? I was not satisfied with the way Argentine films had addressed that.[9]

This speculative approach shows that there may be in Martel's films a goal of avoiding the periphery regarding the viewer's gaze: they are neither exotic nor endogenous, but almost smotheringly local, and they force that localness into the centre of filmmaking, as a production which is material, expensive, complex and sponsored.

One of the most interesting effects in *Zama* is that it pushes us away from Di Benedetto's novel: the important lies not in the elements of the novel that have vanished (the character's rhythmic and invasive sexuality, the anxiety of the absurd created by the smooth and severe style of Di Benedetto, a master of the classical style — whatever that may be: in this case, a Cuyo-based inflection of Argentine prose), but in what is left. And what is left, that which is shared by the novel and the film — as well as by Saer's *The Witness* and some of Aira's works — is that awed interrogation, never fulfilled, of Argentine culture: how might we imagine that ghostly colony from which we emerged? Conversely, what is our link to the living testimonies of its existence, to those Americans who owe nothing to the arrival of the conquistador, those who were there, who dreamt and ate and hunted there, whom we, however, seldom address?

Translated by Juan Ignacio García Fahler

NOTES

* This chapter is based on my participation in the '*Zama:* de la novela al cine' panel discussion, held on 14 February 2018, in Casa de América, Barcelona, for the premiere of Lucrecia Martel's film in Spain.

1. Fanjul, S. (2018), '*Zama*', *ABC*, 26 January 2018, <https://www.abc.es/opinion/abci-zama-201801261048_noticia.html> (last accessed 28 April 2021).

2. Sánchez, M. (2017), '*Zama*, una película como reescritura virtuosa. Entrevista con Lucrecia Martel', *Clarín*, 15 September 2017, <https://www.clarin.com/revista-enie/escenarios/zama-pelicula-reescritura-virtuosa_0_SkPlW6Fqb.html> (last accessed 28 April 2021).

3. See Halperín Donghi, T. (1967), 'Primera parte: Del orden colonial al orden neocolonial', in *Historia contemporánea de América Latina*, Madrid: Alianza Editorial.

4. Llinás, M. (2014), 'Nuestros demonios', *Revista de cine*, 1: 1, pp. 39–46.

5. Oubiña, D. (2007), *Estudio crítico sobre La ciénaga, de Lucrecia Martel*, Buenos Aires: Picnic Editorial.

6. Mirizio, A. (2014), *Los antimodernos del cine: Una retaguardia de la vanguardia*, Madrid: Pigmalión, p. 57.

7. Bernini, E. (2017), 'El hundimiento. A propósito de *Zama*', *Kilómetro III*, 13 October 2017, <http://kilometroiiicine.com.ar/el-hundimiento/> (last accessed 29 April 2021).

8. Saer, J. J. (1983), *El entenado*, Buenos Aires/Ciudad de Mexico: Folios Ediciones, p. 84.

9. Diz, J. and D. Lerer (2017), 'Quiero hacer algo que sea en idioma original en todos los países', *Los Inrockuptibles*, 31 August 2017, <https://medium.com/los-inrockuptibles/lucrecia-martel-zama-d095abf57edf> (last accessed 28 April 2021).

CHAPTER 13

'A kind of bliss, a closing eyelid, a tiny fainting spell': *Zama* and the Lapse into Colour

Deborah Martin

Thirty minutes before the end of Martel's *Zama* (2017), there is a 'stunning, almost blinding' cut which has been compared to the iconic cut 'from stone age to space age' of Stanley Kubrick's *2001: A Space Odyssey* (1968).' *Zama* cuts from the eponymous protagonist's interview with the latest governor, tightly framed against the backdrop of a brownish-grey rock, to a wide open panoramic shot of bright green vegetation in intense sunlight against a turquoise sky, the first time either of these colours has featured in the palette of the film, which in its first part has been dominated by faded ochres and pinks, and in its middle section by nocturnal sequences, browns and greys. It is not only that different, brighter and more intense colours are used here and in the final third of the film, but also that the use of colour itself becomes much more noticeable. The cut signals a temporal and spatial shift, and the beginning of the third and final section of the film which takes the protagonist and a band of men, led by Captain Parrilla, into the hot, swampy forests of the Chaco and away from the relative predictability of life on the outskirts of the colonial city. The way the colour palette shifts over the course of the film echoes Diego de Zama's psychological development, from the relative stability given by his status in the early part (muted ochres, dusty reds, the deep blue of the interiors of aristocratic dwellings), to increased depression, confusion and delirium brought about by his gradual exclusion from power in the middle part (greys, blacks, browns, nocturnal sequences). In the final third, intense and bright colour evokes a new stage of delirium, as Diego de Zama, dispossessed of his former position of *corregidor* (magistrate) and its trappings, is left no choice but to join Parrilla's expedition into the wilderness of the Chaco. Charged by the authorities with capturing a legendary bandit, its members also represent the crazed mentality of those who, here on the extreme periphery of empire, still ventured in vain pursuit of riches.

Figure 13.1 Zama and Parilla's band of men trek through the Chaco wetlands. © Rei Cine SRL, Bananeira Filmes Ltda, El Deseo DA SLU, Patagonik Film Group SA

This chapter argues that a consideration of the use and meaning of colour is vital to the analysis of *Zama*, a film in which intense colour is used to challenge the subjective and corporeal boundaries of the white male colonial position, as well as to inflect its enunciatory position with a subaltern voice. Colour is a neglected area in film theory and criticism, as has been noted by scholars who, from the mid-2000s, have begun to correct this tendency.[2] Wendy Everett argues that colour is excluded from the 'process of meaning making' or ignored in a series of canonical and field-defining studies in film theory and semiotics,[3] whilst Steven Peacock suggests this theoretical and critical neglect may be due to the fact that colour is 'non-representational' or that it 'resists critical classification'.[4] Colour is part of the imagistic, excessive or aesthetic aspect of the image which has traditionally been viewed as separate from or antagonistic to the realms of ideas and meaning by Marxist-influenced film theories, which have tended to align 'the potential to speak philosophically or socially' with visual austerity, and thus to neglect colour, amongst other 'decorative' elements.[5] As Rosalind Galt argues, these tendencies in film theory echo the *disegno–colore* debates in art history, in which line is associated with the intellect and colour with emotion, and with 'the troubling sensuality of the image'.[6] In his book *Chromophobia*, David Batchelor argues that the opposition between line and colour encodes and conceals many other oppositions.[7] Tracing the prejudice against colour through Western philosophy, art history and cultural theory, he shows how Western culture is characterised by a fear of the corrupting or contaminating potential of colour, how the preoccupation with the containment of colour by line and form is expressive of social and cultural anxieties about race, gender and sexuality, and how colour's association with Otherness — feminine, queer, oriental, primitive — is accompanied by a tendency to devalue or diminish its significance through its association with the cosmetic and the superficial.[8] On the one hand, 'colour is regarded as alien and therefore dangerous', while on the other 'it is perceived merely as a secondary quality of experience, and thus unworthy of serious consideration'.[9] Perhaps it is a little embarrassing to give serious thought to something as seemingly trivial, as cosmetic, as colour?

Michael Taussig's discussion in *What Colour is the Sacred?* echoes Batchelor's main contentions, in particular the idea that 'Chromophobia is a "habit" of Western society', and one which 'maintains itself through [. . .] techniques of the body'.[10] He delves in particular into the case for colour as a 'colonial subject':[11] bright colours are associated with the tropics — he notes the evocative similarity between 'color'/'colour' and 'calor'/'heat'[12] — as well as with colonised peoples, and with modes of being — childlike, primitive, quick-spirited — associated with those peoples by colonial power and Eurocentric discourses.[13] He cites the discourse on colour in Goethe, who wrote that 'men in a state of nature [. . .] uncivilised nations and children have a fondness for colours in their utmost brightness', whilst (European and North American) 'people of refinement had a disinclination to colours'.[14] Taussig is particularly concerned with the ways in which colour operates to break down subjective and corporeal boundaries, and especially the boundaries of the masculine, white, colonial subject, a subject which, as Richard Dyer has argued, is characterised by a sense of *boundedness*, clear boundaries being, for Dyer, 'characteristic of things white'.[15] Taussig is interested in colour as a potential means of overcoming or undoing these boundaries, and thus a source of both anxiety and potential pleasure. Colour acts as a magical 'agent of metamorphosis'[16] and is associated with narcotic effects, with pleasure, sensuality and loss of control. For William Burroughs, in the *Yagé* state,

> all defences fall, everything is free to enter or go out, a beautiful blue substance flows into me. You come face to face with reality shorn of these lovely categories with which culture so conveniently provides us for thinking straight and being straight.[17]

In his book *Chroma*, Derek Jarman notes that 'In antiquity, colour was considered a drug (*pharmakon*)', whilst for Barthes, intense colour is akin to '[A] kind of bliss [. . .] like a closing eyelid, a tiny fainting spell'.[18] As Batchelor argues, the movement into colour is often imagined as a fall, a descent, as in perhaps the most famous passage from black and white to colour in the history of cinema, Dorothy's fall into Technicolor in *The Wizard of Oz* (Victor Fleming, 1939).[19]

As the insistent Shepard tones of its soundtrack remind us, *Zama* is also the story of a fall, of 'una conciencia que se abisma',[20] and with the protagonist's repeated attempts to resist his inevitable fall.

Taussig studies the diaries of Malinowski in New Guinea, showing how he 'found in colour [. . .] an escape from the prison of Standard Western Subjectivity',[21] a means of 'opening up [. . .] the bodily unconscious', but also pursued strategies for 'keeping the sense of the white body intact, no matter how hot and humid the meltdown, no matter how wonderfully disorienting the light', as a means of maintaining colonial authority.[22] The more muted colour palette in the early part of *Zama* parallels the protagonist's and colonial administration's more successful attempts to shore up that authority. In the eighteenth century in this region, attempts to protect ethnic boundaries – to keep the 'white' body intact – included 'repeated efforts [. . .] to assign each racial subgroup to specific occupations and a fixed rank', while 'intermarriage among the castes was frequently forbidden'.[23] Shoring up colonial authority was all the more urgent for *americanos* like Diego de Zama, born not in Spain but in the New World, whose claim to superiority and power was thus more tenuous. For Walter Mignolo, this group, when it surfaced, was 'already outside of history', placed 'between the limits of humanity (Indians and Africans) and humanity proper (Europeans)'.[24] The repeated commercial and financial crises of the seventeenth and eighteenth centuries in this relatively backward corner of the Spanish Empire led to a reduction in size of the white ruling caste, which increasingly shed whites of lower social status or those who lost political battles.[25]

Attempts by Zama to reinforce his elite status give the film some of its comic moments, such as when he waxes lyrical to Luciana Piñares de Luenga, the wife of the Ministro de la Real Hacienda (Treasury Minister) and object of Zama's romantic attention, on the subject of Russian furs, carpets and princesses, only to be told curtly that 'Europe is best remembered by those who were never there' ('Recuerda más Europa el que nunca estuvo'). Zama and others attempt continually to shore up his position in the colonial administration with excessive, anxious repetitions of his title, 'el Corregidor' (for example, to announce his arrival or entry), recalling the stylings of the theatre of the absurd.[26] Just as the authority of men and other dominant groups is mocked in Martel's earlier work,[27] Zama is continually mocked by those around him, including women, indigenous and enslaved people, and sees his subordinates and rivals succeed in obtaining or usurping the power and positions he views as his. Even animals, it seems, can upstage Diego de Zama, as in the much-commented moment in which his receipt of the devastating news of his rival's transfer to his own desired location, the city of Lerma, is interrupted by a stray llama wandering into the frame.[28]

As these moments of mocking and contestation of Zama's authority suggest, the project of shoring up his elite status and colonial power is ultimately unsuccessful; indeed, the film as a whole as well as Zama's personal trajectory are best read as means to demonstrate the extent to which (colonial) domination and submission are never complete. Whilst the film ostensibly references 'the narrative structures that belong to the continuing saga of the white man's search for identity'[29] that, as Jean Franco argues, tend to underlie narrative fiction films depicting the colonial era − such as those she examines, including *The Mission* (Roland Joffé, 1986) which is also set around the Paraguay–Argentina border − in fact, the positing of Diego de Zama as a protagonist should itself be understood as part of the joke, since the film ultimately effects, through its narrative and aesthetics, an overturning or deconstruction of (his) white male colonial power and hegemony, as well as of his protagonism.

The expedition Parrilla leads in the third part of the film takes the men far from colonial settlement and into the wilderness, where they are captured by an indigenous group. Colour, composition and *mise-en-scène* shift radically here, with the advent of vivid greens already mentioned, which, when the Indians appear, are punctuated with the bright reddish-orange of their painted bodies, another colour thus far missing from the film's palette. Red-orange and green, which provide a strong contrast to one another, are the dominant colours in the last part of the film. Here, the relationship between ground and figure shifts, too, as human bodies which have in the previous parts of the film been separate from bodies of water (this occurs in exemplary fashion in the film's opening shot, in which Diego de Zama stands erect, proprietorial, on the banks of the Paraguay River, and cuts a figure reminiscent of Caspar David Friedrich's *Wanderer above the Sea of Fog* (1818), thus evoking 'high' European culture and that painting's combination of mastery of the landscape and Kantian self-reflection) now merge into the swamps through which they wade. The white soldiers' bodies first begin to merge with the landscape, and then are captured by the red-painted Indians, who use colour and painting to instigate a further challenge to the boundaries of white bodies, in a strange, enigmatic and highly sensorial sequence which is crucial to the challenging of colonial power, the dissolution of colonial corporeality, and the creation of the film's decolonial voice.

After the sequence in which they are captured by the Indians, we cut to a dungeon-like, dark, enclosed space, in which Parrilla's men appear to be interrogated by the tribe.[30] The nature − function, layout − of the interior space in this sequence is highly ambiguous, and much of what little information we do obtain comes from sound, especially since the naked red bodies of the captives and the Indians are tightly framed and take up most of the frame, blocking much of our view of the space, and suffusing the frame with red. We hear the sound of trickling water, and the movement of bodies seems to generate the sound of wading, whilst the naked bodies of both groups appear to be wet. This dampness and liquidity is a common motif in Martel's work, signifying mutability and the transgression of boundaries.[31] Esther Allen calls this sequence the 'steam bath',[32] and remarks on the 'straight walls and heavy, clanging doors',[33] while Bernini identifies the sound of a guillotine.[34] Martel's work frequently aims to create such a lack of certainty about what we are seeing and hearing, a technique she borrows from horror. Fear and threat, but also sensual pleasure, are suggested here; as well as the threats associated with interrogation, there are allusions to ritual, ceremony and eroticism, as the damp and wet bodies of the white men are painted red, daubed, pummelled and massaged by the indigenous people. One soldier, Gaspar Toledo, lies back in seeming ecstasy under their touch as his body is painted red. His engulfment by colour seems to be experienced as intense pleasure, recalling the 'insidious non-Western sensuality' which Batchelor argues is associated with intense colour in Western thought and art theory.[35] It is Gaspar Toledo, a shapeshifting and ambiguous character who speaks in both Spanish and Portuguese, and who later announces himself as Vicuña Porto, the very bandit the troop of soldiers is charged with finding, to whom the reddish hue clings the longest; after the soldiers are released, the colour wears off most of them, but Toledo/Porto remains red-hued until the end.

The 'steam bath' sequence presents, then, a scene of active and obvious colouring, of painting, as if the film were meditating on its own status as coloured, or would-be coloured artefact. Like some earlier sequences in the film, it lends itself to interpretation as a dream or hallucination, the culmination of the many threats to the protagonist's psychic, and now physical, integrity: uncanny confusions of self and other, reality and imagination. The low lighting, and profusion, confusion and layering of the red-painted bodies of both groups in the background and foreground of the frame creates a composition in which the boundaries between bodies are indistinct. The indigenous, who have until this point often been seen nearer to the edges of the frame, here overtake the image, and this overtaking is accompanied by the engulfing of the frame by the red colour of their bodies, which alludes to colour's potential to overwhelm or annihilate, and which happens at no other point in the film. This moment is Zama's (and *Zama*'s) ultimate descent into colour – a dream, nightmare, lapse, undoing or uprooting of self, a fall into the space and the body of the other, the native, the non-white. As line and form become more difficult to discern, as the subordination of colour to the rule of line is overturned, so is the intactness of the white male colonial body, and so are the colonial project's imperatives to contain, demarcate and control.

Paraguayan art critic and ethnographer Ticio Escobar writes of the 'obsession with colours' of the Chamacoco indigenous of Paraguay, who frequently paint their bodies a number of colours, including using hematite to produce a bright red.[36] As Martel has made clear, the film does not aspire to historical accuracy, including in relation to representing the indigenous past, since this would mean representing the accounts written by Europeans of cultures wiped out by colonisation.[37] Instead, she favours a playful, inventive and anachronistic

Figure 13.2 Zama stands on the river bank, waiting for a ship to arrive. © Rei Cine SRL, Bananeira Filmes Ltda, El Deseo DA SLU, Patagonik Film Group SA

approach to the representation of the past, one aspect of which might be the incorporation of contemporary indigenous body-painting and colour ceremonies into the representation of the indigenous in the final third of the film.[38] Escobar has written extensively on aspects such as body painting in contemporary Paraguayan indigenous cultures. For the Chamacoco, 'colours illuminate the backdrop of myths and set the body alight during ceremonies', colours 'force the object to release hidden meanings, [gesturing] to truths that remain otherwise concealed'.[39] This group uses the practice of body painting as a means of negotiating difference, of 'address[ing] the thorny question that troubles and drives the course of culture: that which confronts the self/same and the other, that which tries to define the frontier of identity and separate the alien'.[40] Colour can shield the wearer from harm or confer power on the wearer. It is also used as a means of identifying with, for example, animals or gods, including 'to imitate the designs on the skins of the gods they killed and whose place they have usurped'.[41] The use of colour and body-painting in the 'steam bath' sequence alludes to these properties and practices of colour(ing) in indigenous cultures, suggesting the usurping of white power by the indigenous, figuring colour as a magical agent of metamorphosis and mimesis.

This mimesis does not only occur between the different groups of bodies represented on-screen, which increasingly resemble one another through colour; in addition, the use of colour and other elements discussed brings about, particularly in this sequence, a mimetic relation between viewer and film. I have written elsewhere that Martel's cinema can be understood as motivated by the desire to 'overcome the solitude of the body',[42] and shown how, as here, haptic and tactile images of rubbing, of skin, and haptic sounds are used as means of eliciting an embodied spectatorship, of inviting an embodied response.[43] Such moments have prominence throughout *Zama*, from early images of women by the river applying mud to their skin, to later ones of Zama's body being washed by servants. This tendency of the film reaches its culmination in the 'steam bath' sequence, in which colour becomes a further means of overcoming corporeal boundaries between spectator and film, and of inviting a mimetic and embodied form of spectatorship. In this sense, the use of colour here brings to mind the 'absorbent' properties of colour, as discussed by Gilles Deleuze, as well as by Taussig. For Deleuze, who directly discusses colour in film, the colour-image has an 'absorbent characteristic' which 'does not refer to a particular object, but absorbs all it can: it is the power which seizes all that happens within its range, or the quality common to completely different objects'.[44] Pure colour can be used to transcend the spatial and temporal dimensions of the frame.[45] Taussig writes of colour's capacity for inviting absorption into the image, for making vision 'less a retinal and more a total bodily activity to the [. . .] extent that in looking at something we may even pass into the image'.[46] As he writes:

> colour dissolves the visual modality so as to become more creaturely and close, so close in fact that the image − or what was the image − becomes something that can absorb the onlooker. [. . . T]he same sensation that Nietzsche described for the Dionysian, meaning absorption into the very being of the Other, as with music, dance and ritual, as contrasted with the Apollonian, meaning controlled vision that holds the Other at arm's length.[47]

Colour in the 'steam bath' sequence 'absorbs' what is around it and what is outside it, both within and outside the cinematic image; red suffuses the frame, and threatens or encroaches on the edges of on-screen bodies, yet through its powerful absorbent properties, as well as the host of other haptic and tactile, wild and Dionysian elements with which it is combined in this sequence, it also functions to reconfigure the viewer's relationship to the image, inducing mimesis, eliciting embodied spectatorship, and overturning visual regimes which associate vision with mastery and separation.

The extent to which colour dominates line and form in this sequence also means that − to a greater extent than elsewhere in the film − there is a shift away from representation, narrative and figuration, and towards abstraction. This use of colour recalls the much more extreme and explicit project of Derek Jarman's *Blue* (1993), which consists visually of a single shot of blue colour filling the screen for its seventy-nine-minute duration. *Blue* emphasises the screen as surface, and situates colour as non-narrative. As Alexandra Parsons argues, his film embodies what Julia Kristeva, in her discussion of the blue on the ceiling of the Scrovegni Chapel, Padua, sees as the ability of colour to 'pulverise', 'multiply' and 'shatter' meaning.[48] A shift away from representation and narrative and towards abstraction, surface and touch can be observed in earlier works by Martel, including in *The Holy Girl/La niña santa* (2004), a film which makes important use of colour. That film's final sequence, which, as I have written, functions as a 'tactile and aquatic space-beyond-narrative',[49] is dominated by the colour blue, and uses a shade similar to that of Jarman's *Blue*. Blue in *The Holy Girl*, too, shifts our attention away from narrative and towards the screen as surface, even whilst enveloping the young protagonist Amalia in its meanings: holiness and mysticism, the blue of the Virgin Mary, the precious and the infinite.[50] These meanings are not to be understood in simple terms but as part of the complex and wry subversion of religious ideology which the film undertakes, in which desire, sensuality and subversion are shown always to inhere in what purports to be pure and holy.[51] Further sequences of *The Holy Girl*, set in Amalia's mother's bedroom, employ a contrasting palette of dark reds, suggesting an interior and womb-like space, a palette and space which strongly prefigures (in aesthetic, rather than narrative terms) the dissolution of boundaries both within the image, and between image and viewer, characterising the 'steam bath' of *Zama*.

I have suggested that colour figures in the meaning-construction of *Zama* in a way that undermines the colonial subject, and privileges the worldview and expressive tendencies of indigenous cultures. The final part of this chapter will address further ways in which the film speaks decolonially through colour. The first of these is the contribution made by colour and its use to the film's general tendency towards anachronism, its refusal of the quest for historical accuracy and authenticity which usually conditions historical filmmaking. In her discussion of 'neo-indigenist' historical film, Franco refers to 'the problem of a historical film which is too faithful to history': summarising this as the fact that 'it cannot represent what has gone unrepresented'.[52] Acutely aware of this problem, Martel favours self-conscious fictionalising, invention, substitution and play, rather than any attempt at the 'authenticity' for which the conventional historical film would strive. Again, the 'steam bath' sequence is itself a good example of this, with the straight walls and metal swing doors that feature in its *mise-en-scène*. These are outrageously fantastical elaborations on the kinds of structures likely to be producible or desirable by eighteenth-century indigenous peoples in tropical regions such as the Chaco, and seem more akin to twentieth- or twenty-first-century architecture. In addition to a refusal of historical accuracy or authenticity, the association of the indigenous in the 'steam bath' sequence with contemporary architectural forms constitutes a refusal of the temporal othering or distancing to which Johannes Fabian argues indigenous cultures tend to be uniformly subject, their association with the past,[53] and can be understood as part of a wider project in Martel's work to disrupt 'the discourse which construes the Other in terms of distance, spatial and temporal'.[54]

Colour, too, plays an important part in *Zama*'s tendency to anachronism and lack of respect for traditional aesthetic means of representing the past. In *The World Viewed*, Stanley Cavell proposes that colour in cinema is a means of invoking both futurity and fantasy: 'I have described certain uses of colour in film – as packaging, as unifying the worlds of make-believe and of fantasy, and as projecting a future.'[55] As in *The Wizard of Oz*, shimmering colour does not announce to us the present or reality, but instead lures us into a world which is yet to come. The vivid greens, turquoises and oranges of the final third of *Zama* recall the advent of Technicolor and are used in the final third of *Zama* to create tropical tableaux accompanied by the extradiegetic music of Los Indios Tabajaras – which is reminiscent of the Hapa Haole genre – recalling films such as *Blue Hawaii* (Norman Taurog, 1961), and popular mid-century US representations of Polynesia and Oceania ('Tiki' culture). Indeed, Martel has commented that 1950s screen culture was one of her aesthetic references for *Zama*.[56] The representation of the 1790s through allusion to the mid-twentieth century not only functions as a means of referencing the 1956 novel on which the film is based (as Esther Allen rightly argues),[57] but also acts as a further way of countering the expected and traditional mode of historical representation, and undermining dominant, Western understandings of linear time. The combined use of music and colour here creates a hallucinatory reality which alludes both to time travel (science fiction, like horror, often haunts the edges of Martel's films), and to the polytemporality of indigenous cosmovisions. Typically for Martel's filmmaking, these allusions remain just that, and are not developed into fully elaborated symbolic systems.[58] If, however, as Catherine Walsh and Mignolo argue, 'coexisting temporalities [are] kept hostage by the Western idea of time and the belief that there is one single temporality: Western imagined fictional temporality',[59] the polytemporality alluded to via music and *mise-en-scène*, including colour, functions to liberate these and thus to create a pluriversal vision of the past, which suggests the inclusion of other, subaltern worldviews, an amalgam of diverse layers of time.

In Martel's work, despite its sustained focus on the mechanisms of oppressive structures, there is always a sense in which the subversion of these structures flourishes, and in which that which they repress pervades and overturns them. Other, repressed or elided forms of knowledge and understanding suffuse her films. This is the case, for example, with the perspective of the child in *The Swamp/La ciénaga* (2001) and *The Holy Girl*, and with that of the indigenous or mestizo underclass in *The Headless Woman/La mujer sin cabeza* (2008) and *New Argirópolis/Nueva Argirópolis* (2010). All Martel's films constitute aesthetic experiments in the incursion of these repressed or elided forms of knowledge into dominant reality; as is well documented, sound is one aesthetic means by which, in all Martel's films, this takes place.[60] *Zama*, despite its ostensible focus on the coloniser, is suffused for its part by the subaltern voice, that of the enslaved and indigenous people who gradually work their way towards the centre of the frame over the course of the film. The film as a whole constitutes an act of overturning of the colonial perspective, the embodied subjectivity of that perspective, an act which is performed in a number of ways, including through sound, but also through the use of colour, especially in the 'steam bath' sequence, in which the boundaries of paramount importance for the colonial endeavour are threatened and in which colour and redness make tangible the eroding of those boundaries on-screen. Likewise, dominant, Eurocentric modes of writing, narrating and cinematically representing the indigenous and colonial pasts are challenged by the use of a bright mid-twentieth century aesthetic; a univocal and Eurocentric discourse which might at first seem to be associated with the subject and the protagonist of this film is queered or undermined; 'history' is imbued with fantasy, dream, time travel and subaltern knowledge.

Emilio Bernini, in his excellent analysis of the film, argues that the subaltern speaking position is articulated from the outset of the film by its opening episode, in which we hear:

> An oracle that seems to address itself to the colonial functionaries themselves, who listen to it, amazed, as if to an (allegorical) description of their own fate in the adverse conditions of the South American colony, delivered precisely by one of its subjects. The importance of this subject's voice, and of his utterance, is that it becomes the introduction to the film, the paradigm of the story about to be told.[61]

In the final third of the film, in which the use of colour becomes more noticeable, in which colours are brighter, and in which the use of colour and corporeal painting in indigenous cultures is portrayed on-screen, the extent to which meaning is organised through colour in this film becomes clear. If, as Taussig and Escobar discuss, colour functions in the thought of some indigenous groups living in the region in which this film is set as a significant means of expressing and ordering reality, and if, as these thinkers argue, colour stands for what is denied by Western culture, then to speak through colour is also to speak decolonially, to speak from the place of the subaltern. For the spectator, the hallucinatory use of colour in the film's final section acts as it does for the captured soldiers in the 'steam bath' sequence, it acts as a drug, or *pharmakon*, inviting absorption by the image, as part of a broader aesthetic in this last part of the film of boundary dissolution, as bodies wade through swamps, and the white men take on the red hue of their indigenous counterparts. Through its elevation of colour to a primary mode of meaning-making, the film not only allows a subaltern worldview to encroach upon the colonial one, it also functions to reinvigorate the role of formalism, and in particular colour, in the service of a political cinema.

NOTES

1. The quotation in the title of this chapter is from Barthes, R. (1986), 'Cy Twombly: Works on Paper', in *The Responsibility of Forms: Critical Essays on Music, Art and Representation*, Oxford: Blackwell, pp. 157–76 (p. 166). References in this sentence are to Gemünden, G. and S. Spitta (2018), 'I Was Never Afraid: An Interview with Lucrecia Martel', *Film Quarterly*, 71: 4, pp. 33–40, p. 35. In *Zama* the cut in question occurs at 1:19:14.
2. See Dalle Vacche, A. and B. Price (2006), *Color: The Film Reader*, New York: Routledge; Everett, W. (2007), *Questions of Colour in Cinema: From Paintbrush to Pixel*, Oxford: Peter Lang; Peacock, S. (2010), *Colour*, Manchester: Manchester University Press; and Brown, S., S. Street and L. Watkins (eds) (2013), *Colour and the Moving Image: History, Theory, Aesthetics, Archive*, New York: Routledge.
3. Everett, *Questions of Colour in Cinema*, p. 17.
4. Peacock, *Colour*, pp. 2–3.
5. Galt, R. (2011), *Pretty: Film and the Decorative Image*, New York: Columbia University Press, p. 183.
6. Ibid. p. 183.
7. Batchelor, D. (2000), *Chromophobia*, London: Reaktion, p. 29.
8. Ibid. p. 23.
9. Ibid. p. 23.
10. Taussig, M. (2009), *What Colour is the Sacred?*, Chicago: University of Illinois Press, p. 12.
11. Ibid. p. 159.
12. Ibid. p. 5.
13. Ibid. p. 5.
14. Ibid. p. 3.
15. Dyer, R. (1988), 'White', *Screen*, 29: 4, pp. 44–65 (p. 51).
16. Taussig, *What Colour is the Sacred?*, p. 8.
17. Ibid. p. 62.
18. Jarman, D. (1994), *Chroma: A Book of Colour*, London: Vintage, p. 38; Barthes, 'Cy Twombly', p. 166.
19. Batchelor, *Chromophobia*, p. 39.
20. Bernini, E. (2017), 'El hundimiento. A propósito de *Zama*', *Kilómetro 111*, 13 October 2017, <http://kilometro111cine.com.ar/el-hundimiento/> (last accessed 29 April 2021).
21. Taussig, *What Colour is the Sacred?*, p. 92.
22. Ibid. p. 94.
23. Rock, D. (1987), *Argentina 1516–1987: From Spanish Colonization to Alfonsín*, Berkeley: University of California Press, p. 59.
24. Mignolo, W. (2005), *The Idea of Latin America*, Oxford: Blackwell, p. 4.
25. Rock, *Argentina 1516–1987*, p. 38.
26. Although 'corregidor' may be translated as 'magistrate' for the purposes of describing Zama's role in the colonial administration at the moment of the film's setting, it refers also to his prior military role as 'corregidor de indios', that is, a commander who enforced colonial power structures onto indigenous populations.

27. Martin, D. (2016), *The Cinema of Lucrecia Martel*, Manchester: Manchester University Press, p. 16.

28. Reviews and academic work on the film frequently discuss this moment. See, for example, Gemünden and Spitta, 'I Was Never Afraid', p. 34; and Galt, R. (2019), 'Learning from a Llama and Other Fishy Tales: Anticolonial Aesthetics in Lucrecia Martel's *Zama*', in C. Grant and T. Cox-Stanton (eds), *The Cine-Files*, 14, 'Beast Fables, on Animals in the Cinema', <http://www.thecine-files.com/galt/> (last accessed 2 April 2020).

29. Franco, J. (1993), 'High-Tech Primitivism: The Representation of Tribal Societies in Feature Films', in J. King, A. M. López and M. Alvarado (eds), *Mediating Two Worlds: Cinematic Encounters in the Americas*, London: BFI Publishing, pp. 81–94 (p. 83).

30. The sequence in question runs from 1:29:46 to 1:31:18.

31. See Martin, *The Cinema of Lucrecia Martel*, pp. 106–21.

32. Allen referred to the sequence in this way in an interview as part of 'The Film Comment Podcast', published by Film at Lincoln Center, 10 April 2018, <https://www.filmcomment.com/blog/film-comment-podcast-lucrecia-martels-zama-2/> (last accessed 9 September 2021).

33. Allen, E. (2018), 'The Crazed Euphoria of Lucrecia Martel's *Zama*', *New York Review of Books*, 14 April 2018, <https://www.nybooks.com/daily/2018/04/14/the-crazed-euphoria-of-lucrecia-martels-zama/> (last accessed 2 April 2020).

34. Bernini, 'El hundimiento'.

35. John Gage, quoted in Batchelor, *Chromophobia*, p. 29.

36. Escobar, T. (2007), *The Curse of Nemur: In Search of the Art, Myth and Ritual of the Ishir*, Pittsburgh: University of Pittsburgh Press, pp. 66, 125.

37. As Mignolo writes, 'Colonization of being is nothing else than producing the idea that certain people do not belong to history – that they are non-beings. Thus, lurking beneath the European story of discovery are the histories, experiences and silenced conceptual narratives of those who were disqualified as human beings, as historical actors, as capable of thinking and understanding. In the sixteenth and seventeenth centuries the "wretched of the earth" [. . .] were Indians and African slaves. That is why missionaries and men of letters appointed themselves to write the histories they thought Incas and Aztecs did not have, and to write the grammar of Kechua/Kichua and Nahuatl with Latin as the model.' *The Idea of Latin America*, p. 4.

38. Martel has commented, 'The natives are Guaraní, Qom-lek, and Pilagá; and working with them was very interesting because everything was an invention – their haircuts, the clothes, the feathers, the colors. Initially, they assumed that they should play themselves, but I explained to them that they should act as if they were somebody else, somebody fictitious [. . .]. Those red-painted natives you see are supposed to be Guaycuru, but they speak Qom. The Guaycuru language, spoken by the natives who attacked in the eighteenth century, is extinct. Nothing of what you hear is real; it is completely anachronistic. No one spoke in that manner at the time. I wanted to capture the beauty of a diverse world. [. . .] The film is not a serious depiction of the past but pure invention. We aimed for a tone that was not too serious, sometimes even slightly parodic.' Gemünden and Spitta, 'I Was Never Afraid', p. 37.

39. Taussig, *What Colour is the Sacred?*, p. 6.

40. Escobar, *The Curse of Nemur*, p. 118.

41. Ibid. p. 138.

42. Martin, *The Cinema of Lucrecia Martel*, p. 125.

43. Ibid. *passim*.

44. Deleuze, G. (1986), *Cinema 1: The Movement-Image*, London: The Athlone Press, p. 121.

45. Everett, *Questions of Colour in Cinema*, p. 109.

46. Taussig, *What Colour is the Sacred?*, p. 6.
47. Ibid. p. 19.
48. Quoted in Parsons, A. (2018), 'A Meditation on Colour and the Body in Derek Jarman's *Chroma* and Maggie Nelson's *Bluets*', *a/b: Auto/Biography Studies*, 33: 2, pp. 375–93 (p. 379).
49. Martin, *The Cinema of Lucrecia Martel*, p. 75.
50. See Parsons, 'A Meditation on Colour and the Body', pp. 377–8, where these meanings and connotations of blue, and their origins, are discussed at length.
51. See Martin, *The Cinema of Lucrecia Martel*, pp. 54–79.
52. Franco, 'High-Tech Primitivism', p. 82.
53. Fabian, J. (1983), *Time and the Other: How Anthropology Makes its Object*, New York: Columbia University Press.
54. Ibid. p. xxxix. See Martel's short film *New Argirópolis* in which a strongly future-oriented indigenous activism circulates via YouTube videos; and Martin, D. (2016), 'Lucrecia Martel's *Nueva Argirópolis*: Rivers, Rumours and Resistance', *Journal of Latin American Cultural Studies*, 25: 3, pp. 449–65 (p. 456).
55. Cavell, S. (1979), *The World Viewed: Reflections on the Ontology of Film*, Cambridge, MA: Harvard University Press, p. 95.
56. Post-screening discussion, Portland International Film Festival, 11 March 2019.
57. Allen, 'The Crazed Euphoria of Lucrecia Martel's *Zama*'.
58. On this tendency in Martel's filmmaking, see Page, J. (2009), *Crisis and Capitalism in Contemporary Argentine Cinema*, Durham, NC: Duke University Press, pp. 180–93.
59. Walsh, C. and W. Mignolo, (2018), *On Decoloniality: Concepts, Analytics, Praxis*, Durham, NC: Duke University Press, p. 3.
60. On sound in Martel's work, see Martin, *The Cinema of Lucrecia Martel*, p. 21 and *passim*; Greene, L. (2012), 'Swamped in Sound: The Sound Image in Lucrecia Martel's *La ciénaga/The Swamp*', *Printed Project*, 15, pp. 52–60, <http://www.lizgreenesound. com/wp-content/uploads/2018/05/LG-Swamped-in-Sound-Printed-Project.pdf> (last accessed 16 April 2021); and Russell, D. (2008), 'Lucrecia Martel: A Decidedly Polyphonic Cinema', *Jump Cut*, 50, <https://www.ejumpcut.org/archive/jc50.2008/ LMartelAudio/> (last accessed 16 April 2021).
61. Bernini, 'El hundimiento'.

CHAPTER 14

Phenomenology of Spirits: Off-screen Horror in Lucrecia Martel's Films

David Oubiña

THE HOUSE FULL OF HORRORS

A 'mock trailer' for *The Swamp/La ciénaga* (2001) is available on YouTube. It is a film school assignment, where some scenes from the film are manipulated, carefully curated, and reconfigured, mixed with disturbing promotional phrases and upsetting music. This fictional trailer is announced with the title *La ciénaga del terror* ('Horror Swamp') and prepares us for a movie which could very well have been the real one. Taking situations to the extreme, coercing them, forcing them to confess, the trailer makes evident what the film merely suggests. Or, rather, it displays explicitly that which the images of *The Swamp* do not show, but which never ceases to intrigue them, because they fear it. What one *does not want to see* is always what one *is afraid of seeing* because one *would not stand seeing it.*

The horror genre is defined by the type of emotion it tries to elicit, and from which it takes its name. That which causes fright is a situation considered by the characters (and, thus, by the viewers) 'as abnormal, as disturbances of the natural order': what horrifies – according to Noël Carroll – is that which threatens and causes repulsion because it is indescribable, unconceivable and inadmissible.[1] That relation is not straightforward, because the fear of seeing often is the fear of not knowing how to see. Naming is always reassuring: language describes, shapes, contains, and thus dominates or at least creates a certain feeling of control. When the unknown acquires an outline, a distance is created as well. Sight replaces touch. Most of all: that which we can see, precisely because we see it, should not be able to touch us. Like a painter who takes a step back to appreciate the landscape captured in the canvas, the real changes its scale and becomes more encompassable when it falls under a gaze.

To see is to compare. Jorge Luis Borges would say that something entirely new would be invisible. Indeed, things become decipherable (understandable) when we can see them against a known reference. That is why, behind our fear of seeing, there are doubts about our ability to see, that is, of controlling the thing through/in our gaze. In Martel's film, that is what happens with little Luciano, who spies on the dog next door because it terrifies him. He needs to check that it is there, a wall away, and in check, as if seeing it turned it into something of this world, which no longer disturbs him. The gaze tames and brings quiet. After all, seeing is always preferable to not seeing. An image is much better than emptiness as a source of shelter. Because when the fear-ful person establishes that there is nothing to fear, all they manage to do is strengthen their apprehension about what is yet to be discovered. In any event, daring to not see is what takes courage, as that action leaves the observer help-less. Momi is the only one who goes to the site of the apparition and admits to not having seen anything. She and Luciano are the ones who try to watch. The rest, instead, content themselves with thinking that it is not necessary to see, or that seeing again what has been seen already is enough.

Of course, *The Swamp* is not a horror film; but it could be said that horror lies off-screen: Martel uses all the mechanisms of the genre that announce the irruption of that which would be unbearable. Something terrible haunts the viewer outside the frame, and turns the image into a place in which, at any time, catastrophe could befall them. We know it from the very start: sooner or later, someone will get hurt. Horror, as a genre, is nothing else but the dark side of curiosity, and unfolds because someone overcomes their resistance and yields to the temptation of seeing; in this sense, the mechanism of horror is defined by the tension between what is shown and what is not. In Martel's films, that which happens off-screen is never realised, and thus remains as an insinuation, as a threat, as a disturbing dimension. Martel refrains (she wants and does not want to see), but her films inhabit a land which is always bordering the universe of horror. As if nothing but a wall separated them.

When asked about her favourite films, the director mentions *Cat People* (Jacques Tourneur, 1942), *Les yeux sans visage/Eyes Without a Face* (Georges Franju, 1960), *Night of the Living Dead* (George Romero, 1968) and *Carnival of Souls* (Herk Harvey, 1962).[2] Martel has pointed out Harvey's film's influence on *The Headless Woman/La mujer sin cabeza* (whose title was once to be *La mujer zombie*, or *The Zombie Woman*) on several occasions. In *Carnival of Souls*, a car falls into the water, seemingly taking the lives of all passengers with it, but Mary Henry emerges from the depths safe and sound. The woman plays organ at a church, and everyone criticises her cold, purely professional, relationship with that music made to elevate the spirit. In the following days, she is plagued by strange apparitions. It could be that the woman who emerged from the water is no longer among the living, and the ghosts haunting her actually want to take

Figure 14.1 *The Swamp.* © Lita Stantic Producciones

her back to where the souls of the dead dwell. Martel's movie also includes a car accident and a woman distressed by it. In the northern part of Argentina, it is a common belief that, after a traumatic experience, the soul escapes the body and leaves the person empty, like the living dead. This is what happens with Vero, who after the crash attempts to resume her everyday tasks, but finds everything strange, as if she had never been there.

Aunt Lala can tell something is not right. 'There is something in your voice', she tells Vero. And, immediately, after hearing noises: 'Don't look. The house is full of horrors. They are leaving. Don't look at them, and they'll leave.' Could Vero be haunted by ghosts, just as in *Carnival of Souls*? However, Mary is a lonely and distant woman, withdrawn, who refuses contact with people and ends up joining the spirits that came looking for her. Vero, instead, is surrounded by protective relatives and friends who defend her from evil thoughts. If *The Swamp* is not a horror film because it stops short of showing what is left off-screen, in *The Headless Woman* horror remains like the negative of the image: there is a resistance to facing that what is feared, and therefore is left behind until it vanishes and is ultimately forgotten. In one case, thus, we have a suggested presence which never materialises; in the other, a threat which loses consistency and disappears. Something different happens in *Zama* (2017), not related to stopping short of seeing or to getting rid of a disturbing vision. For Don Diego, horror lies in the unending wait. As someone tells him, 'A god born old who cannot die. His loneliness is atrocious.'

Just like the characters in *The Swamp*, Diego de Zama also swims in mud: he spends all his time with his feet stuck in a mire, waiting without solace for the ship which would take him out of there, sinking inexorably all the while. The difference lies in that he fails to get used to it. At the beginning of the movie, a story is told about a fish rejected by water, which spends its life trying to cling to that liquid which shuns it. It uses all its energy to remain in that medium which pushes it out, and finally dies of exertion. Zama is like that fish, hell-bent on inhabiting a world that repels him. There is something off in that relationship, something out of place and unnatural. Emilio Bernini describes that colonial space as 'the failed, monstrous, grotesque transplant of the monarchic system of domination into the realm which that very power sees as barbaric'.[3] We are no longer dealing, as in *The Swamp*, with leaving off-screen that which we do not want to see. In *Zama*, everything revolves around a wrongful implantation which cannot be fully eradicated, not even when the story focuses on the real monster terrifying the settlers: 'Vicuña Porto was like the river, for the rains made him bigger. [. . .] Each year – and two had passed already – Vicuña Porto grew: he was a multitudinous man, and the city feared him', Di Benedetto writes in the novel.[4] It is said that he has been executed, but people believe he continues to haunt the region: more than a legend, he is a ghost who never disappears for good. And, when Diego de Zama enrols in the platoon tasked with chasing him, Vicuña Porto travels with them, undercover, mingling with the very men who are trying to hunt him.

This should be the most extreme form of horror: when something feared becomes entrenched in a space considered safe until then and, thus, confrontation becomes unavoidable. In *Zama*, however, that revelation arrives late, because Martel never attempts to exploit the tension created when escape is no longer possible. She is not particularly interested in the thrill it would be to discover Vicuña Porto among the soldiers, but rather tries to install the idea of an absurd quest moving towards disaster, blinded by its own obsession (we could say the template is not *Alien* [Ridley Scott, 1979] but *Aguirre, The Wrath of God* [Werner Herzog, 1972]). Hers is a cruel, merciless gaze. In Silvia Schwarzböck and Hugo Salas's words, as regards *The Swamp*:

> As an aesthetic tool, lack of mercy entails the ability to see characters from their own rationale, to find within the boundaries of their worlds the soothing truth which keeps them locked in. Seen from their own perspective, characters are not worthy of pity, though they do need redemption, because they are not happy.[5]

The double lens of horror make us feel near the characters, but unable to save them; Martel, instead, reveals the mechanism of their behaviour, and that leaves us out. There is no way for us to be in their place.

If horror ultimately remains virtual (as an unfulfilled, thwarted or dispelled threat), it is because, in Martel's films, events fail to happen, or take too long to occur, or lengthen into an endless wait. The camera never abandons its capacity for observation, but it seems to get infected with the perplexed attitude of the characters. That rarefied point of view has an instrumental value: Martel says it is 'useful in a phenomenological sense', because it challenges all certainties. Horror films

> always take you to a place in which you feel safe, only to discover you may not be safe. And not feeling safe is a good way to be a viewer. That is central for someone who makes movies: to be able to express an idea of instability or disturbance with a seemingly calm and peaceful image.[6]

It could be that her movies speak of nothing else: the uneasiness that arises when we notice that the ground we have stepped on is not as firm as it looked. '*Carnival of Souls*', Martel concludes, 'is my school of cinema.'[7]

CINEMA AND THE POST–DICTATORSHIP PERIOD

In Argentina, during the military dictatorship, cinema did not dare show any political conflict, and during the democratic restoration, it did not know how to show those political conflicts. An analysis of filmography during the dictatorship would reveal that any reference to the repressive context appears more as a lapsus than as deliberate off-screen information.[8] That gap is what the cinema of the democratic period attempted to close: the movies of the eighties are movies about/for the seventies. If the period's films, in general, seem to be a decade too late, it is because they appear to be obsessed with making the movies which could not be made during the dictatorship. How to show that which filmmakers could not show or knew not how to show? If during the dictatorship nothing was seen, everything appears obscene now. The directors of the post-dictatorship restoration have inherited a debt and are eager to show: their movies attempt to be retroactive testimonies, chronicles of what happened made up of replacement images. That cinema from the eighties never stopped being the cinema of the seventies: the same directors, the same production methods, the same styles. At most, there was a slight change of topic. Martel's films take distance from the cinema of the eighties and deploy a different visual regime, although not in an openly confrontational manner. Rather, her movies assume the traditional forms of the pact between the viewer and what they see. So it is not about the topics, the narrative models or the grammatical structures. This is not an avant-garde artist: if she uses the classic scheme (with all its mechanisms of hypotheses and expectations), it is because the strategy is to undermine it from within. What we have here is a different way of seeing: a ravaged gaze. From *The Swamp* to *Zama*, the conventional gears have not stopped working, but they have been losing their meaning and have begun moving aimlessly.

The Swamp includes many possible stories, and the film insinuates them all at once, without deciding on one. More than a choral movie (where several plots unfold simultaneously and in parallel), this is an indecisive film, which gets bogged down and lost in the tangle of potential stories. The narrative advances in a zigzag, with alternate steps between what is shown and what is not. Every action, every movement, every gesture is overdetermined by a thickness which lurks off-screen and which persists like a perennial mud underneath the surface of everyday life. The image is only half of what we should see. Behind that seemingly chaotic accumulation of characters and situations, Martel understands the movie as the result of a subtraction. A clipping. As if once the shot is framed, the camera narrows its focus on the action. At all times, there is something left outside. Not eliminated, but there, in the image's outskirts, besieging what we see. Something is always bypassed in the frame or removed from the passage between two shots. In *The Holy Girl/La niña santa* (2004), that unspeakable nature configures the very structure of the shot, because the double dimension containing both normality and deviation takes the centre of the image. We cannot know whether Amalia's reaction to Dr Jano's groping is based on a mystical ecstasy or an erotic overflow. The question no longer is 'what else is there to see?', but 'what should we see?' Spiritual ecstasy or sexual outburst. They both coexist in the same shot. Martel suggests they are superimposed, that one is the flip side of the other. It is not a two-fold image (hinging between what we see and what we do not); rather, the frame itself is two-dimensional. For that reason, what makes the shot unstable is not what was excluded from it: its disturbing nature stems from showing both things at the same time, without favouring one over the other. God or flesh. God and flesh. Can an image be a double entendre?[9]

In *The Headless Woman*, doubt is even more radical. Vero is involved in a car crash. Was it a dog or a child that was run over? She is confused, and in the following days, her circle will make a point of erasing all uncomfortable traces, until the accident itself is called into question. Even though we have seen what we saw, that question which appears absurd at first ends up in the realm of possibility: was there an accident? There is nothing but that terrifying feeling of emptiness that grows inexorably. Now, the act of showing is itself challenged, and the question morphs into whether there is something to see. The image offers nothing but its own perplexity. In *Images of the World and the Inscription of War/Bilder der Welt und Inschrift des Krieges* (1988), Harun Farocki has pointed out that even the sharpest photos can render invisible that which we are unwilling or unable to see: the aerial images captured by the Americans to pinpoint the location of an industrial plant did not reveal that the bordering land was the location of the Auschwitz concentration camp. The photos showed it clearly, but no one paid any attention to it. In *The Headless Woman*, the image is paradoxical because it can show without revealing anything. It is a fallible witness, who does not see clearly or would have preferred to have seen nothing. It does not try to identify something in the landscape, but rather attempts to hide it or disguise it in the folds of the gaze. The world becomes blurry and fades around Vero. According to Sergio Wolf:

> While an accident is what happens when our head is somewhere else, hers has the opposite effect or order: it is not that the accident happens *because* her head is elsewhere; rather, the accident is *what puts* her head elsewhere, or puts her on her head, or leaves her headless, or with a different head. Once the wheels of her car shudder after running over the obstacle, and her body jolts a bit, Vero continues driving for a few metres, but she is somewhere else already, without being there. She is still one, but now she is two.[10]

Vero has run over someone or she has not. That quandary creates tension in the visual regime. However, the possibilities do not entail mere content alternatives, but question the possibility of the image and its right to exist. Having killed someone is not the same as having not. If Vero is guilty, the film has a point; if she is not, her story holds no interest. Why, then, does the movie (and not only the woman's relatives and friends) deploy its plots, but behave as if nothing had happened? Is it possible to tell a story, but reserve the right to state, afterwards, that the goal never was to tell anything? In *The Headless Woman*, conflict is what ends up vanishing as a memory fog, while in *The Holy Girl*, the scandal which unfolds towards the end remains a muted reverberation over the peaceful image of the teenagers in the swimming pool. While it is true that *The Swamp* has a tragic conclusion, in this case we could say that death appears not as a derivation of a narrative development, but as a brutal irruption which paralyses the story and permanently interrupts it. More than telling stories with a clearly defined outline, Martel seems interested in exploring the possibilities of narration: a story of events which could happen, which perhaps happen elsewhere or, even, which stop happening.

Zama introduces a different type of question: 'what must we do to see?' Eager to leave these lands, Don Diego goes to the river and scans the horizon, trying to spot the boat supposed to rescue him, which never arrives. He is restless, because he knows that time passes more slowly in the colonies. However, he will realise too late that Vicuña Porto is travelling incognito with the group of soldiers sent to capture him. Zama is constantly disappointed in his seeing. We are no longer dealing with changes in a habitual world: everything is out of place right from the beginning. The viceroyalty is a deranged universe, and the image appears to adapt to that rarefied atmosphere: the camera does not follow the character, but is as confused as he is. Hiding in the tall grass, the Mbayá natives lasso the explorers like animals. It is impossible to know where the attack will come from: they are ubiquitous, they appear and disappear and rematerialise elsewhere, as if they were able to teleport. They cannot be seen, but they are there. In that human hunt, like in the rest of the film, the camera is taken by surprise. It lacks reaction. It is constantly late. As it fails to anticipate events, it is unable to establish connections, and finds everything unmotivated. Like that strange moment, at the beginning of the movie, when the convict under interrogation jumps off-screen to dash his head against the wall. Does the camera allow him to leave the shot? Or is it unable to follow his movements? The frame fails to contain, because its contents are always overflowing. Or, perhaps, the opposite is at play: the shot tends to be encroached upon by the unbridled forces of that barbaric nature. There we see the termites crawling all over the miserable room where Zama ends up, or the llama which strolls by during his interview with the governor. As time moves on, Don Diego is dragged ever deeper into that barbaric land, as if stepping into a jungle he will not be able to leave.

If Martel manages to rid herself of the debt of post-dictatorship cinema, it is because she does not use movies to answer the question of how to show, but because she understands that it is all about allowing the image to oscillate in an interrogative mode.

THE LOGIC OF CONCEALMENT

The image interrogates itself when it doubts what it shows. In other words, when it shows not because it is fully sure of what it has seen, but in order to find out what it should see. That uncertainty should lead to suspense, and suspense always works in two times. It implies a wait whose resolution fails to come, and, in that lengthened time, the hypothetical becomes certainty (even if it stems from an imaginary conclusion). In the passage from one mode to the other lies the upsetting: if there is tension in that wait, it is because it enables the drive to anticipate what may happen, so what is feared becomes a concrete entity. Hypotheses move faster than facts, and it is anxiety itself which completes the outline of the horror.

However, in Martel's films, we deal with a deceptive form of suspense, because the resolution fizzles out or gets bogged down or happens in a deviated fashion.[11] In *The Holy Girl*, the two-fold erotic-mystical interpretation created by the episode with Dr Jano drifts off towards a proliferation of misunderstandings, which causes the initial conflict to become more and more entangled, like

Figure 14.2 *The Holy Girl.* © Lita Stantic Producciones

in a vaudeville act: impossible to anticipate, because anything can happen. In *The Swamp*, everyone acts as if they were predestined, but it is their inability to escape the swamp they are in that consecrates the repetition. That is what a vicious circle is: what will happen has already happened. Mecha dreads becoming her mother, even though nothing forces her down that path. Fate is nothing other than causing what we fear to happen by means of adjusting our behaviour to our belief. Like a self-fulfilling prophecy, the woman will end up in her room, never leaving her bed. That which will happen in the future is already happening.

In *Zama*, there is no suspense. Rather, there is a deconstruction of suspense. We are left with those temporalities which are mixed, but no longer in tension. Like pure chaos. Or a whim. Ms Piñares de Luenga recounts how her liquor cups were packed for the journey by ship:

> They were wrapped in documents with news from Buenos Aires. And, curiously, in that fleet, the documents we received were older than the ones wrapping my cups . . . My cups brought fresher news than the documents they handed out here. Isn't it charming and sad?

Suddenly, we understand that reality chases the forms of discourse and that events no longer need to adhere to a causal structure. Rita complains because officer Bermúdez has attacked her: 'You have avenged me, Diego, and now that villain is dead.' But Zama admits, 'No, I have not killed.' 'Then you must avenge me', comes her reply. The same action moves indistinctly between past, present and future. It is like a dialogue of the deaf; but that is because the events unfold as if they belonged to parallel universes. What should happen later could take place earlier. Facts need not abide by an orderly chronology. They can happen and, then, not have happened. In the beginning, Vicuña Porto has been executed already; later on, the new governor will say they have just executed him and even display his ears like a brand-new trophy; however, that does not keep a third governor from organising a party to hunt him down. In his way, Vicuña Porto is one of the living dead. And that is why he cannot be killed. They say he is dead ('killed a thousand times'), but they all fear him because he continues to attack their homes.

That is what happens with zombies: they are inhabitants of two times. They are gone, but still there. And that is what happens to Vero, in *The Headless Woman*. After the accident, she suffers a *confusional syndrome*: she is disoriented and unable to think clearly, but keeps some reflexes which enable her to go on as if nothing had happened. The woman who resumes her everyday activities is a zombie woman. She takes no part in gatherings, but only wanders about. She barely speaks. She does not need to, as the others ask her questions and answer them for her. She soon realises it could all continue like this. Vero does not need to be conscious, have a will, or manifest emotions or desires while being guided around by those with her best interests at heart. According to Martel, 'There is a dissolution of responsibility which, for me, is the great invention of social classes: a network in which your individual responsibility is watered down.'[12] The accident is what should not have happened, and, in fact, that circle of protective friends and relatives attempts to erase all traces of it: the highway episode is expelled from memory. It disappears. It is erased. It has not happened. Or, rather, class mnemotechnics are used selectively to keep the positive and exclude the uncomfortable. The accident is an excess. It is unnecessary. That is why it stops existing. No body, no tracks, no evidence. And no traces in Vero's memory either.[13]

As the film progresses, Martel insists on using long focal length lenses to achieve images with little depth of field, where Vero's face stands out and isolates itself from an invariably blurry background. The space around her becomes nebulous, uncertain, vague. That drive which dominates the image (and not only the character) to escape the problem and avoid it implies a reformulation of the modes of realism. Bazinian realism trusted in what the world can reveal about itself when observed with perseverance. The critic's metaphor is quite graphic: 'Reality confesses its meaning like a suspect under the police chief's relentless interrogation.'[14] In *The Headless Woman*, that Bazinian realism adopts a radically different meaning: it is about observing a situation hard enough to, in the end, reveal nothing. The camera is not looking for a confession. Quite the opposite, it tries to silence, hide, disguise. We could speak, then, of a concealing realism. To build on André Bazin's metaphor: rather than pressuring reality into confessing its secret, it is all about prowling around it until it forgets every clue.

The camera acts like a false witness: it tries hard to construct an artificial version of reality, an alibi to dispel every suspicion. Vero confesses to her husband, 'I killed someone on the road', but he − who was not present at the time of the accident − corrects her with a determination that leaves no room for doubts: 'You didn't kill anyone. You got scared. It was a dog.' Just like Marcos, the camera states convincingly, but does not quite manage to show. That is it: Vero probably did not kill anyone. She must have run over a dog. And when she passes with her cousin along the canal road, where the firemen are trying to pull out the body of a person or a calf which is plugging the drain, the camera will remain behind them, as if trying to hide or in fear of being discovered. What does the image show? Not much. In any case, what we can see covers up what we should see: the space outside, where the firemen work to recover the corpse, is but an insinuation in the background of a frame taken up almost completely by Vero's profile draped in shadows.

They all look very articulate when trying to convince her that nothing has happened. However, just in case, someone makes some reassuring calls, someone takes advantage of a trip to Tucumán to mend the dents in the car, someone fetches the X-rays from the hospital, and someone else erases the information on her hotel stay. Vero will not have been in the hotel and will have never gone to the hospital. She will not have crashed. And, of course, she will have never run over anyone. That peaceful and sinister *omertà* of the provincial middle class shows the political vibration of Martel's cinema. What is not said, what is hushed, what is silenced is forgotten and completely erased. And then, everyone is convinced that they are not looking away. Rather, there was nothing to see there in the first place.[15]

THE LESSON FROM HORROR CINEMA

Just like the photos retouched by Stalinists to delete dissidents as if they had never been there, the narrative the family builds around Vero disproves the *verismo* of the image: that which the camera recorded is no longer there and was never there. Constant repetition of a given version of reality ends up instilling that memory, and − just like rust corrodes metal − what the woman might have seen or sensed loses materiality until it disappears completely.

Collusion, concealment, silence, negation, oblivion. It may be tempting to draw parallels between those protocols for disappearance and the sinister crimes of the military dictatorship. However, Martel is never allegorical. The child or the dog Vero has run over is not a case of forced disappearance, and her family does not act like a paramilitary group. That point-for-point analogy, too evident, would appear to be too shallow as well. If there is an inflection of the image colonised by a dimension of the sinister which comes from the dictatorship, it is a different type of reference, one installed at a deeper level of the collective unconscious and less tangible, though omnipresent. It is like an origin marking. The military dictatorship remains totally off-camera, but its consequences persist and go beyond its crimes.

It is a logic which permeates images and is always present, even in the case of events which ignore it or think it has been forgotten. There is a matrix of a horror which is always off-screen but which, precisely due to this fact, is persistent and unavoidable. As Georges Didi-Huberman might point out, no image *says* that. However, since the seventies, all images *speak about* that.[16] Martel is part of a generation which had not yet entered adolescence when the 1976 coup erupted, and which did not take part in the political violence which permeated that decade. Her perception is more linked to the effects the dictatorship had on society: like a social disposition which has, since then, overdetermined behaviours, relationships and bonds.

The universe of these movies is inhabited by a middle class which, subdued by repression, 'learnt to speak not of what it knew'. Martel states:

> I think that the most terrible part of the dictatorship is not the crimes and the murders – I don't mean to say those things aren't terrible – but society's collusion, which is also what affects us all, because it is still at work. The neoliberal policies of the nineties could not have been applied if the citizens' capacity for resistance had not been disabled. And, to do that, you need to bring down intermediate organisations. You need violence, death and fear. How else could you enact a labour flexibilisation law in a context with unions and activists? The plan of the dictatorship came to fruition in the nineties. Before, it was an anecdote of death, but the master plan was completed twenty years after.[17]

That is, both things are connected by a curved line. The neoliberalism of the 1990s was the necessary consequence of the military government. The finishing touch of the dictatorship's work. Its 'master plan', according to Martel.

In this sense, *The Headless Woman* is not a film about the dictatorship, but about what it revealed about Argentine society. Martel identifies that political logic of images. As if there was a shared *habitus* (following Pierre Bourdieu) which defined a socially determined way of looking, which imposed itself naturally as an undisputed opinion.[18] In that way of looking, there are visible things and other things which are invisibilised until they disappear. Its classist perspective, its discriminatory drive, and its disdainful indifference hinge on that selectivity. That is the tragic fate of the child Vero might have run over, but also what happens, in various ways, with the employees, the servants, the *collas*, the mulattos and the natives in all her films. They are the others: the subalterns. They work at their houses, live with their families, and are witnesses to their privacy. Together, but not mixed: everything they share only drives them further apart.

The short feature *Leagues/Leguas* (2015) deals precisely with an issue of boundaries. A group of peasant children suffer the harassment of a landowner who has usurped lands belonging to the Calchaquí Diaguita community. It is a problem of language: how are the original leagues converted into the currently used hectares? The difference leads to 3,000 hectares in conflict. In *New Argirópolis/Nueva Argirópolis* (2010), a group of natives is detained by the police when attempting to cross the river on a raft made of plastic bottles. They speak a language which their captors cannot decode and for which the film provides no subtitles. Deborah Martin refers to the 'contemporary water policy' (during the 1990s, 60 per cent of the water capital fell under private management) and to the relevance 'the unequal access to this resource' as a 'sign of social power' has in Martel's cinema.[19] Lastly, conflicts always pit the owners against the dispossessed. For that reason, in the movie, an activist establishes the association between *indigenous* and *indigent*. She says, 'Do not be afraid to move. We are invisible.' Sarmiento posited Argirópolis as the 'capital of the confederate states of the Río de la Plata' and as a strategy to overcome American barbaric nature; in Martel's new Argirópolis, conversely, indigenous communities – dispossessed of their land – resist and perhaps conspire to 'found a space that works as a new social order'.[20] These communities of 'others' have been criminalised, looked down on or stereotyped: they have always been invisibilised by the discriminatory gaze of the owners.

Until *Zama*, at least, Martel's films had focused on a self-contained universe: *The Swamp*, *The Holy Girl* and *The Headless Woman* are movies about families. About families from a specific class. About families from a specific class in a specific provincial environment. This set of films represents a visual sociolect so accurate and specific that one wonders how much of it was understood outside of Argentina. Even though there are no explicit references, these movies are the best portrayals of the decade under President Carlos Menem and its scars. *Zama* is not a movie about families (in any case, it is about the absence of families, because Don Diego asks to be relocated to be closer to his wife and children). But even here, that socially determined gaze which characterised the previous films persists with slight alterations, derived from a time and a place which are not the usual ones. In this sense, a common thread runs through all the movies.[21] The key lies, perhaps, in the visual regime Martel constructs and the type of bond the camera establishes with the characters. That can be seen clearly both in *The Headless Woman* and in *Zama*: the camera is contaminated by Vero's bewilderment and becomes as confused as Don

Diego. Martel stages a disoriented realism, an obfuscated realism: a realism with its head in the clouds. It does not contrast the character's subjectivity and the objectivity of facts. It is not about identifying two differentiated visual regimes, but rather underscores their cross-contamination.

The former *corregidor* is waiting for a transfer which will never arrive: as time goes on, that possibility grows less and less likely, and everything gets worse. In the end, he no longer knows why he is there, why he does what he does, or what he is waiting for. As if afflicted by that type of aphasia that leaves the patient with words devoid of meaning, images here show but no longer remember what should be seen. If a shot should point out what it sees, in *Zama* that gaze has lost the sense of deixis. Is this a free indirect style, as proposed by Pier Paolo Pasolini?[22] Perhaps. But Pasolini was positing a general grammar, while Martel is attempting to channel a specific poetics. Her movies attempt to depict a localised and non-transferable way of seeing. It is a negligent realism. And just as Vero resists stepping out of her car and drives away without helping her victim, the camera remains inside, watching as if it would rather be elsewhere. Rather than lying, its dishonesty is revealed by its attempt to avoid all direct confrontation with what is happening. The question posited by the movie is: how do we look while escaping? It is about showing while moving away: a last glimpse before leaving something definitively behind. The screen no longer is a window into a world, but rather shows things like a rear-view mirror: when reflecting them, it keeps them at a distance.

How can an image deny what it shows? Martel's films bring forth a biased gaze. The rationale of framing assumes a regime of visual euphemism which, though it shows facts, attempts not to refer to them, or refers to them from a class perspective. However, all perspectives have a blind spot, and conversely, that which happens off-screen makes evident that which the shot refuses to see. That is Martel's 'instrumental phenomenology'. Just as in the horror genre that which is repressed returns in the form of a threat, these movies show a full social scheme which is forced to confront what it fears the most: the alterity that it cannot stand to look at, and that it has tried to annihilate with its gaze.

Translated by Juan Ignacio García Fahler

NOTES

1. Carroll, N. (1990), *The Philosophy of Horror or Paradoxes of the Heart*, London: Routledge, p. 16.
2. Though the idea is not to establish a theory based on this short list, there is a similar pattern. They are stories which reveal the dark side of individuals. Characters are two subjects at once: they are affected by a double entity which is always the product of a metamorphosis. Notably, the short feature Martel filmed as a commission for the apparel

brand Miu Miu is called *Muta* (2011). There, a group of mysterious, faceless women wander about a lonesome vessel, with a disturbing attitude and stylised movements, as if they were the children of Nosferatu in his ghost ship.

3. Bernini, E. (2017), 'El hundimiento. A propósito de *Zama*, de Lucrecia Martel', *Kilómetro III*, 14–15, p. 226.

4. Di Benedetto, A. (1984), *Zama*, Buenos Aires: Alianza, p. 195.

5. Schwarzböck, S. and H. Salas (2001), 'El verano de nuestro descontento. Género y violencia en *La ciénaga*', *El amante*, 108, p. 11.

6. Harvey, S. (2017), 'Finding the "One Miserable Tiny Spark" that Experimental Legend Lucrecia Martel Believes All Creativity Relies On', *No Film School*, 10 October 2017, <https://nofilmschool.com/2017/10/stealing-away-commonplace-experimental-legend-lucrecia-martel> (last accessed 29 April 2021). On the denaturalisation of perception as the central trait of horror films, see Bettendorff, P. and A. Pérez Rial (2014), 'Artilugios de pensamiento: Entrevista a Lucrecia Martel', in P. Bettendorff and A. Pérez Rial (eds), *Tránsitos de la mirada: Mujeres que hacen cine*, Buenos Aires: Libraria, pp. 179–96.

7. Ibid.

8. On this subject, see Wolf, S. (1994), 'El cine del *Proceso*. Estética de la muerte', in S. Wolf (ed.), *Cine argentino: La otra historia*, Buenos Aires: Letra buena, pp. 265–79.

9. About the counterpoint (even in a musical sense) between the sensual and the intangible in *The Holy Girl*, see Kratje, J. (2019), 'Otras muchas voces. Géneros perturbados en Lucrecia Martel', in *Al margen del tiempo: Deseos, ritmos y atmósferas en el cine argentino*, Buenos Aires: Eudeba, pp. 149–70.

10. Wolf, S. (2008), 'Que aparezca un accidente', in M. Panozzo (ed.), *La propia voz: El cine sonoro de Lucrecia Martel*, Gijón: Gijón International Film Festival, p. 42.

11. See Gordon, R. (2017), 'La inacción como acción. La pausa en Diego Meret y Lucrecia Martel', in *Narrativas de la suspensión: Una mirada contemporánea desde la literatura y el cine argentinos*, Buenos Aires: Libraria, pp. 167–226. There, this type of deceptive suspense is described as a 'counter-suspense procedure'.

12. Panozzo, M. (2008), 'La mujer que siempre estuvo ahí (entrevista con Lucrecia Martel)', in Panozzo (ed.), *La propia voz*, p. 17.

13. As regards oblivion in Martel's film, see Christofoletti Barrenha, N. (2012), '*La mujer sin cabeza* (Lucrecia Martel, 2008) y el mecanismo del olvido en el pasado y el presente', *Revista Comunicación*, 10: 1, pp. 643–52, <http://www.revistacomunicacion.org/pdf/n10/mesa4/050.La_mujer_sin_cabeza_(Lucrecia_Martel_2008)_y_el%20mecanismo_del_olvido_en_el_pasado_y_el_presente.pdf> (last accessed 29 April 2021).

14. Bazin, A. (1990), 'La evolución del lenguaje cinematográfico', in *¿Qué es el cine?*, Madrid: Rialp, p. 85.

15. I take these ideas about the erasing power of images from Oubiña, D. (2014), 'Un realismo negligente (El cine de Lucrecia Martel)', in Bettendorff and Pérez Rial (eds), *Tránsitos de la mirada*, pp. 69–82.

16. I reformulate this idea based on Didi-Huberman, G. (2004), *Imágenes pese a todo: Memoria visual del Holocausto*, Barcelona: Paidós.

17. D'Espósito, L. (2008), 'Los noventa son el plan maestro de la dictadura. Entrevista con Lucrecia Martel', *Crítica de la Argentina*, 20 August 2008, <http://criticadigital.com/index.php?secc=nota&nid=9423> (last accessed 29 April 2021). See also Sosa, C. (2014), 'Undoing the Cult of the Victim: *Los rubios*, *M* and *La mujer sin cabeza*', in *Queering Acts of Mourning in the Aftermath of Argentina's Dictatorship*, Woodbridge: Tamesis, pp. 51–80.

18. According to a possible definition, *habitus* are 'structured structures predisposed to work as structuring structures, as principles which generate and organise practices and representations'. Bourdieu, P. (1991), *El sentido práctico*, Madrid: Taurus, p. 92.

19. Martin, D. (2016), 'Lucrecia Martel's *Nueva Argirópolis*: Rivers, Rumours and Resistance', *Journal of Latin American Cultural Studies*, 25: 3, pp. 449–65 (p. 454).

20. In Sarmiento's geographical imagination, 'all cartography is politics'; in Martel's too, though of the opposite sign. See Amante, A. (2007), 'El letrado y el poder', prologue to D. F. Sarmiento, *Argirópolis*, Buenos Aires: Losada, pp. 9–31 (p. 22).

21. In *Chocobar*, the film Martel is currently working on, that dimension would be explicitly thematised. It is no longer a fiction, but a documentary about the murder of an indigenous man from a Chuscha community in 2009. In the teaser trailer prepared by the Locarno Festival, the filmmaker explains, 'What happened throughout history to make that possible? I cannot invoke anything on behalf of the community, because the community is an experience totally alien to me. [The documentary] is about how the impossibility to see the other is constructed [. . .] trying to break down the structures with which white thought justifies its violence and exerts its power.' Locarno Film Festival (2020), 'The Films after Tomorrow: *Chocobar*', <https://www.locarnofestival.ch/LFF/locarno-2020/program-2020/the-films-after-tomorrow/chocobar.html> (last accessed 29 April 2021).

22. As regards the free indirect style, see Pasolini, P. (2005), 'El cine de poesía', in *Empirismo herético*, Córdoba: Brujas, pp. 233–60. As regards the form of subjectivity in Martel's work, see Losada, M. (2020), 'Lucrecia Martel's *La mujer sin cabeza*: Cinematic Free Indirect Discourse, Noise-Scape and the Distraction of the Middle-Class', *Romance Notes*, 50: 3, pp. 307–13.

CHAPTER 15

The Conquest of the Uncomfortable: An Interview with Lucrecia Martel

Natalia Christofoletti Barrenha, Julia Kratje and Paul R. Merchant

On 20 March 2021, Natalia Christofoletti Barrenha (in Hastings, UK), Julia Kratje (in Buenos Aires, Argentina) and Paul R. Merchant (in Bristol, UK) spoke with Lucrecia Martel (in Salta, Argentina) about her career, some underexplored connections between her films, and her plans for the future.

Julia Kratje: In many interviews, you have mentioned that what lies off-camera, as regards framing and staging, is a key aspect of the composition of the *mise-en-scène*, which besieges, disturbs, smothers and jolts both characters and viewers. You have also spoken extensively about an environment of strangeness permeating all your work, which implies challenging the real along the lines of horror cinema or science fiction. But the sense of humour or the traits which link the films with a certain air of comedy have not been considered as closely by the audience or by the critics.

Lucrecia Martel: I have some friends who laugh a lot when they watch my movies; but, well . . . that's probably because these are very close friends, with whom I share codes, certain expressions, little things: it's not about the organisation of comedy as a genre, but about details which disrupt the characters' solemnity. Many of those touches of humour are in the dialogues, but also in the scenes' organisation in visual terms and in terms of sound. As these movies are not strident in auditory terms or in acting terms, it's hard to understand that I should say that there is humour in there. However, humour is something I care very much about, not because I want movies to have humour in them, but because the things that irk me the most, what I find most terrible, what I don't like, are the things which are ridiculous because it is unbelievable that they still work. To oppose power with solemnity, or thinking that power is solemn, is a lost cause. However, if the way in which power seems to uphold itself appears ridiculous, understanding it and finding humour in it becomes easier. It's something that happens naturally to me. However, given what the films are like, given their format and the way they are presented, it can be hard, sometimes, to perceive humour. Even as regards the critics, I often think they ask me questions or go to the cinema with such a degree of seriousness that those tiny details, which fail to make you laugh out loud, disappear. I also think that this humour has a strong basis in Spanish, in the use of regional expressions. I don't intend for that to work universally, for everyone to understand it. Some things are lost, and that is fine. New times will come, new people, and some things will be lost, and some will be gained. I think that a desperate quest for communication, for everyone to realise everything one does, is silly. When I read a book or I watch a movie in a different language, I can feel that inevitable loss, even if they are translated. And that is fine, because that wholeness, that pretence of universality, that desire for everyone to understand even the tiniest details, is a stupid goal. Universality is what the human experience needs the least. Our species itself connects in so many needs and preferences that, to me, aiming for universality, on top of everything else, would be too pretentious. In my workshops with students, or when I help young directors, I stress that they should make their movies for their neighbours. You must not think about anything physically far from you, because then you start betraying the narrative in exchange for things which can supposedly be understood by all, based on an assumption of who that 'all' may be. With your neighbours, instead, you have a relationship, you know what jokes you can make. You must write for your neighbours, shoot for your neighbours, and that is how you get everyone to understand. Of course, some things will be lost, because there is no perfect communication. I trust that if something is not understood now, it will surely be understood later on, or perhaps never. For me, the obsession with perfection in effects, in results, with that idea of universality, is a calamity.

Natalia Christofoletti Barrenha: How do musical experiences, such as those with Juana Molina in *Fish/Pescados* (2010), Björk's New York show, and Julieta Laso's video clip *Ghosts/Fantasmas* (2018), fit against the background of your filmmaking career?

Lucrecia: Everything I did with music was rather fortuitous. Juana and I were friends. I had some footage I had shot in Korea, at a Buddhist temple, and I was invited to direct a short feature, so we got together one afternoon and made it. In the case of Juli [Julieta Laso], we shot at home, and, due to our relationship, I am surrounded by the music. As regards Björk, I did not see it as a challenge. It was lovely to meet her and work with her, using what was available and with very little time. Music doesn't work as a starting point to think for me. It's not that I don't like it. I just don't think my curiosity lies there.

Julia: How did you choose the songs for the films?

Lucrecia: For every movie, I chose songs I used to hear as a girl on the radio, or which my uncle sang with his guitar. There is no song I've chosen that I don't have a temporal relationship with. My relationship with music is that of someone who grew up in Salta: 'Cara de gitana', like the rest of the songs, was a huge hit. The exception is *Zama* (2017), in which the idea was to use something Latin American and rather pretentious, and at the same time related to the time in which the book was written. I feel *Zama* has a stronger connection with the 1950s than with the eighteenth century. While looking for *guaranias*, I listened to Los Indios Tabajaras, who came up with a story about a guitar appearing in the jungle, something a tourist had left behind . . . I'm almost certain that that didn't happen, and that it was a mythical invention. And, even if the viewer lacks the specific connection with a temporality and a region, I think the songs work.

Julia: Perhaps they work because those few but significant songs envelop the viewer in the films' atmosphere: they create immersion in the plot and the world inhabited by the characters.

Lucrecia: Many directors have told me that, in Hollywood, music is chosen for economic reasons. For instance, they have prior arrangements with the distributors of this record or that composer. In those cases, the music is defined before the movie and based on the agreements with labels. In my case, I use music very carefully: music has such a complex organisation in itself that you have to pay the utmost attention. Music injects a large volume of information into the scene. I think that some directors ruin amazing scenes by using music that turns them into posters.

Paul R. Merchant: Let's move on from music to a different type of sound: the voices of certain groups and secondary characters, like indigenous people and domestic workers, who are very prominent in your movies and who sometimes manage to wield power, even if they don't speak very much. We would like to know how that dynamic relates to *Chocobar*, the movie you've been working on in recent months.

Lucrecia: In our history, that is, Argentine history, and obviously in the history of other countries, there is an idea which has worked amazingly well: the idea of submission. Submission is an invention, just as peace is an invention. When someone says, for instance, that 'the world is at peace', I always wonder which country they speak of. Because all countries have poor neighbourhoods, marked by the agony of work (looking for work, not finding any, having to find

some way to survive), full of the kind of businesses which are easy to establish in the places the state has forgotten, and which become a shelter for all
types of dangerous trafficking, and are a source of anguish for the neighbourhoods themselves. There is no peace there. Peace exists for those who can live
at peace. In this sense, believing in submission is believing that you can break
a human being's will. And I think that's impossible, even in Guantánamo, or
under torture. There could be times, perhaps years, in which a woman appears
to be a slave to or subdued by violence, but even that submission, like almost
everything else in the world, is not perfect, in spite of all the Argentine history
and universal history textbooks which speak of conquerors who came, established themselves, and subjugated the people. I understood this for good while
watching a film by Visconti, *The Job/Il lavoro*, the short feature with Romy
Schneider from *Boccaccio '70* (1962). According to my theory, if a gay guy like
Visconti — who back then, and on account of the family he belonged to, would
hide his desire — had a relationship with an employee or someone who worked
in his house, something was challenged. And that becomes evident in that
movie: the servants enact certain gestures which are the gestures of the people
in the street, living their lives, smoking and chatting. That led me to think that
Visconti saw the people who worked around him as sexual objects. One of the
things that submission destroys is the possibility for the other to be a desirable
person: not a rape object, which is something different — an abuse of power —
but someone who can desire and be desired. On that ground, another instance
of the human is established.

In Latin America, when we speak of indigenous people we evoke an image
full of solemnity: the representation of the Indians seems carved out of stone,
based on an idea which has more to do with the Catholic religion than with
our knowledge of their cultures. One of the ideas rooted in Argentine history,
besides submission as a block which falls onto people, is the lack of humour.
Humour makes it possible for any culture to look at itself from a distance and
see its own ridiculous nature, which opens up an instant of liberation and
transformation. That is when you're able to say, 'We're gonna have to change
this, guys. If we're laughing, it means something doesn't work.' Humour is
an aspect of self-criticism and self-awareness. And that is something that
was eradicated from our vision of the indigenous world. Humour is a sign of
too much self-awareness. In this country, I'm strongly against the idea that
an indigenous person has no desire of their own, no humour, facing no dis-
grace, clinging to their customs: a person who is rendered submissive by their
own culture, without yearning for transformation. We legitimise those who
resemble what we want them to be. In northern Argentina, there is an appall-
ing blindness regarding what an indigenous community is, regarding what
being an indigenous person entails today: this is something very prominent
in *Chocobar*.

In the films we grew up with, a submissive person is submissive in all respects: their gaze, their speech. The black man is portrayed as an imbecile of sorts, submissive to his master's will, or the slave appears as someone who is happy because her young mistress fell in love. These are our culture's attempts to, once again, create in the other, whom we make work for us, a certain homogeneity. I'm about to shoot a short feature which has something to do with that; though − in fact − it's part of all my movies. There is no such thing as submission: it's a way of looking at the other. If you break away from that, you realise that no one, in his or her time of silence, of intimacy, is unable to have some kind of thought about him or herself. Even the woman who is beaten by her husband has moments of thought about herself, not as an object, not as a worthless thing, but as a person who exists. And then, those devices we use to teach how not to see immediately collapse through small details. You don't need to read a philosophical theory to understand that. You only need to look around. And if you're unable to see it by looking around, then you have that short feature by Visconti. The servants have a life which matters much more to them than preparing coffee, fetching slippers, and being subservient to their master. They have children, they have problems, they have wives, they have a house, they have a neighbourhood, they have neighbours, they have parties they want to go to: things much more important to them than work.

Julia: In that sense, the sequences at the beginning of *Zama* speak volumes. The protagonist spies from a distance on the women laughing and chatting in the mud. He is discovered. Luciana Piñares de Luenga, who is there, commands Malemba to go see who the voyeur is. Zama slaps her, and Malemba glares at him. I'd like to ask how you think about the distribution of relationships of power between characters. Affectivity between women is very prominent in all your films, and would appear to be distinguished from the treatment received by men, who carry their masculinity as a burden, who are self-centred, vulnerable, made fun of, slighted.

Lucrecia: A journalist in Brazil told me something which is very true: Malemba, who is mute, even without speaking manages to drive into Zama the most painful realisation for him at the time, that Luciana Piñares de Luenga has other lovers. That is something she plotted. Besides, in all scenes with enslaved and black people, I always attempted to include a sign of non-submission. *Zama* as a whole is permeated with a certain weariness of the colonial administration. Here, in the north, it is quite common to use the word *taimado* to suggest that someone may betray you or is always plotting against you. That word was used to refer to those Indians who could speak Spanish and manipulated things a bit, because they translated to their benefit into one language and the other, steering situations with their bilingual knowledge. Nowadays, the expression no longer refers to that, but to someone who makes you believe certain things while plotting to do something else which will not work in your favour. In other words, *taimado* is someone who does not accept submission. When a group shows up saying, 'We're Indians' or 'We are a community', coming from a settlement in the hills which was not organised as a community until then, everyone throws a fit and calls them 'phony Indians', because they dispel that white fantasy about submission. I recently wrote a letter replying to someone who wrote about the Calchaquíes Valleys trying to paint a picture of harmony, order and peace, which couldn't be further from the truth:[1] there are clashes over land all over Argentina. There is no harmony outside of the fantasy of those of us who sit comfortably at home with a full belly. That's why it was important to me for *Zama*, which is a white-centric story, not to include that effective trait of submission which appears when the other, that other, is portrayed. And, as regards women, I have an anecdote from when the film was played in a cinema in Rio de Janeiro: when Zama slaps Malemba, I heard outraged shouts. Even though I felt I was not being disrespectful to anyone, I could understand how fed up they were as regards the portrayal of black people in Brazil. I felt disaster looming. However, afterwards, during the Q&A, that scene was not discussed. Or, rather, that slap was redefined throughout the movie. Something, marginally, was achieved: there were many activists there, and, after the movie, there was no anger surrounding that portrayal.

This is something that has happened with women (white, black, of any colour) throughout the history of cinema. If you take movies produced between the 1930s and the 1960s and show them to an alien (let's assume there is no one left after the pandemic), the alien will say this: 'It would appear there was a species here in which the females were stupid, there were some useless guys, who were black, and there were no Indians.'

Natalia: You spoke of reactions, expectations and changes in the audience during a movie. In this sense, how do those sensations work in your case, from one movie to the next, in the relation between one movie and another, after having built a trajectory, a filmography? February 2021 marked the twentieth anniversary of the premiere of *The Swamp/La ciénaga* (2001) in Berlin. We would like to know what you feel looking back at your own career.

Lucrecia: To be honest, I feel nothing. I only think about how time flies. That's my only reflection: how time flies! Twenty years already! I have no ambition of remaining interesting, or for my movies to remain interesting, if people watch them again. I lack that ambition because that would be asking too much of human existence. Actually, I may have the opposite ambition, that of ultimately disappearing. However, there is something about the path taken by the films which is definitely moving, which I see when boys or girls tell me that they watched my films and decided they wanted to make movies (here, in Salta, that happens a lot). I don't know if being young and wanting to make movies is such a great idea, but at least someone felt motivated to go down this road I took or that they saw I was taking. That is very moving. And, looking back, I started in the same year as directors such as Alejandro González Iñárritu and Guillermo del Toro, among others I met when they were just starting, and in that sense I'm very happy with the path I've chosen, which enabled me to grow as a person. After twenty years, I find myself in the same place of not wanting to feel comfortable. I like movies which put me in a place of discomfort, which lead me to think about my situation, about my position in this country, in the world. That is, I never achieved, through cinema, a position of comfort. For me, cinema is for thinking, for feeling curious: not for comfort. After twenty years, I didn't arrive at a place of comfort: I didn't look for it and I didn't achieve it. I like that. Every time I make a movie, I get as restless as I did with the first one, because there is a lot of time between one movie and the next. I don't see myself as a professional, I don't see my life having a fundamental connection to cinema, but rather a connection to thinking, to expressing an opinion, among other things. So I find it moving, even though I'm not paying attention to the anniversary itself − I found out twenty years had passed since *The Swamp* in a newspaper article. I don't have the idea of having built a career. I don't see it that way because I didn't live cinema that way, but rather randomly. I'm grateful for having been able to do what I did, but I never had and I don't have that idea of a career. I have never felt and I don't feel now that I embrace cinema. I notice that when I see other directors who really love cinema and know a lot about cinema. I don't feel that crazy love, that cinephilia. I don't think cinema has embraced me, either.

Paul: You said you didn't know whether aspiring to make movies nowadays was such a great idea. How do you see the future of cinema?

Lucrecia: For a time, I don't think there will be cinema, because we don't know how this pandemic will end and how the theatres will reopen. Add to that the phenomenon of series, which I find more and more empty. I'm very close to feeling completely left out, because I don't like them. I don't watch them. They are not a format I'm interested in. If all audiovisual narrative is going that way, then I don't know what I'll do. For instance, right now, I have offers related to two books I'm very interested in. But they are dead set on one of them being a series, and I don't know if I'll be able to do it. I'm very sorry that that format makes you have to step down, I'm sorry that that format is, to such a degree, the only thing that can be done. Let's assume I have to do it or that I finally agree to do it: I don't know how I'll deal with that. I'll have to make a huge change in my life, at least to accept one of those projects, or I will try to do it in the format I believe it should have. It's a terrible stalemate. Most of my students, or people who are filming already, are offered that. Or, rather, that is the only way now, because it is a way which is economically clear. It is not that the other way does not exist, but it isn't clear economically. There are very few places left which fund movies. And it's not that I think, 'Oh, it's such a pity that we no longer make movies, which are so important to humanity', or rather, that series suck. No! I simply think that I don't find them interesting. I don't watch series, and it is not a whim, like the people who protested against the disappearance of celluloid, claiming that 'celluloid is cinema'. I never cared about celluloid. However, to be honest, I don't know how to go about the narrative format of series. No doubt there is a generation of people who will know what to do with that format which I find so disappointing. I see it so clearly as a business. You may ask why there were no longer or shorter movies, and that had to do with the business aspect as well. However, in those two hours, I feel that I can organise myself in narrative terms, something I can't do in half an hour or forty minutes. In that timeframe, the script, the plot, become extremely fundamental. As regards what I like about audiovisual narrative, I see it as a serious issue that a format forces you into a plot so resoundingly. So, I could very well take a pass on this project until the opportunity to make movies returns. There will always be human beings who need to communicate with others or exchange experiences; and the audiovisual, however it manifests itself (in film or digital media, with or without music, with or without sound, etc.), will always be an interesting matter for expression. Then, there is the world of business, which is where these things become plausible. Imagine the discussions when movies start to appear starring James Dean or Marilyn Monroe, simply because someone bought the digital reconstruction rights. It will be a long and winding road.

Paul: The issue of what to call it will be interesting. Whether it is cinema or something else . . .

Lucrecia: It won't matter . . . We'll change its name, but the issue will be which human beings are trying to exchange ideas, and with whom. The other day I was asked to participate in a manifesto in defence of cinema. And I told them that, honestly, I couldn't. I cannot take part in that struggle, because it isn't mine.

Julia: The world of series, with such guided narratives, offers an experience of time that is very different from what we see and experience in your movies. Both in short films and feature films, the immersion in sound and time could, perhaps, be more closely linked to the experience of a book.

Lucrecia: Mind you, I think these series are amazingly crafted. There are very talented people involved. They are not for me, that's all. Besides, I do think that someone will make something incredible in that world. I don't think it has happened yet. But I believe all people and all generations ultimately find ways to express themselves in the available commercial formats. Perhaps I'm already out of that generation. I don't feel drawn to the idea of making series or watching them. Particularly because I think it is good that things should come to an end. And, with series, that is not the feeling you get: there may be many episodes and new seasons. Something else is at work. I like things that end clearly, where characters do not reappear leading other lives.

Julia: When writing the scripts for your movies, you worked with other screenwriters at times. How is that detailed and meticulous writing born, for instance, as regards the interwoven dialogue lines?

Lucrecia: When your method, your narrative device, is not based on plot but on upholding the tension in every scene, if you want the viewer not to chase the plot, you are forced to pay attention to details like those. It is not that I did away with plot, but it is never the most important thing for me. I think no one (at least among the people who enjoy my movies) cares about what the film is about. They like the experience of watching the movie, not what the movie is about. As regards what making a movie means, 'what the movie is about' is something very superficial, which enables you to organise time and a series of things, but 'what the movie is about' lies in the experience of the film. It isn't something you can include in the synopsis, or a logline . . . For me, all of that represents the most superficial aspects of cinema. Let's take Visconti's short film, for instance. What is it about? I honestly don't remember. But what that short film taught me, I will keep forever. It pointed out something to me that, as a human being, I perceived, but I had been unable to say, 'Ah, that's it! That's it: everyone has a life that is much more important than work.' That is why I find series so difficult: the plot becomes too important. If you're invited to shoot a series for one of the big platforms, like Amazon or Netflix, they ask you for a second season. I mean, not only must you have a plot for the first season, but one for the second one as well. It's like a desire to keep the business going so, so huge . . . Plot is something very superficial, but it enables something similar to what Greek mythology enables: the important thing is not what is happening, but what you take from the myth. I will say something very extreme now. For me, plot debases time. It would appear that plot is something like 'what this person wanted to say in two hours'. Well, if I had wanted to say that, something which you can read in two minutes, I could have done it this way: it would save me a lot of effort, time and (someone else's) money. So, plot cannot be the reason. Another example, which is also a rather extreme comparison: you read someone's biography and think that is the person's life. No, it isn't! The person's biography is not the person's life: it is a summary which is incredibly different from the person's life.

Natalia: You spent some time in Thailand in 2010. Could you tell us something about that experience?

Lucrecia: Apichatpong Weerasethakul wrote to me when *The Headless Woman/La mujer sin cabeza* (2008) premiered in Cannes, because he was part of the jury, and we have remained connected ever since. He invited me to an event called Film On the Rocks, on one of those amazing islands they have in Thailand. It was a festival, and this was the first edition. Weerasethakul wanted to organise a residency programme of sorts for directors, which entailed a few months in one of those resorts which Brad Pitt and Angelina Jolie could have chosen back when they were together and they had to take all those children on a vacation, one of those places which we cannot even dream about being able to afford. I believe that first experience didn't work for Weerasethakul and didn't work for me either. After spending three days locked up in a resort, however fabulous it is, you get absolutely bored. It is a reality constructed for tourists who spend less time there. I stayed for a month. I couldn't stay for the full four-month stint. It is not that I'm such a hippie that I can't enjoy a seven-star resort: I love it! But not for more than three days. After three days, you've already used the pool, you've had your cocktail, you've eaten your breakfast, and the surprise is over. So, during the third day, I started taking a walk around the island (which you could cover in three hours) and tried to film a short feature with a school. Everything was ludicrous, but, since I was already there, I wanted to make something with the people there and get to know them. It was crazy. It was also nice to share things with Weerasethakul, a friend I have many things in common with, who enjoys people, life, rowing in the sea, and other nice things. So, ultimately, it was an incredible experience. But, of course, isolation doesn't work for me. The residency in Cannes, when I was writing *The Holy Girl/La niña santa* (2004), didn't work for me either. Isolation isn't good for someone who wants to communicate with others. You need to be with people, meet people, speak . . . In part, the tragedy we're going through, the worst bit of this pandemic, is the terrifying experience of isolation. I should point out that I got infected, as did all my family, and it was very hard on us, and you also have all the deaths. The thing that breaks down when a person enters isolation is the contact that gives meaning to cities, to towns. The memory of these pandemic years will be very terrible, and I think the mark left by isolation will be the deepest.

Paul: Let's stay a little while longer with these happy memories of international trips, of the festival circuit, and all that. I can't even imagine the number of Q&A sessions you've been in all over the world during these twenty years. You've spoken a bit about your relationship with critics. I wanted to know if you notice any difference between the questions you're asked in Argentina, or in Latin America, and those you're asked in the rest of the world. Of course, every experience is different. Having said that, do you notice any trend in the various regions of the world where your films have been shown?

Lucrecia: Wherever I showcase the movies, I find more or less the same environment I belong to. Of course, with different customs, different things, but always hovering around an educated middle class. And that speaks of a very concrete issue, of a disease affecting cinema, which is homogeneity. And that's why we shouldn't suffer over cinema, or its death, because there are so many people left outside of this expression, which has represented a very tiny share of the population as regards concerns and reflections. So, should it disappear, I won't shed a tear. It's likely 70 per cent of the world population have never watched a movie. I don't know if that's the exact figure, but a staggering number of people don't watch movies, or, when they do watch movies, find nothing in them they can relate to, nothing about their lives. As regards festival-related trips, I feel that, over time, I've been asked fewer and fewer stupid questions. And I'm grateful to time, to people, for that. And I have a theory, based on my own experience: the generation that asks the best questions is that of people who no longer have certain anxieties, who have used recreational drugs, not in the context of an addiction, but as a perceptual experience (and I should point out I'm no expert when it comes to drugs: I've probably tried more or less what you've tried). There are many people who aren't terrified of not understanding everything. Not understanding is not that terrible. You can yield more easily to an experience you don't fully understand. Before, the questions I was asked were too linked to trying to understand something, as if that was the most important thing we have to share. And, if drugs have nothing to do with it, could it be that humanity is improving? I don't know if that last message is very child-friendly . . .

Julia: Speaking of that, in *Magazine For Fai* (1995–9), the absurd was very prominent as a conception of freedom from certain acting restrictions and certain ways of enclosing the universe of childhood.

Lucrecia: There you go. Children don't have that problem of wanting to understand everything, you see? That problem emerges with time. And that is why many parents can deal with a rainy day by playing any movie to a toddler and knowing they will be interested. Toddlers understand nothing of the plot, but there's something there that they like. They'll find some things scary, some things amusing, and perhaps those things have nothing to do with how the movie was conceived. Take *Toy Story* (John Lasseter, 1995), for example. It's we adults who laugh. Of course, children are entranced, but they aren't included in the jokes or notice secondary or tertiary meanings. And that is incredible. The experience with *Magazine For Fai* was amazing. It was an experience of adults with a healthy relationship with their childhoods. I didn't direct everything there. That was Mex Urtizberea. I dealt with the *mise-en-scène* and things that were shot on location, but I had nothing to do with scripts. And it all happened during a turning point as regards women's participation: often, with Nora Moseinco, we had to say, 'Guys, let the girls star', because they [the showrunners] had a certain trend and affinity with male characters. It wasn't machismo at all, but from time to time we still had to ask them to let the girls act more and give them good characters.

Julia: Are you always involved in casting?

Lucrecia: Not any more, no. I'm involved in stages with a lot of people, but not as much as before, when I dealt with everything. I do have one-on-one interviews with everyone who'll be in the movie. That is, I get know all of them before shooting. That is good, because it also leads you to respect the characters more. If you don't know the person playing a certain character, it's easier to trample the character, think they are not important, put them in, take them out, and so on. There are scenes in which some characters appear very little. But if you know the person playing the role, you feel bad about it and try to give the character a little more action. Sometimes, when you remove a scene, you feel this incredible sadness, because there are people who'll later say, 'Hey, I went to see the movie, and I wasn't in it.' And then you remember you took that scene away. Here, in Salta, I run into the extras from my movies all the time. That's another reason why thinking about your neighbours when making movies is good: if you didn't learn to respect characters in movies, at least your own town will teach you how to respect them. That extra will return and ask you why he wasn't in the movie.

Natalia: At the end of 2019, after more than thirty years in Buenos Aires, you returned to Salta. What do you feel about this return? Are you shooting already? Because *Zama* was filmed in Formosa, and *Chocobar* in Tucumán.

Lucrecia: I associate *Chocobar* with my return to Salta very strongly. It is a conflict which is taking place very nearby, and a conflict deeply connected to the hegemonic power structures of the Argentine north. *Zama*, I think, was like an aftershock of *The Eternaut/El Eternauta*, in the sense of being in another time. But it also had the colonial framework, which continues to be an extremely strong cultural matrix throughout Latin America: for instance, the link between poverty and the colour of your skin. If we fail to notice that poverty is always and very clearly related to an indigenous component in our genealogy, it means the colonial matrix continues to work perfectly. I have millions of projects in Salta, because I'm increasingly interested in the social issues of this region: how to have an impact there, how to collaborate in that, how to teach here. I'd been looking forward to my return for a long time. There are 1,700 km between Buenos Aires and Salta. It isn't a lot. It's not like I'm moving to a different continent. However, this has been, for me, the most important step I've taken in the last few years: returning here to work, situating myself here, and organising things with people. That gives you a different relationship with the place.

Translated by Juan Ignacio García Fahler

NOTE

1. Martel, L. and L. Rodríguez (2021), 'Lucrecia Martel rechaza una crónica de Levinas sobre los "falsos diaguitas" en Salta', *Clarín*, 3 March 2021, <https://www.clarin.com/revista-enie/lucrecia-martel-rechaza-cronica-levinas-falsos-diaguitas-salta_0_UWoSItjDo.html> (last accessed 3 May 2021).

Index